DATE DUE

		PRINTED IN U.S.A.

EAGLE VALLEY LIBRARY DISTRICT
P.O. BOX 240   600 BROADWAY
EAGLE, CO 81631   (970) 328-8800

ATLANTIS
and the
SILVER CITY

ATLANTIS
and the
SILVER CITY

PETER DAUGHTREY

PEGASUS BOOKS
NEW YORK LONDON

For the two bravest people I know,
my wife, Margaret, and my sister, Dorothy

ATLANTIS AND THE SILVER CITY

Pegasus Books LLC
80 Broad Street, 5th Floor
New York, NY 10004

Copyright © 2013 by Peter Daughtrey

First Pegasus Books cloth edition March 2013

Interior design by Maria Fernandez

Library of Congress Cataloging-in-Publication Data is available.

ISBN: 978-1-60598-415-5

10 9 8 7 6 5 4 3 2 1

Printed in the United States of America
Distributed by W. W. Norton & Company

CONTENTS

ILLUSTRATIONS

All other images are in the photo insert.

The photographs are by Peter Daughtrey and the illustrations, maps, and charts are by Peter Daughtrey and Maria Paula Duarte, unless otherwise accredited.

PART ONE

The Quest for the Atlantis Homeland

CHAPTER ONE

The Standing Stone

To this day, I don't know what drew me to it. Most of the other visitors to the delightful little museum in Lagos, Portugal, just walked on by. It was another stiflingly hot day in early June 1991. Everyone else probably wanted to get outside to enjoy a cool drink in the town square. I didn't follow them. Instead, I stepped into one last dusty room. It was stuffed full of all the usual local artifacts from yesteryear. Cabinets of coins and bronze arrowheads leaned against one wall. A box of fossils stood alongside another. I love any and all historical objects. But, charming as the setting was, apart from a broken stone slab described later, little else in that room really grabbed my interest. My wife had already moved on, and I was about to join her, when I saw it. A huge oval-shaped rock lay damaged, broken, and all but forgotten in an alcove. Its pale limestone managed to shimmer slightly amidst the dullness of the room.

For some reason I was captivated.

The noise of the other tourists out in the exit corridor faded away as I approached the exhibit. The museum's curators had labeled it as a *"menhir"*—a standing stone. Had it been standing—as I so wished it had been—at around six feet tall, it would have been my height. Instead this beautiful, ethereal object was resting on its side. I looked closely at the new base. Parts of it had clearly been badly damaged long ago. I can't say why, but that almost broke my heart. If it had remained intact and been pulled up into its original position, the *menhir* would have been a perfect egg shape. It would have been magnificent.

"What are you looking at?" My wife was back at my side. It took me a while to reply.

"Imagine how much work it would have taken to carve this," I said, standing back to take in every inch of it. "Imagine how beautiful it would have been."

"It's beautiful now. Look what's carved on it," she said softly.

I leaned forward. In three places, all around the stone, I could see a long, identical, and captivating motif. It must have stood out proud, through the centuries, on the cool, white shell of this ancient, oversized egg. But the beauty of the rough, worn carving wasn't the most intriguing thing about it. I caught my breath as I looked closer. The motif immediately brought to mind one of the most modern discoveries of twentieth-century science: the carvings on this stone egg bore an astonishing resemblance to the symbol of the DNA helix. How could that be? And what could it mean?

I barely said a word as we left the museum. I collapsed into a chair at the nearest café and ordered a cup of the local strong, black coffee—a *bica*.

"That must be the stone the Bongards told us about," I said to my wife when I finally regained my voice. Many months earlier, we had been dinner guests at a beautiful Portuguese farmhouse that belonged to an elderly Swiss couple. They had befriended my wife and me shortly after we had left Wales and moved to the Algarve in the mid-1980s. The four of us had a mutual interest in antiques, unusual artifacts, and local history. We would talk for hours about our discoveries, our collections, our theories, and our latest research. On the evening in question, our host mentioned a strange object he had seen lying by the side of the road a few kilometers from our new home. He said it had resembled a huge stone egg. As far as he had been able to ascertain, a group of farmers had just unearthed it from a nearby field.

"I went back a few weeks later to try to buy it for my collection," he had said. "But by then it had already been taken to a museum in nearby Lagos."

I kept looking out across the countryside as my wife and I drove back up the coast to our home that night. Dozens of standing stones are scattered across the Algarve. I'd seen plenty of them in the few years we'd lived in the area. But I'd never seen one like the stone egg in Lagos. The other *menhirs* were simply large, naturally formed rocks pulled up and displayed with little or no extra shaping. How long would it have taken, by contrast, to sculpt the egg I'd just seen? With only the most primitive of tools, how hard would it have been to adorn its shell with such an intricate, intriguing design? And was there something else I should be asking as well? Something was nagging away at the back of my consciousness. Was it about a sculpted egg, the ancient symbol of creation since time immemorial? Or was it the image of the DNA helix, the ultimate representation of the very building blocks of life?

When we got home, I stood outside and gazed up into the night sky. Sometimes in the Algarve the stars are so bright that the planets seem alive. This was one of those most beautiful of nights. It was full of mystery and promise. I stood there and breathed deeply. Then I looked down. I stared at the stars' reflection in the blackness of the river just beyond our garden. Then, suddenly, I smiled and my mind cleared. I realized what had been eating away at me. It was a history I'd once read of an ancient Slavic culture. Legend had it that the people had migrated into northern and eastern Europe when their original homeland had sunk into the depths of some unnamed western ocean. More important still was the assertion that in their original homeland, this Slavic culture had worshipped a large white stone egg.

Could this have been the same egg? Had a civilization right here in southern Portugal once sunk into the sea?

Three further thoughts kept me awake that night. They have been in my thoughts for most of the subsequent two decades.

The first was that back in the museum, just before my eyes fell upon the egg, I had been studying a broken slab of rock. Engraved on it in a strange spiral fashion were a number of curious letters. Some instantly reminded me of letters in the Phoenician alphabet, the very same alphabet that long ago had given birth to the one I am using here. This artifact was labeled as being from the Iron Age, around 600 B.C. Why were only some of the letters in Phoenician, and where did the others come from? I asked myself. And, just as intriguing, what was it doing in the Algarve?

My second thought was that my new home is located in one of the most precarious places on our planet. Just like California and Japan, we sit beside a lethal seismic fault line. I had discovered that fact while doing some research into a little-appreciated but truly awful event. Only a few centuries ago, the area was hit by the west's worst-ever known earthquake, followed by towering tsunamis. For some time, I had been wondering why no early civilizations were recorded as having flourished, then perished, in southern Portugal, this most beautiful of lands. That ever-threatening fault line would explain this mystery. Over millennia, huge areas of land were likely to have sunk, and any that remained had been washed clean of evidence.

The third thought came unbidden but refused to go away. Ever since my teenage years, I have been fascinated by stories of ancient lands—and by one ancient land in particular. On it was the civilization that had existed in the ocean the Slavs had described. It, too, had disappeared amidst twenty-four terrible hours of earthquakes and floods. It was called Atlantis.

I was a teenager when I first heard about the legend of Atlantis. I was utterly gripped—and I wasn't alone. The idea of this compelling, long-lost civilization has fascinated people all around the world. There are hundreds of books and an infinite number of Internet pages available to read on the subject. There is also an ever-increasing number of television programs and Hollywood blockbusters covering it. Best of all, there is always something new to learn.

From the start, it was the people of Atlantis who interested me the most. I had sat in my bedroom in Hampshire and imagined an incredible, advanced population that had lived more than 11,500 years before me. I dreamed of the civilization's armies, of its navy and its intrepid travelers. I discovered they must have had extraordinary maps and have walked on American soil thousands of years before we did. They had managed to control rivers, store water, and farm abundant crops. They had built a country of extraordinary wealth. Thousands of residents lived in an island capital city built of multicolored stone, ringed with extraordinary silver-topped walls and surrounded by water. As a teenager, living under the shadow of the Cold War, I was particularly interested in the way these people lived—initially almost entirely in peace. There was a harmony and a dignity in the account of the Atlanteans I read. Their silver city had been the center of a golden age.

I soon learned all the theories of how Atlantis had died, after the lofty principles gave way to greed and aggression; the horrors of a sudden, catastrophic earthquake; the vast, destructive waves that hit a fast-disappearing landmass; and the complete and tragic end of an era that came without warning.

I read my way through all the relevant books in my local library to find out more. Maybe it was just my childish innocence. But I was convinced there were things we could learn from this golden but doomed civilization. I loved the idea that Atlanteans could have left secrets for future generations to discover. I was sure that somewhere, far beneath some distant ocean, there must be hidden knowledge that we could use to prepare for our own terrible challenges.

Throughout my adult life I continued to read widely about ancient civilizations across the globe. I kept on dreaming about that serene, powerful kingdom that had disappeared so very long ago. When I reached my midforties, having left Britain for Portugal, learned about that threatening seismic fault, and found that pale limestone sculpture in a tiny, local museum, I followed the lead of many other academics, historians, and would-be Indiana Joneses around the world: I began a personal quest that would take me through two long, fascinating decades. I began my search for a lost kingdom. Today, against all odds, I believe I have found it.

CHAPTER TWO

Plato and Atlantis

A tlantis is indisputably the world's greatest unsolved historic mystery; most people have heard stories about this fabled lost land. But many don't realize that the only concrete evidence that shows that Atlantis ever existed has come down to us from just one source: Plato, the ancient Greek philosopher.

There are a few hints in other ancient documents, but nothing specific. Many of those who have written or made television documentaries about Atlantis do not appear to have thoroughly investigated what Plato said. As a result, misconceptions are rife and those modern phenomena Internet chat-rooms are buzzing with ill-informed comment.

What Plato indicated was that Atlantis was a substantial civilization in the Atlantic, that it was incredibly wealthy, and that it controlled a sprawling island empire as far as the great continent on the western side of the ocean. The homeland's benign climate, coupled with a bountiful agricultural plain, provided everything needed by the inhabitants for sustenance and an idyllic lifestyle. The central capital occupied a small hill approximately one kilometer wide and only a short way inland. It was a glittering affair with the external walls plated in precious metals and the whole city surrounded by water. An earthly paradise indeed, until it was destroyed in an unimaginable disaster 11,600 years ago.

That is an extraordinarily long time. For instance, it's about seven thousand years before the construction of the great Egyptian pyramids and around six thousand before the zenith of the Sumerian civilization in Iraq, hitherto accepted as the world's first civilization. However, perceptive and persistent investigative authors, such as Graham Hancock, have scoured the globe and drawn attention to many incredible remains indicating that other civilizations have existed in much earlier epochs than historians and archaeologists are prepared to publicly accept.[1] Particularly in South America and Egypt, where undeniable records also exist of tall bearded white strangers visiting from another part of the world and teaching the basic precepts of agriculture, irrigation, and construction, as well as instigating laws. The inescapable conclusion is that these strangers came from the same central source. In South America they arrived by boat from the east and in Egypt they were described as rulers from a land to the west.

So who was this Plato who bequeathed us such precious information about these enigmatic people and their long-lost civilization? Although much criticized for his tendency to elaborate on true accounts, Plato was an extraordinary man. No shrinking academic, he was well traveled and in his youth had wrestled in the Olympic games, fought in wars, tutored a foreign king, spent time in prison, and had close contact with many of the leading men of affairs, both in his home city, Athens, and elsewhere. His contributions in the fields of science, mathematics, and philosophy were immense. The scientific views he propounded were far ahead of his time, and this in itself raises an important question: Allowing for the fact that he sometimes struggled to convey his ideas and theories within the confines of the ancient Greek language, did he actually have access to earlier but forgotten advanced knowledge?

He put forward the idea, for example, that the universe is a single, interconnected, unified creation, which mirrors views held today. Modern physicists are actively searching for a "grand unified field theory of nature." He also distinguished between matter and energy, and submitted that the world was a sphere revolving on its own axis and supplying nourishment from its own decay. It was to be another twelve hundred years, and thanks to Galileo, before society was prepared to recognize that the world is round and in motion.

His most far-reaching legacy, however, which has immeasurably affected mankind for the better right up to current times, was in the realm of education. He founded the first university. It has been the world's model ever since.

It is thought that Plato lived from 423 B.C. to 347 B.C.[2] He opened the doors of his school, which gave us the name "academy" because it was built on land belonging to a man called Academos, in about 387 B.C. The university was devoted to research and instruction in philosophy and the sciences. Plato ran it until his death some forty years later.

His ambition was to train young men, enabling them to make better contributions, especially in the world of politics. Dabbling in that field earlier in his career, he had been appalled by the low standards of those holding public office. As an aside, one cannot but wonder what he would have made of today's worldwide crop. Plato certainly managed to train men well. One of his pupils was Aristotle, who in turn became tutor to Alexander the Great. Ironically, it was Alexander who abolished the Athens democracy so beloved by Plato, and made Greece a dictatorship.

Plato's academy ran continuously for nine hundred years, which to date remains the longest period ever sustained by a university. It was finally closed in A.D. 529 by the Christian Emperor Justinian, who claimed that it was a pagan establishment. How many times in the last two thousand years, I wonder, have the knowledge and written records of past civilizations been destroyed in the name of religion?

Plato is central to my investigation, as he is the only direct source of information about the legendary Atlantis. His writings usually took the form of debates between several well-known people—but he never included himself. They are called Plato's Dialogues. The most famous of these is called *Laws,* but those that concern us here are *Timaeus* and *Critias,* both of which contain information about Atlantis. He claimed that the material had come down to him from yet another famous Greek: Solon, "the law-maker," who was a friend of Plato's great-grandfather, Dropides. He had passed it on to Critias, Plato's ninety-year-old grandfather, who then related the story to Plato when he was about ten years old.

Solon had stayed for some years in Sais, an ancient Egyptian town on the Nile delta. This was not unusual, since the two countries involved were on friendly terms. There were many Greeks in Egypt, including a host of mercenaries in the Egyptian army. One day, while conversing with the priests of Sais, Solon started sounding off about the grand history of his native Athens. This rankled the very old and reputedly wisest priest, who admonished him and retaliated, saying that the Athenians were but children in comparison with the history of mankind.

Following my earlier comments about the advanced knowledge I believe Plato possessed, it is pertinent that the priest began by saying that there had been many races and civilizations of humans, each having been destroyed by huge natural disasters. Similar legends persist all over the world, particularly in South America and India. It is possible that other knowledge was passed on to Solon, in addition to the information about Atlantis—which Plato later claimed for himself.

The elderly priest then proceeded to make his point by recounting to Solon the astonishing story of Atlantis. The relevant parts of the two dialogues that resulted from the conversation can be read at the end of this book, but a précis of the circumstances and facts surrounding them may suffice here.

According to Plato, the priest claimed that the constitution of Sais was around eight thousand years old, but that of the Hellenes (Athenians) was older still, by a thousand years. He went on to relate how a mighty power came forth out of the Atlantic Ocean and launched an unprovoked attack against the whole of Europe and Asia. This power was Atlantis; it was overrunning the entire region before being heroically repulsed and defeated by the brave Hellenes. Subsequently there were violent earthquakes and floods and the whole Hellenic army was swallowed up by the earth. Atlantis then disappeared under the sea in a single awful day and night. As a consequence, the sea in those parts, previously navigable, became an impenetrable shoal of mud, stirred up from the sunken land. (SEE IMAGE 1, PAGE 21.)

Plato went on to give many other facts and extraordinary details about Atlantis. They are distilled and summarized at the end of this chapter to allow us to investigate further. You will see from the clues that he is talking about a country and its empire. It is surprising how many think Atlantis was just a city. The capital itself was relatively small and there would inevitably have been many other towns and regional capitals. The initial information was given in *Timaeus,* but the bulk is to be found in *Critias,* which, unfortunately, was never finished and comes to an abrupt end. No one has been able to fathom why, although by this stage Plato was certainly of quite an age.

Several times in his accounts, Plato stresses that he is telling the truth—which he never felt the need to do with his other writings. He must have realized that much of the story would sound a tad far-fetched. He was right—and it caused an uproar! Some of Plato's contemporaries were openly skeptical, though others were convinced of the story's veracity.

As mentioned earlier, however, Plato did have a reputation for over-embellishing stories and had, at one point, been admonished for overstepping the mark by Socrates, his mentor. To try to assess this point, it is worth analyzing a few facts.

- In *Timaeus,* Plato admitted that he had been only ten years old when he first heard about Atlantis and, before setting the story down in the Dialogues many decades later, he had to spend a night thinking about the subject and recovering the facts. He stresses, however, that even at such a young age, it is amazing how some things can make a lasting impression.

- Later, in *Critias,* he appears to contradict this by saying he still possessed original writings from his great-grandfather, Dropides, and had carefully studied them as a child. Solon was also reported to have started to write an epic poem about what he had been told.

- Plato stated that the war had occurred nine thousand years before. That is a daunting amount of time for information to be retained intact and recorded correctly.

- There are inconsistencies in some of his facts, including those statements that Athens had been founded nine thousand years previously, and that Atlantis had also disappeared nine thousand years previously after a defeat by the Athenians, leaving no time for Athens city, its civilization, and its army to develop.

- Conversely, the accounts contain some facts that were indubitably true—and quite astounding for Plato's era—such as that Atlantis lay outside the Pillars of Hercules (Straits of Gibraltar) in the Atlantic Ocean and that the Atlanteans were rulers of other islands stretching westwards from it across the Atlantic to a vast continent on the other side. So, long before its eventual "discovery," Plato was, of course, referring to America. He also says that compared to the sheer enormity of the Atlantic Ocean, the Mediterranean, which represented his known world, was but a small harbor.

So was Plato essentially telling the truth? It was recorded by Proclus in the fourth century A.D. that Kranter of Soli (335 B.C.–275 B.C.), who was later a head of the Academy, thought the story was historically correct and even claimed to have had this confirmed by Egyptian priests who had shown him temple columns on which the story was inscribed. Unfortunately, these columns have yet to be discovered.

My conclusion is in agreement with many others before me: that Plato was indeed privy to information about Atlantis and that this information probably came from Egypt via Solon. The facts must, however, inevitably have been sketchy after so long a period. Like others, I do believe there is evidence that he padded the story to help him present the message he wanted to convey to his Greek audience. He was not recording the event to arouse our curiosity a few thousand years later, but to put forward his views on how the perfect Greek state should be organized. For example, one broad hint that he embellished the story to make it more colorful is provided by Plutarch (A.D. 45–120) in his book *The Life of Solon.* He wrote: "Plato, willing to improve the story of the Atlantic Island, as if it were a fair estate that wanted an heir and came with some title to him, formed, indeed, stately entrances, noble enclosures, large courts, such as never yet introduced any story, fable or poetic fiction. . . ." So what exactly did Plato say—and how can it help us in our search for Atlantis today? Here is the complete list of clues derived from the two dialogues.

From *Timaeus,* taken from the widely used translation by Benjamin Jowett:

1. A mighty power which, unprovoked, made an expedition against the whole of Europe and Asia and to which your city [Athens] put an end.

2. This power came forth out of the Atlantic Ocean.

3. . . . for in those days the Atlantic was navigable.

4. . . . and there was an island situated in front of the straits. . . .

5. . . . which by you are called the Pillars of Hercules.

6. . . . the island was larger than Libya and Asia put together. . . .

7. . . . and was the way to other islands. . . .

8. . . . and from these you might pass to the whole of the opposite continent which surrounded the true ocean. . . .

9. . . . for this sea which is within the Straits of Hercules is only a harbor, having a narrow entrance, but that other is a real sea. . . .

10. . . . and the surrounding land may be most truly called a boundless continent.

11. In this island of Atlantis there was a great and wonderful empire which had rule over the whole island and several others and over parts of the continent.

12. This vast power, gathered into one, endeavored to subdue at a blow our country and yours and the whole of the region within the Straits.

13. She [Athens] was the leader of the Hellenes . . . and when the rest fell off from her, being compelled to stand alone . . . she defeated and triumphed over the invaders.

14. But afterwards there occurred violent earthquakes and floods, and in a single day and night of misfortune all your warlike men in a body sank into the earth.

15. . . . and the island of Atlantis in like manner disappeared in the depths of the sea.

16. For which reason, the sea in those parts is impassable and impenetrable, because there is a shoal of mud in the way, and this was caused by the subsidence of the island.

17. . . . became an impenetrable barrier of mud to voyagers sailing from hence to any part of the ocean.

From *Critias:*

18. In the days of old, the gods had the whole earth distributed among them by allotment.
19. They all of them by just apportionment obtained what they wanted. . . .
20. . . . and peopled their district.
21. Poseidon receiving for his lot the island of Atlantis.
22. He begat children by a mortal woman and settled them in part of the island.
23. Looking toward the sea, but in the center of the whole island, was a plain which is said to have been the fairest of all plains and very fertile.
24. Near the plain again, and also in the center of the island at a distance of about fifty stadia, there was a mountain not very high on any side.
25. Breaking the ground, enclosed the hill all round, making alternate zones of sea and land, larger and smaller encircling one another. . . .
26. . . . there were two of land and three of water, which he turned as with a lathe, each having its circumference equidistant every way from the center.
27. He himself, being a god, found no difficulty in making special arrangements for the center island, bringing up two springs of water from beneath the earth, one of warm and one of cold.
28. . . . and making every kind of food to spring up abundantly from the soil.
29. He also begat and brought up five pairs of twin male children. . . .
30. . . . and dividing the island into ten portions, he gave to the first-born of the eldest pair his mother's dwelling and the surrounding allotment which was the largest and best and made him king over the rest.
31. The others he made princes, and gave them rule over many men, and a large territory.
32. And he named them all; the eldest who was the first king he named Atlas.

33. . . . and after him the whole island [Atlantis] and the ocean were called Atlantic.

34. To his twin brother, who was born after him, and obtained as his lot the extremity of the island toward the Pillars of Hercules, facing the country which is now called the region of Gades in that part of the world, he gave the name in the language of the country which is named after him, Gadeirus.

35. [He then lists the names of the other sons.] All these and their descendants for many generations were the inhabitants and rulers of diverse islands in the open sea.

36. . . . and also, as has been already said, they held sway in our direction over the country within the Pillars as far as Egypt and Tyrrhenia.

37. Now Atlas had a numerous and honorable family, and they retained the kingdom, the eldest son handing it on to his eldest for many generations.

38. . . . and they had such an amount of wealth as was never possessed by kings and potentates, and is not likely ever to be again.

39. . . . and they were furnished with everything they needed, both in the city and country. For because of the greatness of their empire, many things were brought to them from foreign countries. . . .

40. . . . and the island itself provided most of what was required by them for the uses of life.

41. In the first place they dug out of the earth whatever was to be found there, solid as well as fusile. . . .

42. . . . and that which is now only name and was then something more than a name. Orichalcum was dug out of the earth in many parts of the island being more precious in those days than anything except gold.

43. There was an abundance of wood for carpenters' work.

44. . . . and sufficient maintenance for tame and wild animals.

45. Moreover there were a great number of elephants in the island.

46. . . . for as there was provision for all other sorts of animals, both for those which live in lakes and marshes and rivers. . . .

47. . . . and also for those which live in mountains and on plains, so there was for the animal which is largest and most voracious of all [i.e., the elephant].

48. Also whatever fragrant things there are now in the earth, whether roots, herbages, or woods, or essences which distill from fruit and flower, grew and thrived in that land.

49. Also the fruit which admits of cultivation, both the dry sort, which is given us for nourishment and any other which we use for food— we call them all by the common name pulse. . . .

50. . . . and the fruits having a hard rind, affording drinks and meats and ointments,

51. . . . and a good store of chestnuts and the like. . . .

52. . . . and are fruits which spoil with keeping, and the pleasant kinds of dessert, with which we console ourselves after dinner.

53. Meanwhile they went on constructing their temples and palaces and harbors and docks. And they arranged the whole country in the following manner:

54. First of all they bridged over the zones of the sea which surrounded the ancient metropolis, making a road to and from the royal palace.

55. And at the very beginning they built the palace on the habitation of the god and their ancestors . . . which they continued to ornament in successive generations . . . until they made the building a marvel to behold for size and beauty.

56. And beginning from the sea they bored a canal of three hundred feet in width and one hundred feet in depth and fifty stadia in length [nine and a quarter kilometers] which they carried through to the outermost zone, making a passage from the sea up to this.

57. . . . which became a harbor and leaving an opening sufficient to allow the largest vessels to find ingress.

58. They divided at the bridges the zones of land which parted the zones of the sea leaving room for a single trireme to pass out of one zone into another.

59. . . . and they covered over the channels so as to leave a way underneath for ships.

60. . . . for the banks were raised considerably above the water,

61. Now the largest of the zones into which a passage was cut from the sea was three stadia in breadth and the zone of land which came next was of equal breadth, but the next two zones, one of water and the other of land, were two stadia, and the one which surrounded the central island was a stadium only in width.

62. The island in which the palace was situated had a diameter of five stadia.

63. All this, including the zone and the bridge . . . they were surrounded by a stone wall on every side, placing towers and gates on the bridges, where the sea passed in.

64. The stone which was used in the work was quarried from underneath the center island, and from zones on the outer as well as the inner side. . . .

65. . . . one kind was white, another black, and a third red.

66. . . . and as they quarried they at the same time hollowed out double docks, having roofs formed out of the natural rock.

67. Some of the buildings were simple, but in others they put together different stones, varying the color to please the eye.

68. The entire circuit of the wall which went round the outermost zone, they covered with a coating of brass . . . the next wall they coated with tin . . . and the third, which encompassed the citadel, flashed with the red light of orichalcum.

69. In the center of the citadel was a holy temple dedicated to Poseidon and Cleito [his mortal wife] . . . which remained inaccessible . . . and was surrounded by an enclosure of gold.

70. Here was Poseidon's own temple which was a stadium in length, and half a stadium in width.

71. All the outside of the temple, with the exception of the pinnacles, they covered in silver, and the pinnacles with gold.

72. And around the temple on the outside were placed statues of gold of all the descendants of the ten kings and of private persons, coming both from the city itself and from the foreign cities over which they held sway.

73. In the next place, they had fountains, one of cold and another of hot water, in gracious plenty flowing.

74. They constructed buildings about them and planted suitable trees. . . .

75. Also they made cisterns, some open to the heavens, others roofed over to be used in winter as warm baths.

76. Of the water which ran off, they carried some to the Grove of Poseidon, where were growing all manner of trees of wonderful height and beauty, owing to the excellence of the soil.

77. . . . while the remainder was conveyed by aqueduct bridges to the outer circles.

78. . . . gardens and places of exercise, some for men, and others for horses in both of the two islands formed by the zones.

79. . . . guardhouses at intervals for the guards, the more trusted of whom were appointed to keep watch in the lesser zone, which was nearer the Acropolis, while the most trusted of all had houses within the citadel.

80. The docks were full of triremes and naval stores.

81. . . . a wall which began at the sea and went all around: this was everywhere distant fifty stadia from the largest zone or harbor, and enclosed the whole, the ends meeting at the mouth of the channel which led to the sea.

82. The entire area was densely crowded with habitations: and the canal and the largest of the harbors were full of vessels and merchants coming from all parts. . . .

83. I have described the city and the environs of the ancient palace NEARLY (author's capitals) in the words of Solon.

84. The whole country was said by him to be very lofty and precipitous on the side of the sea. . . .

85. But the country immediately about and surrounding the city was a level plain.

86. . . . itself surrounded by mountains which descended toward the sea.

87. It was smooth and even, and of an oblong shape, extending in one direction three thousand stadia, but across the center inland it was two thousand stadia.

88. This part of the island looked toward the south, and was sheltered from the north.

89. The surrounding mountains were celebrated for their number and size and beauty, far beyond any which still exist. . . .

90. Having in them also many wealthy villages of country folk, and rivers, and lakes, and meadows supplying food enough for every animal, wild or tame, and much wood of various sorts.

91. I will now describe the plain as it was fashioned by nature and the labors of many generations of kings through the ages.

92. . . . for the most part rectangular and oblong and where falling out of a straight line followed the circular ditch.

93. The depth, and width and length of this ditch were incredible, and gave the impression that a work of such extent, in addition to so many others, could never have been artificial. Nevertheless I must say what I was told.

94. It was excavated to a depth of a hundred feet and its breadth was a stadium everywhere. It was carried around the whole of the plain, and was ten thousand stadia in length.

95. It received the streams which came down from the mountains and winding round the plain and meeting at the city, was there let off into the sea.

96. Farther inland, likewise, straight canals of a hundred feet in width were cut from it through the plain and again let off into the ditch leading to the sea. The canals were at intervals of a hundred stadia, and by them they brought down the wood from the mountains to the city, and conveyed the fruits of the earth in ships, cutting transverse passages from one canal to another, and to the city.

97. Twice in the year they gathered the fruits of the earth, in winter having the benefit of the rains from heaven, and in summer the water which the land supplied by introducing streams from the canals.

98. Each of the lots in the plain had to find a leader for the men who were fit for military service . . . four sailors to make up the complement of twelve hundred ships . . . such was the military order of the royal city—the order of the other nine governments varied.

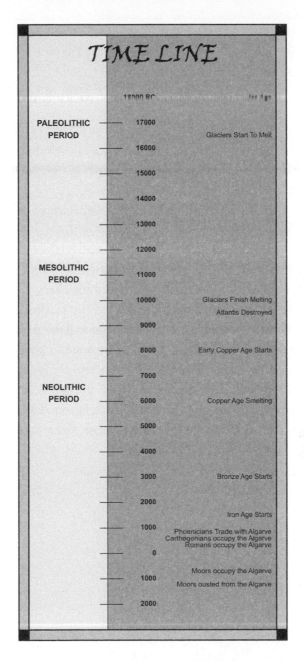

(IMAGE 1) *Timeline covering the period from the date given by Plato for the sinking of Atlantis up to the present day.*

99. There were bulls who had the range of the temple of Poseidon . . . the ten kings . . . hunted the bulls without weapons but with staves and nooses.
100. These [laws] were inscribed by the first king on a pillar of orichalcum at the temple of Poseidon.
101. There follows an amazingly detailed discourse on how the kings sacrificed the bull, and the ceremonies and contemplations to arrive at decisions and judgments, even down to the putting on "most beautiful azure robes."
102. Plato then discourses on the people's debasement.

It's a long, complicated list. I've read and reread it countless times. I will return to each section of it as I lay out further evidence in this book. I'll admit that from the first time I fully examined the clues, I could immediately see parallels between them and southwest Iberia. But, containing my excitement, I decided to reexamine the other major Atlantis theories first to ascertain whether any of them are relevant or, more importantly, whether any of the reasoning behind them would be useful for my own analysis.

Hopefully, this will also help readers who are not very familiar with the Atlantis phenomenon to understand the background and, particularly, the confusion that surrounds it. It's time to think about location, location, location.

CHAPTER THREE
Location, Location, Location

The story of Atlantis has intrigued, entertained, and puzzled millions of people for more than two millennia, and at least two thousand books have been devoted to the subject. All over the world, people have a subliminal hankering for a lost golden age, when life and its pleasures were simpler, everyone was provided for, and there were no wars or major confrontation. There is an inexorable fascination for civilizations whose knowledge has been buried for thousands of years. Knowledge that is time-worn, mysterious, and coded.

Many authors have stimulated interest and awareness by pulling together the myriad of evidential strands from various continents and legends indicating the one-time existence of a worldwide maritime civilization, but none have been able to pinpoint it. Some of the books on Atlantis have enjoyed huge success, the first being *Atlantis: The Antediluvian World,* published in 1882 by Ignatius Donnelly[3] and, more recently, three books on the subject written by Charles Berlitz between 1969 and 1984.[4] Some of the plethora of titles presented theories that were just plain wacky, but most of them are by intelligent researchers or academics who believe that they have finally located the site of Atlantis. But that is precisely what continues to fuel the debate: not one of the books or any of the clutch of television documentaries has convincingly nailed that location. None of them has produced a theory, let alone evidence, that can be accepted as plausible in the light of what Plato wrote. So the debate rumbles on and the books keep rolling off the presses.

Russian, French, German, and Italian authors have contributed to the debate, as well as a host from the English-speaking world. Some of the books are incredibly detailed and scholarly. To this day, Ignatius Donnelly's book is still much quoted. He examined evidence and legends from old civilizations all over the globe, as well as the coincidences of certain plants and place names, for example, that are found on both sides of the Atlantic, defying any explanation other than that they emanate from a common source. As I suspected, however, on serious analysis not a single hypothesis passes the "Plato test" by matching a good percentage of his clues.

In many cases, deliberately or otherwise, I found that clues that don't sit comfortably with specific theories are simply ignored. One example is to be found in a recent book, *Discovery of Atlantis,* proposing Cyprus and its surrounding seabed as the site.[5] The author, Robert Sarmast, gives a list of Plato's clues but omits key ones that would definitely preclude Cyprus, such as the one about Cádiz. To support the theory, an expedition was mounted and resulted in a claim to have discovered a hill on the seabed with a surrounding man-made wall. After the book's initial publication, a second expedition discovered that the wall was a natural formation.

The theory that has probably had the most academic support in recent years claims that Atlantis was the Greek island of Santorini, which used to be called Thera and supported a Minoan population. Some decades ago, an archaeological team led by Spyridon Marinatos excitedly began to unearth a whole town buried under volcanic ash there. It is called Akritori and had been covered when, in around 1620 B.C., a volcano blew its top in spectacular style. It ripped the mountain apart, leaving only the caldera as a reformed island in a completely new bay. The explosion was heard all over the eastern Mediterranean basin, and the ensuing tsunami is even attributed with having wiped out the main Minoan civilization on Crete. Significantly, Plato used the words "violent earthquakes and floods" (clue 14)—definitely not volcanic eruptions.

Clues 16 and 17 refer to the sea being "impassable and impenetrable" after the catastrophe because a shoal of mud, caused by a subsidence of the island, was in the way. The Santorini explosion would have deposited a thick layer of volcanic ash on the sea, and it has been claimed that this complies with these clues. This is nonsense: any mariner encountering and recording it would have been able to tell the difference between the color and consistency of volcanic ash on the one hand, and mud caused by land sinking on the other. Plato was emphatic about this and twice used the word "mud." Much of Akritori is still buried, and work still continues. In the meantime, it has become a fashionable port of call for cruise liners, helped in no small part by the Atlantis claims. Strangely, it is reported that not a single body has been unearthed in the excavation, yet Plato indicated that the disaster struck without warning.

That the disaster occurred on Santorini is not in dispute—but, as already indicated, much else is. There are no indications or records that the Minoans were aggressive or warlike until after the eruption when they had to defend themselves against the attacking Mycenaeans. They did not conquer parts of the Mediterranean, or even invade Egypt as the Atlanteans supposedly did. Like the Phoenicians, who appeared on the scene about half a millennium after the explosion, the Minoans were traders. Archaeological finds have led some historians to believe that they traded as far away as southern England. Recently, it has been claimed that some of the cargo of copper found in a Minoan shipwreck off the coast of Anatolia indicates that they were also trading as far afield as Canada. This intriguing discovery has fueled the theory that the Minoan civilization was the great maritime one Plato referred to as Atlantis.

More significantly for me, it is thought that Minoans also traded with southwest Iberia. This would hardly be surprising; it would have been much closer than Canada, for copper—or England, for tin. Southwest Iberia was already producing bronze, the much-prized alloy made from copper and tin. The Minoans would also have been attracted by the prolific amounts of silver, copper, and gold mined there. This trade was mostly carried out by the Minoans on the much larger island of Crete, which comprised the dominant part of the same confederation as Santorini. The Cretans also produced some bronze at Gournia, a town on the north coast, where there was a substantial port for the island's extensive fleet of ships. As was the case later with the Phoenicians, southwest Iberia could have contributed mightily to the growth and wealth of this unique seafaring civilization, as you will see in later chapters. Archaeological records indicate, however, that despite the scale of the eventual disaster on Santorini it did not completely kill off the Minoan civilization on Crete. It differs from Plato's account of Atlantis in that it existed, although probably badly wounded, for at least another 150 years before succumbing to an assault by the Greek-speaking Mycenaeans.

The timing is also hopelessly wrong. The eruption occurred around 8,000 years after the date given by Plato. It has been suggested that when converting from Egyptian to Greek, either Plato or Solon got the figures wrong, inflating them by a factor of ten. But that has to be a contrived argument as it would also imply that the Egyptian civilization has only been in existence for a mere 800 years, a ludicrous notion that would certainly not have been uttered by the venerable priest. So many of the other clues don't tie up either. Santorini was far too small and in the wrong part of the world altogether. Plato made it abundantly clear he was referring to the Atlantic, as will be explained in Chapter Seven. And where is the large lush plain, where are the heavily wooded mountains and valleys and the elephants he was so insistent about? The eruption was so cataclysmic the memory of it would have been embedded in the area's psyche and inevitably documented. Plato would almost certainly have had knowledge of it and if he intended to imply it was Atlantis he would have been specific about the spot and the type of disaster.

A further strand of the argument for Santorini is that yet another piece of information from the Egyptian priest was misunderstood by Solon. It is suggested that the priest could really have been referring to straits at the *eastern* end of the Mediterranean, but that Solon thought he was indicating those at Gibraltar. There is as much evidence to support this theory of Solon's misunderstanding as for the moon being made of cheese and inhabited by white mice. If Solon knew of several straits by the same name, surely he was intelligent enough to have queried it at the time. Also, the clue about "coming out of the Atlantic" to invade Egypt came out of the same priest's mouth. In fact, the Atlantic is mentioned more than once, so Solon would have had to fudge the information several times.

One BBC documentary, shown on television in May 2011 and repeated in January 2012, stated that Plato claimed that Atlantis was surrounded by concentric rings of water and land. This was sloppy and simply not true, as it was only the capital—a very small part of a substantial country—that was ringed in this way. Sadly, such errors are typical of many books and television documentaries proposing Santorini or other sites as Atlantis—all following the same well-worn path. They treat Plato's clues like a "pick and mix" sweet display: very selective about the Plato clues with which they agree, but completely ignoring the many that would preclude Santorini. They imply that poor old Solon or Plato got completely the wrong idea about where Atlantis was, when it sank, what the topography was like, how old it was, and much else. About the only thing they got right was that Atlantis, or somewhere like it, once existed. The authors' and documentary makers' own "correct" information is presumably a result of divine intervention. The reality is that it is fiction, nothing but a fanciful theory. It is incredible that so many historians and academics have embraced it while turning a blind eye to more than ninety percent of what Plato actually wrote. I suspect that they feel the need to adopt a theory that fits in with their accepted model of civilized human history and that also offers them an excuse to dissociate from something that suggests much earlier significant events. The thought of having to rewrite history simply terrifies them.

So, where else should we look for Atlantis? Over the years, the most suggested location has been in the middle of the Atlantic Ocean, with the Azores Islands often cited as the remaining mountaintops of the unfortunate sunken island. It will become obvious from analyses later in Chapter Seven that these islands are, again, in the wrong geographical position for the main part of Atlantis. In geological terms, the Azores are currently rising, not sinking. There is, however, evidence that land in this region has consistently been heaved upward by as much as a thousand meters and subsequently sunk by six thousand meters.[6] The Azores were once much larger and there were more of them, but that itself is not an argument for their being the Atlantis homeland.

Some other more extreme examples about Atlantis put it in the North Sea between Britain and Scandinavia, or southwest of Britain or Ireland. The mythical lost St. Brendan's Isle is frequently trundled out as a possible location. The fact that the climate around Britain is and was far removed from that indicated by Plato is conveniently overlooked.

In 1996, a scholarly book by Peter James was published.[7] His hypothesis was that a city in Anatolia was swallowed by a lake and that this was the Atlantis capital. A submerged city may well be there; but for much the same reasons as I have already marshaled about Santorini, it could not possibly be the ancient Atlantis capital.

Another more recent and intriguing theory revolves around crustal plate science. Rand Flem-Ath has carried out meticulous research on the subject over a long period and claims that startling, substantial movements of individual earth surface plates have occurred. His theory had many members of the academic community foaming at the mouth, but he does make some telling points. He cites precise evidence proving, for example, that the magnetic North Pole has moved dramatically and substantially several times. To learn more on this subject, consult *The Atlantis Blueprint* by Rand Flem-Ath and Colin Wilson.[8]

The link with our quest is their theory that Antarctica was Atlantis and was once much farther north in a more temperate zone, before suddenly and dramatically moving south to its current position. However, even allowing for the possibility that Antarctica did suddenly move enormous distances in a very short time span (rather than the few millimeters per year that continents now move), it would still originally have been a long way from where Plato indicated Atlantis was.

More recent claims by Dr. Sunil Prasannan and others propose large submerged areas in Southeast Asia as the Atlantis location. They make a strong case for a lost civilization in that area, and I have little doubt that there are many of these submerged around the globe.[9] This doesn't say, however, that any of them are Plato's Atlantis. One, a large city recently discovered off the west coast of India in the Gulf of Cambay, must be at least seven to eight thousand years old, due to its depth under the water and rising sea levels since the last Ice Age.[10] Initial carbon dating from artifacts of wood, beads, teeth, pottery, et cetera, confirms a date of around 9500 B.C. This discovery has caused a very public spat between archaeologists who were not involved in the discovery and the Indian authorities. The archaeologists, mostly Americans, pointed out that the finds had not been confirmed with the usual rigorous, painstaking research required. The Indians had discovered the site using side scanners when examining the area in a pollution survey. Subsequently, the authorities instigated a dredging operation to see what they could trawl up. Unfortunately, this method can also destroy a lot of the surrounding evidence. They excused themselves by pointing out that the quality of water there is so bad that conventional, careful examination by divers was just not possible.

The archaeologists, who the authorities suspect are somewhat miffed to have to reconsider their accepted view of where the first ancient civilization materialized, say that the artifacts found could have been washed there in far more recent times and that the pottery shards could be no more than an aggregate of naturally formed materials. The extraordinary accounts of ancient Indian civilizations in some of their old Vedic literature, however, would seem to support the Indian case, as would the position of the site on the banks at the mouth of a great river submerged by rising meltwater at the end of the Ice Age. It is exactly where you would expect an old city to be. Remains of another submerged city, including ancient temples, have been discovered elsewhere in India. Graham Hancock has contributed significantly to this development.[11] These intriguing discoveries certainly demonstrate that Atlantis was not the only ancient civilization. Indeed, Plato alludes to this when he talks of the ships from other places crowding the harbor front of the Atlantis capital. His many other clues, however, completely rule out a site for Atlantis in the Far East.

Andrew Collins has written many fascinating and groundbreaking books. He recently added an exhaustively researched one propounding Cuba as Atlantis.[12] The basic location arguments again rule it out as the main part of the Atlantean Empire, but, as will be revealed later, it does have a definite link with the conclusions of this book. The same applies to the predictions of the famous American "sleeping prophet," Edgar Cayce. His family and their foundation are the most active continuous searchers for firm evidence of Atlantis, particularly around the Bahamian islands of Bimini and Andros, where Cayce predicted that remains of Atlantis would be found.[13] Among what they have claimed to discover are submerged harbor installations and breakwaters not far beneath the water's surface. I will return to these later, in Chapter Fifteen; like Cuba, they have a definite resonance with this book's hypothesis.

Intriguingly, closer to home, the area around Cádiz has been suggested. Dr. Rainer Kuehne from the University of Wuppertal, in Germany, claimed to have spotted, on a NASA satellite image, rectangular-shaped buildings beneath the land surface—and maintained that these formed the famous Atlantis citadel. The area cited, the Marisma de Hinojos, is north of Cádiz and is also very marshy. Old maps indicate that it was once a huge lagoon extending inland. At the time of this writing, it has been widely reported that Spanish archaeologists have started excavations in the area, based on aerial photography showing outlines under the surface. The National Geographic television channel made a documentary about it, fronted by an American, Professor Freund. He also made sensational claims that they had found the Atlantis capital, much to the consternation of the archaeologists involved. On analysis, all these claims simply do not pass the Plato clues test. Let's apply just three of them.

- Plato said that the citadel was close to the center of Atlantis, an area quite a bit bigger than this eastern extremity. This corner of the supposed kingdom couldn't possibly have been in the proximity of the center of the country.
- The area around the citadel was given to Poseidon's first-born, Atlas. The area close to Cádiz was given to the second-born son and could, therefore, hardly have housed the capital.
- As mentioned earlier, the citadel was reported by Plato to be backed by a huge swath of mountains. The area north of Cádiz is as flat as a drum skin for kilometer after kilometer. There are mountains to the east, but none at all close to the north.

Dr. Marc-André Gutscher and Georgeos Diaz Montexano had also both earlier picked up on the very obvious clues referring to the same Gades region of southwest Spain and formulated theories that this narrow area, the immediate seabed, and part of neighboring Morocco were the combined site of Atlantis. I realized that they could be partly correct, but the area was far too confined, as it does not take into account exactly what Plato said about Gades, that it was only the eastern extremity of the lost civilization.

Another suggestion has been that Atlantis was a large island, once incorporating the Canary Islands and Madeira, which subsequently broke up as parts of it subsided. Like the theory put forward by Andrew Collins about Cuba, I think there is a definite link with Atlantis, as will be revealed as this book develops.

Other theories, though, are soon shot down. In the spring of 2009, for example, an unusual grid pattern was spotted on a Google Earth image, in the seabed off the coast of west Africa. This made headlines around the world in the press, on television news channels, and on the web. "It's Atlantis," was the cry. "It must be the street grid of the citadel." Google pulled the shutters down on that theory by explaining that the grid was merely a by-product of the imaging system and no such layout existed. Furthermore, even if it had existed, such was the scale that each street would have been a few miles wide.

Those, therefore, are the main rival theories for the true location of Atlantis. Those, too, are the reasons why the theories don't stand up to serious examination. Could my own ideas take matters further? I was impatient to move ahead with my research. And while these were early days, I was excited by my discoveries. I had thrown up several leads for further inquiries. I particularly wanted to look again at the Cuban and Bahamian connection, for example, although my main feeling was simply that Atlantis, as Plato had described it, had not yet been found. But I did have some vital information; I was convinced that I knew what had probably destroyed it.

CHAPTER FOUR
Destruction of Paradise

I t was Sunday, November 1, All Souls' Day, and by 9:40 A.M. the capital city's cathedrals and churches were packed with devout Catholics. They were, perhaps, aspiring to heaven, but instead were suddenly pitched into an unimaginable hell.

The entire city began to shake violently and there were simultaneous unholy growling and groaning noises. The phenomena persisted for an incredible six or seven minutes.

Eyewitness accounts tell of whole buildings swaying like saplings in the wind, and of terrified people throwing themselves from upper floors in the desperate hope of escaping the horror. Others, clinging on to something—literally for dear life—watched incredulously as people in the same room were flung across it, smashed through windows, and fell flailing to the street below. So immense was the force of the quake that an unbelievable eighty-five percent of the city was destroyed, including all the churches, entombing the pious at prayer and leaving them little time to question why God had forsaken them. Even today, a few hundred years later, the city's largest convent at the time remains roofless, in ruins . . . a memorial to the dead.

Soon after the first tremor, at around 10 A.M., a second struck. Even more buildings, already badly damaged, were reduced to rubble.

Yet a third violent tremor followed at noon. Horrifying fissures, up to fifteen feet wide, tore through the city center, swallowing those unfortunate enough to be in their path.

Thousands gathered on a recently constructed quay on the waterfront, hoping to board boats to escape the catastrophic episodes. Without warning, the entire quay sank beneath their feet into the angry waters, like a high-speed elevator descending to hell. Nothing of the quay or its milling occupants was ever seen again. The seabed at that spot was later said to be six hundred feet deep.

(IMAGE 2) *Western Europe and North Africa.*

A firestorm raged through the city for days afterward, consuming everything in its path. It was estimated that at least thirty thousand souls perished in the city alone; some reports indicate more than double that many fatalities. Most of the towns and coastline villages of the surrounding region were flattened, and many were flooded. In some areas closest to the quake's epicenter, the resulting tsunamis were estimated to be as high as thirty meters—the height of a modern ten-story apartment house.

It is believed that the earthquake would register nowadays as a colossal 8.9 to 9 on the Richter scale, and I have seen estimates as high as 10. That is at least equivalent to the fateful Japanese quake on March 10, 2011, and possibly up to ten times stronger. Most earthquakes resulting in severe carnage are a maximum of Richter 6.0 to 7.5. This was the largest earthquake in the known history of the Western world.

Two major aftershocks on December 11 and 23—and many more in the following weeks—further terrified the survivors; the population lived in constant fear.

The current worldwide perception of this disaster is minimal, yet it only happened surprisingly recently—in the era of Haydn and Handel, a year before Mozart's birth, in 1755. It didn't occur in Turkey, Asia, or South America, but in the capital city of Portugal: Lisbon. As I was to discover, similar events had frequently happened before and will almost certainly occur again in this most unstable of zones. (SEE IMAGE 2, PREVIOUS PAGE.)

Despite the magnitude of the catastrophe, it had some enduring benefits for mankind as it kick-started, among other things, the study of earthquakes. Previously, little had been understood about seismic activity or what caused it.

I first researched this event more than twenty years ago for an article in a magazine. It is enshrined in the annals of history as The Great Lisbon Earthquake, but that is a misconception. In fact it was The Great Algarve Earthquake. In 1755, mass tourism was unheard of and had not yet thrust Portugal's southernmost province onto the world's stage. Few had heard of The Kingdom of the Algarve, as it was known. Back then, anyone found exposing their nipples on a beach and worshipping the sun would probably, at the behest of the Pope, have been lashed to a stake in the town square and burned alive as a witch. Plenty of poor souls suffered such a fate for less erratic behavior.

Today the Algarve's golf courses, stunning golden cliffs, and sundrenched, sandy beaches are famous, forming a backdrop for many a television commercial. The region has taken its place as one of Europe's most popular tourist destinations, with millions of sun-seekers arriving through the airport at Faro every year.

This all began back in the 1960s, when stars like the Beatles and Cliff Richard discovered the area's charms. Little had changed since 1755, apart from the rebuilding of the shattered towns. There was no airport, there were few made-up roads, and the common mode of rural transport was the donkey cart—all part of the attraction of the region: celebrities could lose themselves in paradise, away from the prying eyes of the press. Overexposure on the beach, however, was still viewed with distaste by the locals.

In 1755, Lisbon was one of the world's richest and most famous cities; its devastation and the associated huge death toll resulted in global alarm. This is hardly surprising, since such was the awesome power released by the earthquake that tremors were felt throughout Europe—to be exact, over a total area of 1,300,000 square miles. There were ground motions in Spain, France, Italy, Switzerland, Germany, and North Africa. In Italy, locals were amazed—and mightily relieved—when a violent eruption of Mount Vesuvius stopped abruptly. Tens of thousands perished in Morocco, and Algiers, a thousand kilometers away, was completely destroyed. Even Scandinavia was affected—the Dal River suddenly overflowed its banks— and, bizarrely, church bells suddenly started ringing in Paris.

Scientists now believe the epicenter of the earthquake was several hundred kilometers southwest of Cape St. Vincent, itself the most southwesterly point of the Algarve, and of Europe. It was near a large seabed zone known as the Gorringe Bank (or Ridge), which is much closer to the surface than the surrounding seabed. The exact point was on the now-notorious fault line where the African plate, one of nine forming the earth's crust, collides with and grinds against the Euro-Asian plate to the north. Each is inexorably trying to invade the other's territory, which has produced, shaped, and folded the contours and mountains of Africa and Europe over millions of years. (SEE IMAGE 3, NEXT PAGE.)

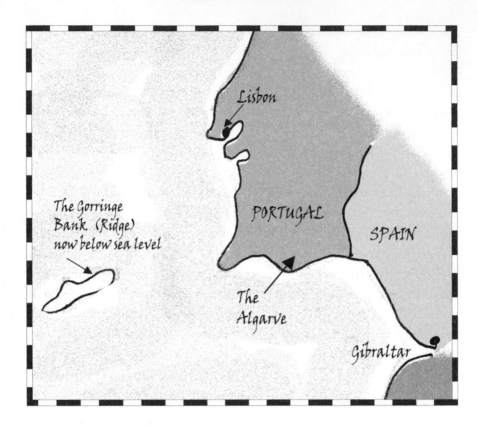

(IMAGE 3) *The position of the Gorringe Bank, now submerged in the Atlantic.*

Plate tectonics is a twentieth-century science, and exactly when and where earthquakes will occur is still not predictable with any certainty. We do know, however, that enormous pressure builds up and is eventually released by one plate suddenly moving over, under, or along another.

This particular fault starts way out in the Atlantic at the Azores, travels east toward Europe, where it meanders in front of the Algarve and the Costa de la Luz in Spain's southern province of Andalucía, and then runs under the Mediterranean Sea and moves on to Italy and Mount Vesuvius. It is a recipe for disaster on a gigantic scale, as witnessed by the destruction of Lisbon, despite its location some four to five hundred kilometers from the quake's epicenter.

Unfortunately for the Algarve, at the moment, the crustal plates seem to be most in conflict in the epicenter area of the 1755 quake. Having just learned what happened to Lisbon, try to conjure up what it was like in the Algarve, considerably closer to the quake's origins. It is almost beyond imagination. All the ports and coastal villages of the region, and of Costa de la Luz in neighboring Spain, were destroyed by the initial tremors. Earthquake-proof building methods were as yet nonexistent. Anyone fortunate enough to have survived on the coast and its immediate hinterland was quickly inundated by the terrifying tsunami. As we said earlier, waves reached heights of thirty meters in places, far higher than the tsunami in Thailand on December 26, 2004, and three times the height of that which struck Japan in March 2011. The one that caused havoc and mayhem in Samoa in September 2009 reached barely five meters.

Every inland settlement and town was also reduced to rubble. It was reported that in Silves, the Algarve's opulent capital during the Moorish occupation, nothing but birds stirred among the debris and rubble for many years.

Much of the coastline was changed as the brittle sandstone cliffs were shaken and torn apart, before being battered by a succession of great waves. There were huge landslides in the mountains that sweep across the north of the Algarve. It has been estimated that, extending from the Algarve, the total area shaken was four times that of Europe.

The tsunami reached Britain by the afternoon and all the way across the Atlantic Ocean to the Caribbean on the same evening—albeit with a reduction of the staggering height. Research has revealed that about 282,000 square kilometers of the seabed sank by as much as 30 meters over a radius of 300 kilometers.[14] These figures beggar belief, but they are the result of painstaking surveys of the seabed by marine geologists. Recently, other parts of the seabed have been discovered to have thrust upward, and this has been attributed to the same event.

The three individual earthquakes lasted for a considerable time—some reports say one went on for as long as nine minutes. That is an inordinately long period. It is known that on some geological faults, a destructive ripple effect can occur along a large section, lasting many minutes and resulting in devastation over extensive areas. According to experts, one such susceptible fault running up the west coast of America from Seattle to Canada is overdue to fracture.

Living in the Algarve, it would be an understatement to say that I was perturbed on discovering this. Was I to live with the possibility of all hell breaking loose at any moment? I resolved to find out whether this was a one-off or part of a sequence of similar events. The answer was to be found in the findings of several recently conducted surveys.[15]

In one, core samples were drilled out of the Atlantic seabed between Cádiz and Gibraltar. This is well within the zone this disaster has been traced to. It seems that tsunamis cause characteristic sediment to be deposited on the seabed. By analyzing the depth of each layer, the strength of the event can be accurately deduced, and its depth in the overall strata indicates when it occurred. The bad news is that events of the ferocity of the 1755 earthquake happen regularly and will continue to occur. The good news is they only occur infrequently—every 1,250 to 2,500 years. This means the next one should not be troubling the area for at least another thousand, or even two thousand, years. I breathed a big sigh of relief, but still I made sure that I had quake insurance.

A survey, by Dr. Marc-André Gutscher of the University of West Brittany in France, looked for layers of turbidite (sand and mud) shaken up by underwater avalanches caused by earthquakes; the survey was published in the journal *Geology*. He found a 50- to 120-centimeter-thick sedimentary deposit, left by a huge tsunami around twelve thousand years ago.[16] That is very close to the date given by Plato for the destruction of Atlantis.

A combination of my natural curiosity and imagination kicked in. What momentous changes must have taken place in the Algarve over these past twelve thousand years? In 1755 alone, there was a 30-meter subduction (lowering) of the seabed over a 300-kilometer radius. It almost certainly reached as far as the Algarve, with the seabed dropping about 100 feet. Some dry land was most likely affected too. A few of the events may have been even stronger than the 1755 quake, and the occasional epicenter could have been farther east, more directly in front of the coast.

A short time before I started this book, in September 2009, there was an earthquake in the Algarve measuring 4 on the Richter scale. It wasn't strong enough to cause serious damage and was just one of innumerable small quakes, causing absolutely no problems, experienced there every year. According to experts, these frequent minor quakes are advantageous, since pressure is released in small doses rather than building up. This recent example, however, was ominously in front of Faro, the Algarve's capital city, plumb in the middle of the coastline and therefore much closer than the 1755 quake.

Having always been fascinated by ancient civilizations, I had often wondered why none are recorded to have flourished in this corner of Europe where conditions are about as ideal as it's possible to get: a perfect climate, productive plains, plentiful rivers, wooded mountains, and rich, verdant valleys, all skirted by bountiful seas. It would also have provided a superb refuge from the Ice Age and, lying at Europe's most southwesterly point, offered a natural departure point for maritime exploration.

Now it was becoming apparent to me why no records exist. If there had been any flowering of civilization here, it would probably have been annihilated subsequently, over millennia, by earthquakes, tsunamis, and floods. Buildings would have been shaken down, buried under huge alluvial deposits, and the debris would have been sucked out to sea. Any rare survivors in the mountains would have gotten the hell out, terrified that they might be engulfed again. The Algarve's coastline could well have once extended much farther out into the Atlantic but could also have progressively sunk in successive violent tremors, as well as being engulfed by rising sea levels.

I sensed there was something tantalizingly hidden here; my antennae were twitching. An urgent visit to the local harbormaster's office was called for; I wanted to find out what the seabed in front of the Algarve was like.

CHAPTER FIVE

A Forgotten World

"**A**re you serious?" I stammered. A local historian and friend, Jonathan Wilson, could not have stunned me more if he had suddenly heaved me in the river. We were sitting outside a café on the long estuary promenade in Portimão, a port town at the mouth of the Arade River in the Algarve. He had agreed to let me tap into his considerable knowledge of the area's history over the past twelve hundred years. Jonathan, a former London barrister, now lives in Silves, the old Arab capital, a few kilometers up the Arade. Soon after arriving in the Algarve, he developed a passion for the town's tumultuous history and the conflicts that took place there between the Arabs and the Crusaders. The latter helped to free it from the Moors on their way to the Holy Land.

We were verbally rummaging around the earthquake phenomena when he casually asked whether I'd heard of the submerged city. While translating a centuries-old Portuguese book about the Crusaders' assault on the Algarve—and on Silves in particular—he'd come across a throw-away comment indicating that in 1755, as the sea had receded from the coast before the impending tsunami, a settlement standing on the seabed was clearly visible. Jonathan knew of no other reference to these remains, and my own subsequent research also drew a blank.

It appeared that there had been no local legends about anything being swallowed by the sea.

I was elated: this supported my fledgling hypothesis that the area must at some stage have developed and supported an earlier civilization.

Having mulled it over for a few days and made further inquiries, it became obvious that this submerged settlement must have been of considerable age. If it had suddenly sunk, with the possible exception of a few grander stone edifices, the building style of ordinary dwellings in the Algarve over the past two thousand years would not have survived under the sea for long. Walls were made from clay, mud and bits of pottery debris, and small stones mixed with lime and left to dry, compressed tightly between planks of wood. This dried to a hard consistency and, if the outside was regularly coated and the roof maintained, withstood the elements well. Permanently submerged under the sea and washed twice a day by the strong Atlantic tides, however, it would have deteriorated quickly.

If, on the other hand, the settlement had been engulfed over time by slowly rising sea levels, the pounding of the tides would have wreaked havoc. My inquiries, however, produced no local records, legends, or folk memory of a sunken settlement. It all indicated that the buildings must have been of a great age, disappearing below the water before living or recorded memory, and probably built from large blocks of hewn stone in a similar manner to that used by ancient civilizations. For it also to have withstood the effects of the 1755 quake, and perhaps others before it, indicated that the structure was quite possibly in the very ancient polygonal cyclopean style, with large, irregular, different-sized blocks carefully cut and fitted snugly together. This is recognized to be a highly effective way to absorb serious tremors. The buildings of the Maya people in South America are just some of the ancient examples. Others can be found in Egypt, Malta, Iraq, even Morocco.

The only other known peoples who had possibly built in a sufficiently durable way would have been the Romans. It is known that the Algarve coastline has been eroded since their era, two thousand years ago. But if this settlement had been Roman, I doubt whether that would account for the current position of the submerged remains in an area famous for its cliffs. If it was on land being inexorably eaten away by the sea, it would have collapsed as the cliff below it avalanched onto the beach. Parts of Roman remains have been discovered on cliff edges, the missing parts having been consigned to the sea long ago. The exact distance from the shore was not disclosed in the old history book, but the evidence would appear to indicate these remains are farther out to sea with subsidence appearing to be the more likely cause—and who knows how large an area was affected? I have just discussed an estimated 30-meter drop over a radius of 300 kilometers as a consequence of the 1755 earthquake, and there were many others of similar or greater intensity before it.

If here was evidence of one sunken town, it was most unlikely to have existed in isolation in such a fertile area. My excitement barometer rose: cities could be dotted all over the seabed out there. What enlightening surprises could be in store from ruins that have lain unnoticed and forgotten for many thousands of years, finds that might change our whole perception of the world's history!

After leaving Jonathan, I visited the harbormaster's office just along the seafront and purchased a large bathymetric map showing the levels and contours of the seabed in front of the Algarve.

Arriving home, hardly able to contain my curiosity, I grabbed a Bible and a dictionary, the two heaviest books to hand, to weigh down each end of the map as I unfurled it on the dining table. This was turning out to be quite a day; I was in for my second major surprise. The seabed directly in front of the coast was pretty well flat and extended way out to sea, to a distance varying from 6 to 30 kilometers, with only a gentle slope. It looked like a large plain had been flooded. Interestingly, it finally reached a depth of around 120 meters before plunging sharply to around 200 meters. One possibility was that the original plain had once been fronted by cliffs, much as most of the western end of the Algarve is today. Dotted around this submerged plain were gray spots marked as "rocky areas." I doubted whether any of these had been examined to determine whether they just might be submerged ruins.

A second flat area, sloping by roughly the same gradient as the first, continues out for a distance varying from 2 to 6 kilometers. Again this falls over a much steeper drop. There is then a third plain, only gently rising and falling in parts, as it is also mostly very flat. It extends from a farther 20 kilometers out in front of Portimão in the western Algarve to 47 in front of Faro in the center, before again culminating in a drop that, like the others, is much steeper in some areas. The most precipitous part is at its extreme distance from the existing shore, where it finishes in what must have been a cape almost due south of Faro. It ends in a much higher area topped by a couple of rock-outcrop mini-peaks, not far below the surface.

The submerging of one of these plains could be explained by the melting of the glaciers that used to cover much of the northern hemisphere. This happened from around 16,000 B.C. to 11,000 B.C. (estimates vary). As a result of this meltdown, the sea is thought to have risen by around 100 to 120 meters worldwide. The submerging, however, could equally well be a result of sinking during a serious earthquake like that in 1755, or the combined effects of several of them. (SEE IMAGE 4, NEXT PAGE.)

The seabed map showed one more fascinating aspect. The bed of the Arade River, beside the mouth of which Jonathan and I had chatted, was clearly shown extending way out under the sea, with its original wide mouth at the point of the third submerged cliff, clearly indicating the limit of an earlier coastline. The first part of the riverbed closest to the existing coast appears to have been filled with drifting sand and alluvial deposits; but the old, original bed farther out to sea is clearly shown. This was evidence that the seabed on either side, between it and the current coast, had once been above water. Intriguingly, this old riverbed reached incredible depths compared to the surrounding land: as deep as four thousand feet. Indeed, the map names it the Portimão Canyon.

A few thousand years ago, there would have been huge volumes of water flowing from it into the sea, as just upstream it was joined by two other, then mighty, rivers. Today, the Arade and one of the other rivers, the Odelouca, are dammed to provide freshwater reservoirs. I assumed that the sheer volume and speed of the flow would have worn this deep chasm in the soft sandstone bed. From later discussions with a local geologist (detailed in a later chapter), it appears that it is a natural geological phenomenon caused by the pressures of that fatal fault line farther out to sea. Not surprisingly, the river found and enlarged it.

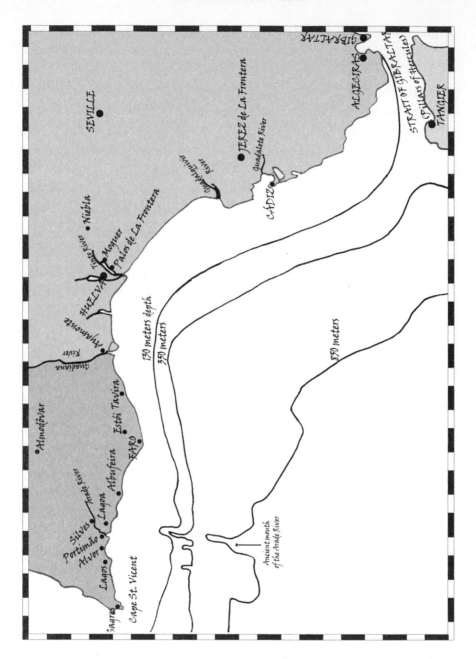

(IMAGE 4) *The seabed off the Algarve and the Costa de la Luz, showing the extent and ultimate depth of each of the three old plains.*

It had been quite a day, and that submerged settlement might yet provide the first physical evidence. There were lots of pointers indicating that it was certainly worth continuing my inquiries. It was time to ramp up the investigation and examine the history of the area as far back in time as I could trace. Maybe the region's remote past would throw up more lines of inquiry.

CHAPTER SIX
Untold Wealth

"In the morning the Pagans were led away from the gates of the city in a more disciplined manner; and thereupon, we first saw their enfeebled condition, for instance they were extremely thin and barely walking. Many were crawling, some were held upright by our men, others were lying in the streets either dead or half alive."

This quote is from the hand of an anonymous Crusader from Bremen, Germany, who, together with his own countrymen and others from Britain and all over northern Europe, helped the Portuguese king lay siege to the occupying Moors in the Algarve city of Silves. These Crusaders were on their way to reclaim Jerusalem and the Holy Land from the Moors in A.D. 1189. The fascinating account furnished by the crusader from Bremen is published in a book written by Jonathan Wilson titled *The Siege and Conquest of Silves in 1189.*[17]

While investigating the area's history, this was the first book I turned to in the hope of finding anything that hinted of an earlier civilization. My intention was to explore chronologically back in time as far as possible, emulating archaeologists who have to dig ever deeper in search of remains.

Muslim forces had first arrived in the Algarve, as well as across the border in Spain, in A.D. 711. They called their kingdom al-Andaluz and occupied it for more than five hundred years. The grand capital, Córdoba, soon became the largest in Europe. A hundred thousand citizens thronged the city's streets, alleys, and bazaars, taking advantage of three hundred public bathhouses and seventy libraries, as well as roads and street lights. Private dwellings had running water and enclosed sewers, while cities like London and Paris were mainly impoverished settlements, consisting mostly of thatched wooden houses, with open sewers.

By A.D. 1110, another Muslim dynasty, the Almovarids, had invaded and taken over al-Andaluz. From North Africa, this was a fundamentalist federation of Berber tribes from the Sahara. It was eventually overthrown by yet another group of Berbers, the Almohads, mainly from the high Atlas Mountains. By this time, Muslim Portugal was ruled from Seville, in Spain. The capital of the western region, Algarve—called Al Garb by the Moors—was Silves. By all accounts, it was a fine city of tinkling water gardens, well-stocked bazaars, and attractive buildings, with a well-mannered and eloquent populace, many of whom were particularly fond of writing poetry.

The Crusaders brought this utopia to a savage end. Paradise became purgatory. They may have undertaken the Crusade in God's name, but for the most part they were a bloodthirsty, unprincipled lot with a passion for plunder. Many of them had joined because they had been told that they would be absolved of their taxes back home and they could strike it rich in the Holy Land.

Portugal's geographical position inevitably meant that passing Crusaders from the north put into the country's ports for provisions or when seeking shelter from Atlantic storms. In 1189 the fleet, including our man from Bremen, docked in Lisbon. The king of Portugal, Dom Sancho I, seized the moment and convinced them that one set of Muslims was just as bad as another and persuaded them to help him oust the Moors from Silves and help unify Portugal. No doubt a promised share of the loot appealed to their lofty Christian principles.

Silves' mighty fortress was practically impregnable, and the Portuguese, along with some of the Crusaders, had to be persuaded several times to persevere rather than abort during the six-week siege. They tried every-thing: ladders to scale the walls, siege catapults lobbing lethal stones inside, fiery missiles, and tunnels under the walls to destabilize them. The Moors reacted by pouring boiling or flaming oil on the attackers, firing the missiles back, and breaking through from inside the fortress into the Crusaders' tunnels to repel them.

A friend who owns a house overlooking the river a short way downstream from Silves recently unearthed a cache of roughly formed stone missiles, ready for the siege catapults but, in the event, obviously not needed.

The end came when the Christians succeeded in cutting off the town's water supply. The Muslim defenders were dying from thirst and finally offered to surrender. The quote at the beginning of this chapter is the anonymous Crusader's description of their pitiful state when they were finally allowed to leave.

The Moors did not take the loss of what they regarded as an earthly paradise lightly, and the following year a fleet arrived from Seville to reclaim the city. The famous English monarch Richard the Lionheart was passing through on his crusade to the Holy Land at the same time and dispatched a contingent of men who helped to send the Moors scuttling back to Spain.

During the subsequent summer, however, while Richard was otherwise occupied in Palestine, the Moors returned and, after a month, the castle capitulated. It remained in their hands until, some forty years later, the Portuguese were strong enough to retake it—along with the rest of the Algarve's Muslim strongholds—on their own.

So goes the most recent saga of Silves. No one has invaded the Algarve since—apart, that is, from thousands of north Europeans—English and Irish in particular—who over the last thirty years have bought homes there, from which to enjoy the peaceful countryside as well as three hundred annual days of azure skies.

Not much meat, then, to support my developing theory that an ancient civilization once existed in the Algarve, except for the revelation that the Moors had a port and a shipyard nine kilometers upriver at Silves. This confirms other reports that the rivers of the region were navigable far deeper into the hinterland than they are today, and were used to transport goods and people.

The Moors had originally come to power in the Algarve at the expense of the Visigoths and local tribes. In truth, the Visigoths do not seem to have ever made the same headway in the south of Portugal as they did in the rest of the country and across the border in Spain.

I obviously needed to dig deeper; perhaps the Roman era would prove more fruitful. The Romans first invaded with the intention of blocking Carthaginian reinforcements in southern Iberia from reaching and helping their famous general, Hannibal, who was fighting the Romans on the Italian peninsula. It was, however, some time later, early in the second century B.C., that the Romans, having realized that the area had vast precious metal resources, set about conquering it and quelling all resistance from disparate tribal groups in Iberia.[18] The Lusitanians, who hailed from central Portugal, put up the stiffest resistance. One leader, who appeared out of the ranks when his tribe was encircled by Roman legionaries and led his fellow tribesmen out of the trap, became the biggest thorn in the side of the invaders—and one of Portugal's greatest heroes. Viriato to the Portuguese and Viriathus to the Romans, he took over leadership of the various tribal groups and embarked on a guerrilla campaign of harassment. He later defeated one Roman general after another in pitched battles, to the extent that he was the most successful general ever to fight against them.[19] Rome found that it had a serious crisis on its hands—morale was affected, and legion recruitment rates dropped.

Eventually, the Romans typically reverted to treachery and bribed three of the hero's peace emissaries to murder him in his sleep—then refused to cough up the promised reward with the weasel words "Rome doesn't reward traitors."

The Lusitanians turned against the local tribe in the Algarve (variously referred to as the Conii, Konii, or Cynetes), who had decided it was preferable to bend the knee to the Romans and pay their taxes rather than face slavery or oblivion. The Lusitanians regarded them as turncoats and swept down from central Portugal when the Romans were occupied elsewhere, gave them a fearful beating, and reportedly razed the Conii royal capital, Conistorgis, to the ground. The site of this city has never been found but, according to a Roman map, it was not far to the north of Faro, the current capital of the Algarve. We will return to it in a later chapter. Intriguingly, they also had a city where modern-day Silves stands; its name was Cilbes.

Julius Caesar, arguably the most famous Roman ever, set up his western Iberian base, Pax Julia, near Beja in Portugal's Alentejo province, just north of the Algarve. There was a huge gold and copper mine close by at São Domingos, and Caesar used the wealth of the area to finance the maintenance of his legion and his initial grab for power as a consul in Rome. If it had not been for this, he would merely be a passing mention on the pages of history today rather than bestriding them.[20] Unfortunately, apart from a few records about the Conii and the mines, I could find no evidence that the Romans inherited or discovered anything from any great earlier civilization.

Few readers are likely to have heard of the Conii, but evidence is accruing that this was a very old race indeed, one that had occupied the area since way back in the mists of time. It would appear that they had developed a script but, sadly, it was out of general use long before 1000 B.C. It seems to have only been kept alive for the next few hundred years by priests to somewhat crudely incise memorials to the dead on funerary stones. That broken slab with letters on it, in the museum mentioned in Chapter One, is an example. This script does hint at an earlier, more sophisticated civilization having originally developed it, but historians and academics do not generally agree. They have been quick to pigeonhole it under the name of the "Southwest Script" and assert that it could only have developed from Phoenician around 900 B.C., then died out a few centuries later. I quickly discovered that this was nonsense. It stemmed, I suppose, from a desire to quickly shoehorn it into existing historical dogma, as it possessed the potential to warrant a complete reappraisal of the origins of our Western alphabet. Chapter Eighteen will deal with this mysterious script and will agree with the opinions of a few other dedicated researchers that it is extraordinarily ancient and that Phoenician and Greek developed from it.

Some historians believe that during the first millennium B.C., the Conii were infused with a migration of Celtic people. The academically approved view is that they came from north of the Pyrenees. Principally pastoral people, these Celts were also skilled in working with metals. Exactly who the Celts were, however, is nowadays exciting conflicting theories. It seems there were two completely different groups, both called Celts by historians. Hitherto, the classic textbook claim has been that they originated in the Hallstatt region of Austria and migrated from there. Yet toward the end of the last century, research into blood groups generated a whimsical headline in a highbrow English national newspaper . . . "Taffy Gaddafi." "Taffy" is, of course, the nickname given by English people to the Welsh, indisputably a proud Celtic nation. The research proved that their principal blood group was of Middle Eastern origin. Unlikely as that may seem, ancient tradition in south Wales and England claims that the Welsh ancestors were Trojans (of wooden horse fame). As they fled from persecution in Troy under their leader, Brutus, southern Portugal would have been on their route as their boats hugged the coast all the way up to Brittany in France and, eventually, to Britain. Anyone interested in exploring their story further should read the excellent book *The Holy Kingdom* by Adrian Gilbert, Alan Wilson, and Baram Blackett.[21] As my research developed, it became apparent that the Conii and the Celts may well have been one and the same—originating in southwest Iberia and migrating in several directions from there. See Chapter Seventeen and the latest research from the University of Wales.

The so-called Celts who it is thought migrated down from Hallstatt principally occupied the central area of Portugal and Spain, around the Guadiana River but well north of the Algarve.

Apart from the alphabet, other research threw up yet more startling information. I referred earlier to the mining wealth exploited by the Romans; but they were not the first to do so. It may surprise readers to learn that southern Iberia was the largest producer of metals in the Western world during at least the last three millennia B.C. Much copper, as well as silver and gold, was mined in southern Portugal, but the real El Dorado was over the current border in the Spanish Sierra Morena mountain range north of Huelva, a large Spanish port. There, the Rio Tinto mines alone produced slag heaps comprising many millions of tons.[22] Even the Romans were taken aback by the obscene wealth that awaited them there.

Accepted history has it that this metal trade had first been exploited by the Semitic Phoenicians from the eastern Mediterranean, who exchanged it for goods with the locals, then traded it back into the Mediterranean. They were followed by the Carthaginians, the last invaders before the Romans. So important was this trade to them that they imposed an embargo on any ship trying to muscle in by sailing out of the Mediterranean through the Straits of Gibraltar. They enforced this restriction by permanently stationing forty war galleys in the straits. Any passing sea traffic from another nation was unceremoniously rammed and sunk, no questions asked.

The Carthaginians were more ambitious, ruthless, and cruel. They were the heirs to the Phoenicians, formed largely from the remnants of their broken and defeated state. Their ambitions went far beyond mere trade. They wanted to control the entire area and, with it, the metal production. They swept through the territory from Cádiz to Cape St. Vincent, cruelly wasting any cities that opposed them. Surviving nobility fled to the hills, while the hoi polloi were enslaved to work the mines.[23]

Contrary to contributing to my research, their dubious achievements would have hindered it. They destroyed cities, towns, and records.

Before them, the Phoenicians had developed into one of the Old World's greatest-ever maritime nations. They first appeared as a cohesive group toward the end of the second millennium B.C. along the coast of modern Lebanon.

They did not try to conquer, but reached agreements with local inhabitants to allow them to establish trading posts, often at the mouths of rivers such as that at Cádiz, and initially enjoyed a virtual monopoly on the trade with southwest Iberia. Centuries before they arrived, the area was already one of the biggest producers of bronze, an alloy of copper and tin, which was much sought after for making weapons, being considerably harder and more durable and more suitable for warfare.

At one time so much silver was shipped from the area by them that it flooded the Babylon bullion market and caused it to crash.[24]

Some historians think that much earlier, prior to 1500 B.C., long before the Phoenicians and Carthaginians, the Minoans had traded in the area's metal wealth, bronze in particular, and wholesaled it en masse back in the Middle East from their empire based on Crete.

One way or another, this semiforgotten area of southern Iberia exerted massive influence over the rise and fall of city-states, countries, empires, and individuals. This fact is little appreciated and not adequately credited in the "standard" annals of European history.

But during the Phoenician era, there was another mysterious power at work in southwest Iberia: Tartessos. The Tartessians, as the inhabitants were called, crop up in several historic accounts, particularly those by ancient Greeks. But that is all we have: enigmatic references and allusions—no firm facts about how big their territory was, where the capital city was located, or how long their state had existed.

Other accounts refer to a place called Tarshish, but there is even disagreement about whether it was the same territory as Tartessos or was the name of the capital city of Tartessos or whether it was somewhere quite different, located at the other end of the Mediterranean.

It must have been of some importance, as it carries the unique distinction of being the only place outside the Middle East mentioned in the Old Testament—and several times—as follows:

- 1 Kings 10:22: "Ships of Tarshish brought gold, and silver, ivory, and apes, and peacocks."
- 1 Kings 22:48: "Ships of Tarshish to go to Ophir for gold that were broken at Ezion Geber."
- Jonah 1:3: "But Jonah rose up to flee unto Tarshish from the presence of the Lord."
- Isaiah 23:1: "Howl, ye ships of Tarshish for it is laid waste, so there is no house, no entering in."

There is, however, very little hard fact upon which to build any persuasive hypothesis about this mysterious state and its capital.

As these Tartessians were thought to have been the font of much of the metal production, their territory is generally assumed to have been the area around Cádiz, west to Huelva and inland to Seville. This trade, however, was not exclusive to them; there are a few reports of a legendary king who ruled somewhere west of the Straits of Gibraltar at the end of the Phoenician era and during the period when the Carthaginians were beginning to flex their muscles. It must have been considerably west of Cádiz, as it is recorded that he defeated that city in a sea battle when it may have been no more than a city-state, populated largely by remnants of the Phoenicians. It has been suggested that his capital was Huelva, but this is uncomfortably close to Cádiz. His name was King Arganthonius, and he is reported to have had a particular fondness for the Greeks. According to the ancient Greek historian Herodotus, a mariner named Kolaios from the Greek island of Samos was reputed to have been hopelessly blown off course through the Straits of Gibraltar into the Atlantic and, eventually, have made port at Arganthonius's capital. He enjoyed the king's hospitality for a few months before being sent home, loaded to the gunwales with a fortune in silver.[25]

Apparently old Arganthonius, who is said to have lived to be 120 years old, was famous for owning huge amounts of the metal. The reason behind his generosity with Kolaios was an attempt to entice footloose Greeks to settle in his kingdom. Wisely, he saw the Carthaginians as the rising power and their greed as a serious threat, and he probably wanted men and allies to bolster his defenses. It proved a well-founded fear: some time after his death, his kingdom was overrun by the Carthaginians. How he died and the fate of his city are not known. This occurred around the sixth century B.C.

It has been speculated that at the time he may even have been the ruler of Tartessos and that it extended west into the Algarve. Perhaps it overlaid the area of an earlier civilization. Cádiz was almost certainly just a remnant Phoenician city-state sitting in one corner of the kingdom and a thorn in his side competing for the metal trade.

If his kingdom was that extensive, Tartessos would also have embraced the Conii and the Turdetani. The history is confusing and our knowledge imprecise. The latter were reported by the Romans to have inhabited the Spanish Costa de la Luz (Coast of Light) over the Portuguese border with Spain, but it is thought that they were also Tartessians.

It has often been proposed that Seville was Arganthonius's capital; but in that case, that mariner from Samos would have made port first at Cádiz, which is many kilometers downriver on the coast and unavoidable, before reaching Seville. This again indicates that the elusive city was farther west.

Interestingly, the famous Strabo (circa 63 B.C. to circa A.D. 24), known as The Geographer, stated that the Turdetani had written records dating back to 6000 B.C.[26] So they had invented (or inherited) an alphabet and writing. Could the ancient script mentioned earlier be one and the same? That would imply that they were a very old race, certainly ancient enough for memories of them to have been muffled by the mists of time. It would seem that they and the Conii were one and the same. This investigation into the area's past was starting to prove very worthwhile.

Whatever, it is undeniable that great wealth existed in the area—and had done so for a good few thousand years. It would be surprising, with the amount of trade and outside contact that this generated, if it had not inspired a power of some significance.

Facts were becoming increasingly hard to come by, but I persisted in digging ever deeper. There is a superb museum in the Algarve, on Portimão's waterfront, housed in a refurbished sardine-canning factory. The area once dominated that industry throughout Europe, until the shoals of sardines—like tuna—inexplicably migrated farther out to sea. A significant part of the museum is dedicated to an exposition about a large necropolis (burial chamber) and the community that lived around it, built in approximately 3500 B.C., long before the Romans, Phoenicians, and Carthaginians. The necropolis lies about fifteen kilometers northwest of Portimão. Archaeologists have discovered evidence that the inhabitants who lived in the settlement surrounding it were well organized under a hierarchy, with centrally pooled storage facilities for grain and other essential goods. It was active around a thousand years before England's Stonehenge was constructed. The southwestern Algarve is particularly rich in standing stones (*menhirs*) and other relics from this period. They are indistinguishable from others found all the way up Portugal's west coast, around Brittany in northwest France, and in the British Isles. As elsewhere, who exactly the people living near the necropolis were, where they had come from, and exactly how their society was organized and related to others still have historians and archaeologists scratching their heads.

The similarity of these monuments throughout the entire Atlantic seaboard of western Europe indicates that they were all erected by the same culture—or at least by closely related cultures. Their knowledge of astronomy was extraordinary and could only have been gleaned from many previous years spent observing the night sky. Could they have sprung from the remnants of an earlier knowledgeable race that had been largely destroyed in a great disaster?

At some stage, the "Libyans," as they were then called, from the now-Moroccan Atlas mountains, were also present in southwest Iberia and probably merged with the local population.[27] One of their most distinguishing features was the hairstyle of the ruling classes. They wore a lock of hair falling down as a side lock on one side of their head, curling in front of the ear. They also wore one or two large ostrich feathers at an angle from the top of the head. We know this from clear illustrations of them in the Mortuary Temple at Medinet Habu in Egypt, as prisoners of Pharaoh Rameses III. They had invaded and overrun the Mediterranean as part of a loose confederation of other peoples, largely from the eastern Mediterranean (Cyprus, for example). Collectively dubbed "The Sea Peoples," in 1178 B.C. they were decisively defeated by Rameses III in epic battles on land and at sea.[28]

It has been suggested that some members of this confederation were southern Iberians. This has not been proved, but I mention those Libyans here because, a few years ago, a large stone funerary slab was unearthed just over the northern mountains of the Algarve. Circling its perimeter is writing in the ancient alphabet mentioned above; but, uniquely, there is a crude depiction of the deceased in the center. He holds a spear in one hand and a shield in the other—and has a simple representation of the Libyan side lock. It has been dated to the Iron Age, around 600 or 700 B.C., clearly indicating a Libyan presence in southern Portugal at that time. (SEE IMAGE 5 BELOW AND 37 IN THE PHOTO INSERT.)

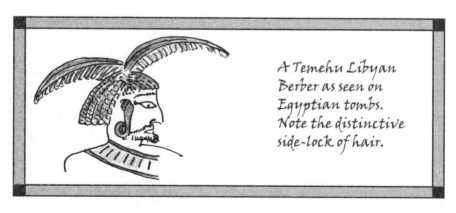

A Temehu Libyan Berber as seen on Egyptian tombs. Note the distinctive side-lock of hair.

(IMAGE 5) *A drawing of a Libyan Temehu chieftain.*

I now felt that I had dug down to the bedrock, that nothing else could be discovered about the Algarve's ancient past; but as my theory also embraced Spain as far as Gibraltar, I was keen to extend my history search there. It seemed logical that any ancient civilization would have included the two regions. The combined coastline is only around 360 kilometers long, and the natural boundaries seem to be from the entrance to the Mediterranean at Gibraltar in the east to Portugal's Cape St. Vincent in the west. The Atlantic seaboard is the bond, coupled with all that wealth from metals.

I had heard of a little-appreciated Spanish fortress town called Niebla about a half-hour's drive over the border into Spain—not far north of Huelva and toward the mountains where those vast quantities of metal were mined. Nothing I had read prepared me for its imposing presence when, turning a final corner, I saw Niebla for the first time. The walls are immense, encompassing no less than fifty towers. It is not on a hill of any great height and cannot be seen from the Huelva-Seville motorway that passes close by. It was built on a bluff overlooking the now-sluggish Rio Tinto, obviously sited there for a specific purpose. (SEE IMAGE 6 IN THE PHOTO INSERT.)

Its importance was revealed thanks to the efforts of an intrepid English archaeologist, Mrs. Elena Wishaw. She spent more than fourteen years, during and after the First World War, suffering great hardships in a small house adjacent to Niebla's mighty walls. Initially she worked in tandem with her equally eminent husband, Bernhard, from Oxford, but he died not long into the project. The couple had already published several classic books on Spanish history. Both of them were fascinated by the awesome grandeur of Niebla and what little was then known of its history. They were determined to uncover what they suspected was a tumultuous past.

Mrs. Wishaw almost achieved sainthood in the eyes of the impoverished townsfolk by discovering and restoring a fresh water supply into the town square, via a very ancient conduit, built many millennia ago to link to a supply in the hills. Before this achievement, the locals had an arduous trip outside the walls, down many steps to a well across the river, to avail themselves of water that, at the best of times, was of inferior quality. The existence of the conduit alone indicated that the town was of great age.[29]

I will return to Elena Wishaw—and Niebla—in later chapters, but I mention both here because it was she who originally drew attention to the amazing volume of metals mined in the region and to the important role Niebla played in that. She arranged for a well-respected mining engineer to examine the slag heaps at the huge Rio Tinto mine; he confirmed that they represented many thousands of years of toil. Significantly, he was emphatic that the oldest slag, at the bottom of the heaps, showed clear evidence that its extraction process was the most sophisticated of all. Amazingly, those very early miners were extracting gold at levels of only half an ounce per ton. The sophistication and efficiency of the process slowly deteriorated with time. It may seem extraordinary, but this was a clear indication that the people who worked these mines originally, many thousands of years ago, were far more advanced than those who worked them later. Clearly, their civilization had declined for whatever reasons, and their knowledge dissipated with it.

Elena Wishaw had written all this up and published it in a book in 1928. In it, she makes a compelling case for Niebla existing as a collection point and inland port for the onward transportation of ore, possibly as far back as 10,000 or even 15,000 B.C. The book was originally titled *Atlantis in Andalucía* but has recently been reprinted as *Atlantis in Spain*.[30] After twenty years painstakingly sifting evidence, she was convinced that the area around Niebla had been part of Atlantis. That really kicked in with me. The thoughts I had been harboring about Atlantis received new impetus and urgency. I had already determined to reexamine Plato's original accounts in detail, since they are the only records we have of the fabled lost kingdom. Now that intention became my priority.

This whirlwind trawl through local history had revealed sufficient fascinating facts and a good many hints to justify my thinking the area certainly had a hidden, forgotten past. It was clear that I now had to sharpen the focus of my quest. I needed to start examining Plato's detailed pointers to the exact position of Atlantis.

That meant confronting the most awkward clues first, which coincidentally were also the most important and had already been the subject of much debate and argument in recent years.

Was Atlantis inside or outside the Mediterranean?

Was it really a huge island?

CHAPTER SEVEN

Inside or Outside
the Mediterranean?

This was the first and most important question. If the answer went against me, then all my theories about Atlantis being in the Algarve and neighboring Spain were wrong. I would have to give up my quest—or pursue a new quest elsewhere. For two thousand years, it has been generally assumed that Plato was referring to a region outside the Mediterranean, in the Atlantic—and the weight of evidence has always supported that supposition—but recent proponents of the Greek island of Santorini have sought alternative interpretations to back up their theory. Their quest has failed to reveal any fresh facts to substantiate their case. Plato actually wrote the following:

"... and there was an island situated in front of the straits ... which by you are called the Pillars of Hercules" (clues 4 and 5).

To support the Santorini theory—and others—for Atlantis to have existed in various parts of the Mediterranean or Aegean Seas, it was suggested that the ancient Greeks referred to several different locations as "The Pillars of Hercules." The Straits of Gibraltar, at the entrance to the Mediterranean, was but one of them, and Solon was confused about which location the Egyptian priest was referring to. I have already laid out comprehensive arguments against this in Chapter Three. Analysis of the other clues bequeathed to us by Plato clarifies beyond doubt that he was referring to the Straits of Gibraltar. (SEE IMAGE 7 IN THE PHOTO INSERT AND 8 BELOW)

(IMAGE 8) *Southwest Iberia and the Straits of Gibraltar.*

In *Timaeus*, when talking about the invasion by the Atlanteans that was repulsed by the brave Hellenes, Plato wrote:

"This power came forth out of the Atlantic Ocean" (clue 2).

Unambiguous. Specific.

He also mentions a true sea (the Atlantic), that the Mediterranean was but "a little harbor" in comparison, and that there were islands in this sea, enabling the seafaring Atlanteans to "island-hop" to a vast continent on the other side. There is little doubt that the vast continent was America; it could be no other (clues 7, 8, and 9).

It was an astonishing statement for that era, suggesting that the Atlantis inhabitants knew the New World well, voyaged to it, and most likely had colonies there. Greeks of Plato's era, as far as historic records show, were certainly not aware of the existence of America, so this incredible comment—unique in its time—lends credence to the rest of the philosopher's accounts. He was not making it up, as others have suggested.

Andrew Collins, in *Gateway to Atlantis,* sets out to prove that the Phoenicians, from their Iberian port bases *outside* the Mediterranean—Cádiz, for example—had regular contact with America via the Atlantic islands, Cuba in particular.[31] His case is built around various archaeological finds and innumerable myths and legends, but little if anything from the Phoenicians themselves. As is usual with Collins, he has carried out exhaustive research. He cites odd items discovered in the New World, including Phoenician coins, amphorae, and stone carvings of heads with beards (indigenous South Americans cannot grow so much facial hair) and features that appear more Semitic than South American. These had already been brought to general attention by other authors but do back up the theory that contact had taken place. It was thought, however, that there was no evidence that this was part of any regular trade pattern by the Phoenicians or, later, the Carthaginians. It has been assumed more likely to have been the odd merchant or adventurer blown off course. Crucially, evidence has recently come to light showing that some of them probably made it back to Europe. Traces of tobacco and cocaine were found in recently examined Egyptian mummies, spawning a television documentary, *The Cocaine Mummies.* With the exception of a different wild strain of African tobacco, both were only available from South America.

This puzzling discovery could be explained if Collins is correct and the Phoenicians had known of America and the Atlantic islands, especially the western ones like Cuba and Hispaniola; but it would have been against their policy and instincts to divulge the knowledge to any other race—and the Greeks were the last people they would have gossiped to. Plato would certainly not have discovered anything from them. The Phoenicians were renowned for keeping maritime information secret in order to benefit from it, at the same time spreading the most outrageous and fearsome stories about what lay beyond Cape St. Vincent, at the southwesterly end of the Algarve. Anyone who passed on cartographic information to another race did so at the risk of death. Later, the Carthaginians were equally ruthless in this respect. Plato's knowledge could only have come from an alternative source with earlier privileged access to it—and that was almost certainly the Egyptians.

But the most crucial clue indicating the Straits of Gibraltar is the one referring to "Gades." Plato says, without any scope for misinterpretation, that the extremity of Atlantis reached as far as, or close to, Gades (clue 34). He did not specifically say it was the eastern extremity, but it is obvious that that is what he meant. If Atlantis was in the Atlantic, it had to be the eastern end. Historians unanimously agree that Gades is today's Cádiz, the large Spanish city sitting at the mouth of the Guadalete River, not far outside the Straits of Gibraltar. It is Plato's marker beacon for Atlantis and "black box" combined.

It has been flashing away in his narrative for more than two thousand years, directing us straight to the site with all the other critical identifying clues stored in his writings.

In Plato's time, the city's position would appear to have been farther south to southwest, as the sea has steadily encroached over the intervening centuries and there is the distinct possibility of land subsidence. Some years ago, archaeologists confirmed this when they discovered other submerged remains just out to sea. Inevitably, familiar cries of "the Atlantis citadel" were heard, but they could hardly be relevant when Plato said the capital was in the center of the kingdom, not in the extreme easterly corner.

When referring to his sons, Plato's clues 32 and 33 read:

"the eldest who was the first king he named Atlas . . . and after him the whole island (Atlantis) and the ocean were called Atlantic."

He was clearly referring to the sea around Atlantis. It is final proof, if any is needed, as it would hardly have been relevant if the kingdom was in the eastern Mediterranean.

To summarize:

- It is irrefutable. If what Plato said is analyzed, he was unambiguously referring to the area starting immediately outside the Straits of Gibraltar—in other words, the Atlantic.
- There was no evidence in his account to support any other location—and this is the only account we have. Those putting forward theories regarding other areas referred to by the Greeks as "Pillars of Hercules" completely ignore some of the other clues he and the Egyptian priest gave.
- The suitability of all of the other sites put forward over the years, such as the North Sea, southwest of Ireland and England, Antarctica, Santorini, Anatolia, or off Cyprus in the Mediterranean—even various sites in the Far East—is a fiction that Plato had no hand in.

After I had finished drafting this chapter, along with the rest of the book, I discovered a superb web site about Atlantis run by American R. Cedric Leonard.[32] I was astonished; it mirrored much of my research, even including that mysterious alphabet. The site is by far the best and most comprehensive source of background information I have found, although he doesn't agree with my conclusion about the actual Atlantis site. Had he been living in the Algarve rather than operating from America, he probably would have. I said the site mirrored my own research but that is really an understatement. Cedric's site is far more detailed and scholarly, apart from a few areas where I have the advantage of local knowledge. He has delved exhaustively into every possible area and one section, headed "Pre-Platonic Writings Pertinent to Atlantis," provides further evidence that Atlantis was definitely in the Atlantic. Cedric has scoured manuscripts from many ancient writers to find several references to Atlantis that predate Plato. Many refer to the Atlantic Ocean or the Western Sea. One example is from the famous Greek Herodotus, known as "the father of history." Cedric gives his own translation from a portion of Herodotus's *Clio*, thought to date from around 450 B.C. It refers to the ocean in which Atlantis sank.

". . . but the sea navigated by all the Greeks and the one outside the Pillars called the Atlantis sea and Erythraean are called one and the same."

The Greeks knew of an island in the far west known as Erythraea, the name deriving from the color of the setting sun. The quote is crucial, as it not only refers to Atlantis itself but clearly positions it outside the Mediterranean.

Among other examples, Cedric draws attention to something noted in 1946 by the Cambridge scholar and explorer Harold T. Wilkins.[33] On column 8 of the great hall of the temple of Rameses at Karnak in Egypt was displayed a text referring to "the loss of a drowned continent in the Western Ocean." The Egyptians identified the Western Ocean with the Atlantic.

My developing theory that Plato was referring to a now-sunken portion of southwest Iberia was massively reinforced. There was, though, still one substantial question mark. Plato referred specifically to an island, and a huge one at that.

Or did he?

CHAPTER EIGHT

Was Atlantis a Huge Island?

ollywood blockbusters and common knowledge all hold that Atlantis was a mystical, mythical island. Dozens of historians have taken the same view. But what if everyone was wrong? I had to forensically re-examine exactly what Plato wrote.

According to the translation from his Dialogues, there was an island in front of the straits, and it was huge: larger than Libya and Asia combined. This island had rule over a great empire that included other islands in the open sea and parts of the continent on the other side of the ocean. It also held sway inside the straits as far as Egypt and Tyrrhenia. It disappeared under the sea in a day and night, after a period of violent earthquakes and floods (clues 4–8 and 15).

Ever since I had considered including Atlantis in my hypothesis, this island business had niggled away at the back of my mind. So far, I had unearthed no evidence to prove that a large island starting immediately outside the Straits of Gibraltar had ever existed, although there had once been a scattering of small islands. Indeed, if this large island was anything like the size Plato appeared to indicate, it would hardly have fit in between Portugal and America—and certainly not between southwest Iberia and the north coast of Africa. Many researchers had come to the conclusion that either Solon or Plato was simply confused about the size. With so many other clues pointing to southwest Iberia—the one about Cádiz, for example—it is not surprising that so many people have been baffled.

I discovered that the English translations had not been made from the original, and some were from translations already made into Latin. Could there have been errors? I soon ascertained that in recent years, scholars had indeed begun to question the standard English text—on several important points.

The key to answering the island conundrum revolves around the original Greek word used by Plato to describe what Atlantis was.

That word was *nesos*.

The first English translation assumed *nesos* meant "island." In recent decades, it has been pointed out that, at the time Plato used it, *nesos* had three alternative interpretations. The standard reference work for ancient Greek, *The Greek Lexicon* by Liddell and Scott, for example, gives three distinctly different meanings:

> One was "island"; another, "the mouth of a river with mud shoals." Critically, the third meaning was "peninsula."[34]

There does not seem to be any reason why "island" was the preferred initial translation, but all subsequent translators have followed suit—despite other specific facts given by Plato that do not justify its use.

For instance, he only ever mentioned one coast—the south. In clue 23 he explains there was a vast productive plain facing the sea and expands on that in clues 84 to 88, intimating that it faced south with a high coast overlooking the sea. It was sheltered to the north by mountains "celebrated for their number, size and beauty." Significantly, no reference was made to the north, east, or west coasts. If an island was being described, surely these would have warranted at least a passing mention? Look at clue 84 again: "The whole country was said by him to be very lofty and precipitous on the side of the sea." Note that it refers to the whole country and the "side" facing the sea. An island has *all* sides facing the sea, not just one of them.

Clue 4 includes another subtle misinterpretation. In ancient Greek, Plato did not write "an island situated in front of the straits," as in the accepted translation by Benjamin Jowett, but "because there was an island/peninsula in the mouth or lobby of the Gulf, that you consider the columns of Hercules."[35] The clear implication is that the Straits of Gibraltar formed the throat, and the area outside the Atlantic where the sea broadened out was the mouth (that is, the area outside the straits that was still confined on the north by the southern coast of Iberia and on the south by the North African coast). A lobby is clearly the area of sea you pass through before entry through the straits of Gibraltar into the Mediterranean.

In clue 35, Plato wrote that the Atlanteans were also the inhabitants and rulers of diverse islands *in the open sea*, clearly somewhere different from where the homeland was. He would appear here to be referring to the Atlantic Ocean beyond any such land as Portugal, Spain, and Morocco, consequently reinforcing the descriptions of Atlantis being in the mouth of the Gulf before the Straits of Gibraltar, therefore not in the open sea.

Previously, a popular assumption has been that Atlantis was situated way out in the Atlantic; but the middle of that vast ocean can hardly be described as being "in the gulf outside the Straits of Gibraltar." If so, it could equally well be claimed, for example, that New York is too; a ludicrous theory—even the original translation of it, to be "in front of," implies proximity.

It now appeared that the original translation of *nesos* as "island" was what had bedeviled, impeded, and misdirected the centuries-long search for Atlantis. Until recently, everyone had taken that description for granted and looked for a large sunken island, big enough to have been a continent; yet it is apparent that Plato may not have wished to convey that meaning at all.

Others have noted that the ancient Greeks even used *nesos* to describe the *Peloponnese* Peninsula. In fact, that very name is a combination of two words. The first, *Pelopos*, is the ancient name of a Greek mythological hero who supposedly conquered the whole region. The other is *nesos*, giving the original Greek spelling "Peloponnesos."[36] Although technically now an island, since the construction of the Corinth canal, it was a peninsula connected to mainland Greece by a nine-kilometer-wide strip of land when it was named. This confirms that the Greeks tended to lump islands and peninsulas together under the same word.

Reginald Fessenden, once head chemist to Thomas Edison and a professor at the University of Pittsburgh, had papers published by the Massachusetts Bible Society in 1924 and 1927.[37] He had made an intense study of the Egyptian *Book of the Dead*. The papers were titled "The deluged civilization of the Caucasus Isthmus." In order to complete the works, he closely studied ancient terminology, including Greek. He categorically stated that *nesos* was never regarded by the early Greeks to mean solely "island." Instead, it was often a more encompassing term meaning "land." He quotes such examples as "Nesos Arabia" and "Nesos Mesopotamia."

In the light of the other clues Plato gave, the inescapable conclusion is that he meant the area of land immediately outside the straits, the Iberian Peninsula.

He was probably referring only to the southern part of Iberia, west of Gibraltar, which would have been familiar to visiting mariners from the Mediterranean. The northern area had been affected by the Ice Age, and the chances of any significant civilizations developing over a long period of time in those conditions would have been remote. Nor would that region have fit the clues Plato provided regarding climate, crops, flora, and fauna. This also partly explains why he fails to mention other coasts, or anything beyond the mountains. In time, however, the civilization would almost certainly have stretched up the west coast, at least as far as Lisbon.

The continuous southern coasts of Andalucía and Portugal's Algarve curve around, protruding southwest into the Atlantic at Cape St. Vincent as a peninsula in its own right. If this was the area Plato was referring to, it must mean that the major civilized area, principally the great southern plain he mentioned, was the part that sank 11,600 years ago. Before this disaster, the peninsula would have protruded much more, with more dry land also right up to and around the mouth of the Straits of Gibraltar.

But I do not think the solution is that simple. As already discussed, the seabed map for the area off the Algarve coast shows several large, very flat areas that are separated by sudden drops in levels and are called *planalto* (plains). In the sea off the western end of the Algarve, 210 kilometers southwest of Cape St. Vincent, is the area known as the Gorringe Bank (or Ridge). It is a substantial area, 60 kilometers by 180 kilometers, and is much shallower than the surrounding seabed, parts of it only 30 meters deep. There are other similar areas to the west and south before the Canary Islands, some of which could have been above sea level before the great glacier melt—as would parts of the Gorringe Bank.

At some time in the past, all these could possibly have been linked as one or several landmasses above water. Maybe they even connected to Cape St. Vincent; but in this case, some areas would have to have sunk considerably, as the sea plumbs great depths in parts. Geologists are now beginning to accept that sudden movements up or down, of thousands of feet, have taken place in various parts of the world (see Chapter Fifteen). The area around the submerged Gorringe Bank is a highly volatile seismic region. This is where the 1755 earthquake originated and, combined with others, caused the dramatic sinking of parts of the seabed, with some parts thrust upward.[38]

The possibility cannot be discounted that there was once also a long island, or what could have been mistaken for one, off part of the Algarve and Andalucía, which housed the great Atlantis plain. In front of the Algarve, particularly, and stretching east in front of the Costa de la Luz as far as Huelva, there are many narrow tidal lagoons from 100 meters to around 400 meters wide, fronted by long strands of sand bearing some fauna. A few of these strands are connected to the mainland by narrow isthmuses, particularly at river mouths. The central Algarve, from the capital, Faro, for 30 kilometers or so east, also has substantial offshore sandbank islands farther out to sea beyond the lagoons.

Some of these islands have shanty settlements inhabited by hardy fishermen, with the occasional café and bar to welcome the hordes of sun-worshipping tourists who are ferried across to the pristine sands in the summer months to enjoy their calming, away-from-it-all atmosphere. The sea in front of Faro is also a cobweb of mud shoals and narrow, treacherous channels, as anyone flying into Faro airport can see as the plane circles before making its final approach.

These islands and sandspits may well have been much larger and more prevalent in 500 or 600 B.C., when Greek mariners started venturing that far, during the period between the demise of the Phoenicians and the rise of the Carthaginians. There are several historical accounts by Portuguese and Spanish authors stating that there were once more islands than there are now.

The area has been seriously affected by large earthquakes and tsunamis since Plato's era, which must have resulted in significant changes to the coastline and islands in the immediate coastal waters.

It is also credible that other areas of the western end of the Algarve coast, in the few places where there are sand dunes rather than cliffs, once had similar lagoons or straits. One example runs west from Galé to Armação de Pêra. An inland lagoon still exists, and part of the eastern end of Armação de Pêra is built on land below the level of the beach, which was reclaimed at some stage. Another runs from Alvor west to Lagos. Part of this has several pure links-style golf holes on it and is within the Palmares golf course. Any of these low-lying islands and spits would have been devastated by the 1755 tsunami, let alone all the earlier ones. Their size and shape would have been significantly altered. Layers of the sandy topsoil would have been successively ripped off.

The visiting Greek sailors may only have been afforded glimpses during their brief stay—not daring to journey into the straits between these islands and the coast—and brought back tales, which Plato picked up and wove into his story. If the islands and sandspits were much larger then, they may also have supported considerable habitation. The mariners could have been told by the locals that they were the remnants of a much larger combined area.

Dr. Ulf Richter has perceptively pointed out that Plato never used the words "high cliffs," although the general assumption has been that this is what he meant.[39] Clue 84 reads: "very lofty and precipitous on the side of the sea." Dr. Richter suggests that the coast could just as easily have been composed of high dunes. These can be formed by persistent westerly winds at a slight angle to the shore. The southwest Iberian coastline is perfectly situated for that, with a prevailing southwesterly wind almost every day.

Dunes, such as those near Arcachon on the west coast of France, can reach more than a hundred meters in height. The area behind this huge dune wall is normally lower and features a series of lagoons. Seen from the sea, the dunes would give the impression that the coast rises sheer from the sea. Perhaps the existing offshore Algarve islands and lagoons are remnants of such a phenomenon, and the original coastline involved a combination of high dunes and cliffs. (SEE IMAGES 9, 10, AND 11 IN THE PHOTO INSERT.)

While mulling this over, I was agreeably surprised to discover yet another error in the translation of Plato's original account. It made the hairs rise on the back of my neck, as it substantially supported my hypothesis.

It is in the section of Plato's account where the sea is described as being navigable before Atlantis had sunk, but not after (clue 3). The accepted translation reads: "The Atlantic was navigable" (referring to before the sinking). This has been disputed. The critical word here is *pelagos,* which Plato specifically used to denote the actual area of the sea, past Gibraltar, where Atlantis sank.

Pelagos means, literally, "A strait of low bottoms and islands" ("archipelago" is derived from it).[40] It was also used at that time to refer to "salt marshes and lagoons." Plato's Dialogue should have been translated as "then the strait was passable (or navigable)." I must reiterate that he is not referring here to the Straits of Gibraltar, but to an area starting outside.

This lends significant support to other facts indicating that Plato was referring to the area immediately in front of the Andalucía and Algarve coasts as the area that sank. Even today, "straits" would exactly describe the channel or channels between the many existing offshore islands, sandbanks, and the mainland and is accurately depicted by the precise meaning of *pelagos.* That the strait was originally passable implies that it separated two pieces of land.

It is not unusual for a narrow strip of water to separate an island from the mainland. I am fortunate to have once lived in a house perched on a large rock outcropping overlooking the beautiful Menai Straits that separate the Island of Anglesey from mainland Wales, in Great Britain. These straits vary in width but are never very wide, being only a hundred meters or so across at their narrowest. Anglesey is indisputably an island, and a similar situation could have existed in southwest Iberia.

There are other references by classical writers to the area of the sea being blocked by mud shoals in the vicinity of the southwest Iberian coast:

- The geographer Scylax described in his *Periplus:* "the ocean beyond the Pillars of Hercules is not navigable because of shoals of mud. . ."[41]
- The Phoenician administrator Himilco mentioned having to avoid them during his voyage around Iberia to Britain. This is significant,

as he was reported to be sailing specifically "around Iberia." In other words, he would, as usual, have been keeping close to the coast, and therefore clearly encountered the obstacles not far offshore.[42]

- The Roman author and administrator Pliny the Younger referred to sandbanks immediately outside the Pillars of Hercules.[43]
- Plutarch also described the ocean just outside the Pillars of Hercules as "difficult of passage and muddy."[44]

These reports are far more recent than 9,600 B.C. and most likely indicate that the whole area did not sink completely at the same time. We know earthquakes of sufficient immensity to cause serious subsidence were repeated every few thousand years or so after 9,600 B.C. and could have accounted for recurring problems.

All these accounts of mud and impediments in the area also confirm that Plato was referring to this region rather than the volcanic ash around Santorini.

Further hard evidence tying in with the use of the word *pelagos* is provided in the area immediately to the north of Cádiz, starting at Puerto Real and El Puerto de Santa María, which initially consists of waterways before giving way to marshy land. An old Roman map shows a large lagoon there, penetrating deep inland. The famous protected Doñana nature reserve, northwest toward Huelva—now one of the few refuges for the almost extinct Iberian lynx—was also once underwater.

As mentioned earlier, it is also accepted that there was once a smattering of small, low-lying islands immediately outside the Straits of Gibraltar, all of which are now submerged. Spartel Island, the best known, has been explored for evidence that it was Atlantis by the team that discovered the *Titanic*. In such a critical position, commanding sea traffic in and out of the Mediterranean, it would inevitably have been part of the Atlantis Empire, but in no way could it have qualified as Atlantis per se. If, however, this and other islands close by sank or were inundated with the rest of Atlantis, they could well have formed very low-lying blockages or shoals of mud and precisely fit with Plato's use of the word *pelagos*.

In those days, mariners would not have sailed or rowed straight out into the open sea, quickly losing sight of land. They would invariably have kept a coast in view. Spartel Island and the rest of the cluster of little islands (or their sunken remains) would also have forced navigators up the Iberian coast or south along the African one. If they were under sail, the prevailing southwesterly winds would have made the African coast a hazardous option. It would have been far easier to tack up the Iberian one. But the submerged plain extends right up to the entrance to the Mediterranean; so if it initially just sank a little below the surface, anyone trying to sail northwest up to Cádiz would have encountered mud. Land on the north coast of Morocco would also have sunk or been inundated at the same time as Atlantis disappeared, and that would have caused mud and sediment problems.

So, if the main plain described by Plato was the part that sank and now forms the seabed south of the Algarve and southwest of Andalucía, perhaps it was originally largely separated from the coast by a narrow strip of water, a strait, and the current islands and sandbars are the remnants of what would have been its north coast. Another possibility is that this narrow strait could have only extended partway west in front of the Iberian coast, as far as a great river such as the Arade, which it then joined to wend back out to sea. The result would have been a low-lying island that stretched back to Cádiz and Gibraltar, but which could have had high dunes on its south coast. Judging by Plato's account, mentioning a swath of protective mountains immediately to the north of the plain, he was referring to the whole area (that is, the submerged part together with the remaining Algarve and Costa de la Luz), whether or not part of it was technically an island by virtue of a narrow strip of water. The mountains are still there today, starting from around three to thirty kilometers inland in the Algarve but farther inland as you travel east into Spain. Plato indicates that they survived by stating that they are not now as numerous or as large as they were, presumably as a result of the original upheaval that destroyed Atlantis with earthquakes, erosion, and subsidence. Clue 89 reads: "The surrounding mountains were celebrated for their number and size and beauty, far beyond any which still exist. . . ." (SEE IMAGES 12A, 12B, 12C, 12D, AND 13 IN THE PHOTO INSERT.)

If, as others have suggested, Plato was referring here to a comparison of the original Atlantis mountains to any existing in the whole of the then-known world, then the Atlantis mountains would presumably have disappeared together with the rest of the land. That would have meant subsiding the enormous amount of more than ten thousand feet, as the Greeks were aware of mountains elsewhere of that proportion. There are none on the region's existing seabed until well out into the Atlantic and the Gorringe Bank, and even then they are nowhere near as deep.

Judging by Plato's description of the huge area of mud and low bottoms where the land sank, it did not subside to any great depth. This would presumably have applied equally to the mountains, leaving them still visible—evidence again that Plato was not referring to just a large island, as the mountains are on the mainland.

The mysterious land of "Tartessos" is discussed in several parts of this book. It is broadly accepted that this was somewhere in southwest Iberia, but there is no historical account pinpointing it exactly. In Chapter Sixteen, the hypothesis is put forward that it was the whole region from Gibraltar to Cape St. Vincent and therefore mirrored the remnants of Atlantis. Reginald Fessenden pointed out that at some stage in ancient Greek, *Ta* also roughly translated as "the land of." Combine that with *nesos* to give *Tanesos*, which could credibly have evolved into *Tartessos*. The meaning would then have been "the land of the islands/peninsulas," which also accords well with Plato's use of the word *pelagos* to describe that area.

To add to the confusion and uncertainty, there is one other intriguing possibility thrown up by the famous ancient "Piri Reis" map. Controversy rages over claims made by Charles Hapgood who, together with his students, made a prolonged and exhaustive study of it. Turkish admiral Piri Reis, the man who made it, indicated that he used parts of several other much-older maps to make a complete chart of the Western Hemisphere, including Europe and the Americas. Hapgood pointed out that the coast of South America is shown in reasonably accurate detail, apart from an area where two of the source maps for South America overlapped. Amazingly, Antarctica's ice-bound coast is also shown, plus inland mountain ranges now indistinguishable, buried beneath thick ice.[45] Hapgood claims that the mountains shown on the map have been proven to be more or less accurately placed by a survey conducted by a U.S. Navy exploratory team, thus indicating that the original source map was drawn many thousands of years ago when the ranges were last ice-free. This has frequently been cited as an argument for a lost civilization which had the ability to sail the oceans and produce maritime charts. The professor has a letter from the leader of the team to prove the existence of the mountains and that they concord with the map. This could possibly place the original map *before* Plato's date for the sinking of Atlantis, yet it shows no large island off Portugal, in the region of the Canary Islands or the Azores.

It does appear to show Cape St. Vincent extending farther out into the sea, but the map's scale is too small to assess whether the southern Iberian coast is also farther south. It must be remembered that Piri Reis produced it from an amalgam of maps. He was trying to produce a map of the world as it was then and did not know that the ancient source maps he used for Antarctica were rendered out of date by a layer of ice that was many thousands of years old and miles deep. He could, however, have used more recent maps of Europe, including Iberia, drawn by his contemporaries. The map does, though, show two very wide rivers on the Iberian Peninsula. One of these is the Tagus, which flows east to west and out to sea past Lisbon, Portugal's capital. The other is the Guadalquivir, flowing north to south into the sea by Cádiz. On the Piri Reis map, they are shown to meet up in midwestern Spain at a series of lakes, effectively making all the land to the south and west of them an island, completely surrounded by water.

That it could have been considered as such is not so far-fetched. Today, for instance, just over the border from the Algarve, in Spain at the mouth of another large river, the Guadiana, is an area called Isla Canela. It now boasts golf courses and a marina, as well as kilometers of beaches backed by drifted dunes. *Isla* means "island" in Spanish, and Isla Canela effectively is one, by virtue of a waterway that cuts across it from its west coast and winds south to join the sea again.

Yet one further translation correction is critical, as the original error has led to the search being for an island of huge proportions, thus narrowing the choice of potential sites. The English translation reads: "the island was larger than Libya and Asia put together" (clue 6). Even allowing for the fact that, in Plato's day, the regions referred to as Libya and Asia meant areas somewhat different from the ones we recognize today, it still meant a mighty chunk of land, almost too large to fit in any ocean. For an island, or land, of that vast size to have sunk completely in only twenty-four hours is just not credible.

It is like America disappearing. Imagine boarding a flight headed there and when you arrive there's nothing—just sea. It would have been a catastrophe that would have had unthinkable effects on the rest of the planet.

Yet the translation into Latin by Chalcidius, one of Plato's students at his academy who, it must be assumed, was more competent in ancient Greek than any modern-day professor translating from later question-able versions of Plato's Greek manuscripts, reads: "a peninsula/island, at the same time, of Libya and of Asia, the greater (or hugest) one."[46] In other words, he appears to be intimating that the peninsula/island was "larger than any that existed" *in Libya and Asia at that time.* With that more logical complexion, the Iberian Peninsula accords well with that description.

Other researchers have pointed out that in using the word *meson,* which translates as "greater," Plato may have meant "of much greater importance *as a power,*" not in size. The word was often used in that context.

Another very plausible theory has been put forward by researcher Georgeos Diaz-Montexano. He translated fragments of the oldest samples of Plato's works he could find in universities and European libraries. He came to the conclusion that Plato meant that Atlantis was an island/peninsula outside the Straits of Gibraltar, that was bigger than Asia and almost joined to Libya (Morocco).[47] Like others, Georgeos pointed out that to the Greeks, "Asia" only referred to Anatolia (Turkey, approximately, also known as Asia Minor), which was not a very large area. If Atlantis was southwest of Iberia and it ruled other islands and lands, northern Morocco would inevitably have been included. It is apparent that large areas of its coast were also inundated and sank, forming part of today's seabed. Before the disaster, the straits would have been longer and the two shores even closer together, making a hop across to Morocco a routine event.

Let's pull the evidence together and summarize the conclusions.

- It indicates that Plato was referring not to an island on its own but, more likely, to a peninsula, possibly with a large flat area to the south being separated—or partially separated—by a narrow strip of water, making only that area an island.

- The Iberian Peninsula, embodying the southern Costa de la Luz, part of Spanish Andalucía, and the whole of Portugal's Algarve, starts immediately outside the Straits of Gibraltar in precisely the right position. Stretching south from its coast are large submerged plains.

- Apart from the probable mistranslation of *nesos*, Plato clearly stated that the country had only one side facing the sea.

- Plato's description of "straits" in front of this coast, where navigation was difficult due to many islands, mudbanks, shallow (tidal) waters, marshy areas, and lagoons, even today perfectly matches the area from Cádiz in Spain to beyond Faro in the Algarve. More than two thousand years have passed since he wrote his Dialogues, with the inevitable geographical changes caused by momentous earthquakes and tsunamis. Today the straits between the offshore islands and the coast are navigable, aided by well-marked charts; but because of the shallowness of the water and the strong Atlantic tides, there's a risk of running aground when venturing into the inner lagoons and the sea around Faro.

- This area could be the result of the southern part of Atlantis sinking, leaving a few remnants in the sea off the coast or the remains of the northern extremity of a long, flat offshore island that had originally only been separated—or partially separated—from the mainland by a narrow strait.

- Most of the western half of the Algarve shoreline is different from the east but exactly matches Plato's description of the original dramatic Atlantis coast, with high cliffs.

- Plato was not referring to a huge island bigger than Libya and Asia combined, but a peninsula that was bigger than any existing at that time in what he understood as "Libya" and "Asia," two of the largest other landmasses known to him that he could cite in comparison.

- He also indicated that the swath of mountains to the north of the Atlantis plain still existed, although they were not as impressive as they had been before the great calamity. This is contradictory if he was referring to them being on an island that had sunk. The mountains do still exist, but on the mainland peninsula, not on the remnants of an island.

There is another solution that is perhaps the simplest and most telling of all. Several experts have suggested it was the Egyptian vocabulary that was at the root of the confusion.

Jonas Bergman, for example, firmly believes that the original Egyptian word for "island" also meant "lowland" or "coastland."[48] If this was the case, then one can easily see how confusion could have crept into the information given to Solon and his translation into Greek. It must be considered doubtful whether the priest knew the precise intended meaning of the inscription on the temple columns. He had not been there when it was put there nine thousand years earlier. It is far more likely that he was only able to pass on the geographical position of the sunken civilization.

This view is supported by Eberhard Zangger. He maintains that the ancient Egyptians did not have a specific character for "island." The hieroglyphic used was the same as for "sandy beach" or "coast," and it was also used for "foreign countries."[49]

Perhaps, therefore, Plato only knew the supposed position of Atlantis but, not being familiar with the area himself and only having a few tales from mariners to go on (which could have confused him), he was uncertain as to whether it was partly an island or islands, an island by virtue of being cut off by rivers, or simply the citadel on an island, or the whole southern flank of the Iberian peninsula—or a combination of them all. He was struggling to describe it and hedged his bets with *nesos,* which could ambiguously and conveniently have meant the whole lot.

Nevertheless, they all amounted to different descriptions of the same area, and I thought I had uncovered enough evidence to prove that Plato was not talking of a gigantic island, but this southern part of Iberia immediately outside the Mediterranean.

Progress was solid, ample justification to closely compare all of his other clues with southwest Iberia to see if they supported my case, starting with its fabled wealth.

CHAPTER NINE

Follow the Money

Plato was emphatic: Atlantis was the wealthiest civilization ever.

Clue 38 reads: ". . . and they had such an amount of wealth as was never possessed by kings and potentates, and is not likely ever to be again."

This means it had to control a vast amount of natural resources. I already knew that my target area, from Gibraltar to the southwest tip of the Algarve, had been prized by everyone from the Phoenicians to the Romans. It had been the largest producer of precious metals in the known world for many thousands of years before Plato's era. Mind-boggling amounts of gold, silver, and copper ore had been mined and processed there to produce millions and millions of tons of slag. Were Plato's comments and these facts mere coincidence? Or did they compellingly lead to one conclusion: that they related to one and the same place?

In Chapter Three, I briefly discussed the work and findings of that remarkable lady Elena Wishaw. As a result of her painstaking explorations over two decades, she was convinced that Niebla had existed as a fortified inland port to facilitate this metal trade for between ten and fifteen thousand years. That puts it in the timespan given for the Atlantis Empire, which Plato stated had been destroyed nine thousand years before Solon was given the information by the priest.

Adding the last two thousand years A.D. makes it around 11,600 years ago.

The old priest's assertion that civilization had existed that long ago is corroborated by the Greek historian Herodotus (c. 484 B.C.–c. 425 B.C.), who wrote of a long, unbroken line of Egyptian kings and priests. He was shown 341 wooden statues in the great hall of a temple as proof of the immense age of the Egyptian nation.[50] Each statue represented a generation's king and high priest in continuous lineage. Calculating on the premise of three generations spanning 100 years, they represented a total of 11,366 years. Alternatively, allowing for shorter life spans of three generations every 80 years, the total would be 9,092 years.

It is a well-known fact that the Egyptians recorded that the first of their "god kings" came to Egypt after first having ruled in a western land.[51]

Intriguingly, the Egyptians also said that the sun had changed its usual position several times within this period, twice setting where it normally rose and twice rising where it normally set. Legends from other parts of the world—South America and Scandinavia, for example—also refer to this phenomenon. The events that could have caused it and the effect on all life on earth hardly bear thinking about. If, for some awful reason, the earth's rotation had suddenly stopped, what would have happened to the oceans? Would they have kept moving in a giant wave around and over the world?

Returning to Mrs. Wishaw's conclusions in southern Iberia, these were not mere intuition: they were based on hard evidence. Early in her explorations, she had been befriended by a local man, the owner of the area's quarry, who showed great interest in her work. He took her around the quarry, which he was convinced was just as old as she had concluded that Niebla had been. She was fascinated by his knowledge of the different quarrying techniques. He demonstrated the current methods, then explained how the process had been carried out in different eras: by the Romans, by the Carthaginians, and during the Neolithic, Stone Age, and Paleolithic periods.

This information proved invaluable. Whenever she unearthed old stone walls—or even the odd separated quarried stone—she could now establish the period when it had been hewn.

One example was the *desembarcadero*. From her earliest time at Niebla, she had been fascinated by what transpired to be a large harbor quarried out as an extension of the Tinto River, directly below the city walls. *Desembarcadero* loosely translates as a pool where goods were loaded and unloaded; this one, however, was long out of use. Mrs. Wishaw was never able to conduct the detailed investigations she would have preferred, the major obstacles being the water, the deep silt, and working on her own with primitive tools and local peasant labor. She was, though, able to examine it sufficiently well to become convinced that it was Stone Age work and dated back ten to fifteen thousand years.

Progressively back upstream on the river were innumerable mills for grinding flour, many of them ancient. There were far too many for merely supplying the surrounding area. Mrs. Wishaw concluded that the ore was brought down from the mines in the mountains about thirty miles to the north, initially on mules over mountain tracks and then by river. The mills would have been needed for the provision of sustenance for the many people involved in the large volume of transportation, who would also have required a considerable amount of policing.

From Niebla, the ore was floated a further two kilometers on a canal she discovered, to a point where the tide on the Rio Tinto provided enough clearance for larger boats to carry it down to the ports of Moguer and Palos, close to Huelva. Palos, incidentally, was where Columbus sourced his ships and crews before embarking on his epic voyage of discovery. If Atlantis had ruled parts of America, it was ironic that more than eleven thousand years after the demise of the Atlantis civilization, seamen from the same region rediscovered it.

Old mines, mostly copper, are dotted all over the Algarve's hinterland. The biggest, at São Domingos in the northeast corner of the region close to the Guadiana, was one exploited by Julius Caesar, initially for gold. It lies on the same metal-rich seam that runs through the Algarve mountains to the Rio Tinto mines and beyond, in Spain. Until last century, the mine, owned by an English company, was still in production. The gold had long been exhausted, but it had become one of the largest copper mines in the world. The site now boasts a hotel and a museum and is marketed as a tourist attraction.

Early in 2009, a company was granted permission to examine the mountainous areas of the Algarve for valuable ores such as gold and silver, since the region was known to have produced such substantial amounts in the past.

One of the Romans' favorite activities was plundering the treasures of the local Portuguese tribes they had conquered. They were often astonished by the amounts they gleaned. Between 209 B.C. and 169 B.C., the haul totaled a staggering eight hundred tons of silver and four tons of gold.

It was not until I was putting the finishing touches to this book that I discovered another unique fact linking southwest Iberia to Plato's Atlantis account. One of his most debated clues is the one related to the mysterious metal orichalcum. He stated that it was no longer mined and only known by its name but was regarded by the Atlanteans as the most valuable metal after gold. Clue 42 reads: ". . . and that which is now only name and was then something more than a name. Orichalcum was dug out of the earth in many parts of the island being more precious in those days than anything except gold."

Exactly what orichalcum was has captured imaginations and occupied learned minds ever since. Different theories have been proposed, mostly suggesting that it was a naturally formed alloy comprising copper and another metal. The main reason for this is that the Greeks had two words for copper. One of them was *kipros,* from which the name "Cyprus" probably derived, as copper was extensively mined in the island's Trudos Mountains. The other word was *chalcos,* which could mean "copper" or "brass." As *ori* was also similar to a Greek word for mountains, it was presumed that Plato was referring to something called "mountain copper or brass," but that uses the Greek vocabulary, and Solon's information came from the Egyptians.

What appears to be the definitive solution came out of the blue when I was ruminating around Plato's clues with Carlos Castelo, a local Portuguese expert on the ancient Kunii people and their alphabet (see Chapter Eighteen). "It was obvious," he declared, "*ori* or *oro* was the word used for gold in the ancient local Kunii tongue at various times." Even today, *ouro* is gold in Portuguese. During the same ancient period, *calcos* meant copper and, like other ancient Iberian words, it found its way into Greek. The current Portuguese word for copper is *cobre.*

So the very name used by Plato that had been passed on by the old Egyptian priest originated in southwest Iberia, a combination of *ori* and *calcos*. It graphically described a metal that was a natural or manufactured alloy of gold and copper. Its gold content would explain why the Atlanteans valued it so highly. It is logical that its origin would have been in the same place as the name.

Carlos supplies ample evidence that this old language and script long preceded others, including Phoenician, Greek, and Latin (see Chapter Eighteen). It must be presumed that, as the metal was unknown to the Greeks, its name had been preserved by the Egyptians for thousands of years and was not invented by Plato. It is a unique, exciting, and telling link between southwest Iberia and Atlantis.

Interestingly, the inhabitants of the Andes in South America also had an alloy of gold and copper, which they called *tumbago*.[52] If this area was influenced by the Atlanteans (as discussed later, in Chapters Fifteen and Seventeen), then the same alloy appearing there would not be a surprise. It is reported to have consisted of a fifty-fifty ratio of gold to copper. The alloy was harder than copper but retained its flexibility even when hammered; consequently, it was very useful in the making of intricate objects with the appearance of gold.

The Spaniards were reported to be somewhat enraged when melting down what they thought were gold objects, only to discover that they were made from this alloy.

There are very few other historic reports of this enigmatic metal. One recounts that it was used for the vessels in Solomon's Temple and another that the wand, the ancient symbol of authority and office, had been traditionally made from it. Chapter Nineteen briefly discusses wands and rods of power; after reading it, you will appreciate that this offers another intriguing link with southwest Iberia. It would, coincidentally, also be an extremely good conductor of electricity. King Solomon is also thought to have obtained some of his gold from southwest Iberia—Tartessos. Maybe a small amount of this unique alloy was still available then, or even other objects made from it existed. Perhaps his merchants obtained some for use in the temple simply because of its rarity.

There is one other clue that chimes with the importance of the area around Niebla. Clue 34 relates to the area that the second-born son was given dominion over. "To his twin brother, who was born after him, and obtained as his lot the extremity of the island toward the Pillars of Hercules, facing the country which is now called the region of Gades in that part of the world, he gave the name in the language of the country which is named after him, Gadeirus." Plato did not say "eastern," but elsewhere he made it very clear that he was talking about the Atlantic, so it must have been the eastern extremity. "Gades" is today's Cádiz, across the bay from Niebla. Many people have wondered why Plato specifically mentioned the inheritance of this son and not those of the others—apart, that is, from his firstborn: Atlas.

It is now clear. If southwest Iberia was where Atlantis was situated, apart from the citadel itself, this eastern zone was the next most important area of the kingdom, the font of much of its vast wealth . . . precious metals. Certainly a fitting area of responsibility for Poseidon's second born.

Gades is the only specific place name quoted by Plato for anywhere in Atlantis.

So far, so good. The most implacable cynic could not argue against southwest Iberia's conformity with Plato's description of immense wealth. This was all starting to get very exciting indeed.

In view of my comments in Chapter Three, wealth was one of the most promising and obvious clues to examine first. But would the others prove more problematical? What, for instance, about the climate, the plants, and the animals?

CHAPTER TEN

Mysterious Fruit, Warm Sun, and Big Beasts

Twenty-one of Plato's clues give information about what the climate was like, the rainfall, which crops and fruits grew there, what the landscape looked like, and a limited amount concerning animals. Taken together, they are crucial in helping to place the legendary land accurately in the right latitude—and are also the basis for ruling out so many sites suggested over the years. If previous authors had noted them, they might not have plunged into writing their hypotheses for some far-flung spots.

Climate

Most of the information is interlinked like a giant spider's web. The weather details, for instance, are not only given directly but can also be deduced from a study of the crops and fruits listed. Perhaps the most pertinent climate clue is that regarding bathing. Clue 75 reads: "They made cisterns, some open to the heavens, others roofed over to be used in winter as warm baths." It was obviously too cold for open-air pools to be used in the winter. This information is reinforced by the disclosure in clue 97 that it was warm enough for two crops annually and, although there was plentiful rainfall in the winter, water had to be carefully conserved in a hugely ambitious storage system for irrigation in the summer. "Twice in the year they gathered the fruits of the earth, in winter having the benefit of the rain from heaven, and in summer the water which the land supplied by introducing streams from the canals." This clearly indicates a climate of hot, dry summers and mild, wet winters. Any resident of the Algarve or southwest Andalucía, asked about the local climate, would describe it exactly thus.

In southern Iberia, summer lasts from May to the end of September, with hardly any rain. The temperatures vary between 27°C and 35°C, with occasional heat waves causing spikes up to 40°C.

October is often glorious, with little rainfall and sufficiently strong sunshine to still quickly bring a red glow to unprotected skin. Autumn colors continue beyond the end of November and any serious rain immediately heralds the first sprinkling of wild flowers. In late December, early almond blossoms break bud and wild narcissi and dainty daffodils nod in the fresh breeze. The lemon yellow as acacia (mimosa) blooms, completely covering the trees, is synonymous with January, as autumn blends seamlessly into spring.

There is no real winter, apart from a few frosts in places in early January, when the night skies are so clear that you yearn for a telescope.

The most satisfying months are from February to May. It is a joy to be alive, bathed in warm sunshine and breathing alpine-like air, for an average of twenty days each month. The fields and trees are swathed in blossom and, before March is out, the heady perfume of orange blossom is all-pervading.

From November to April there is usually rainfall, sometimes torrential, interspersed with spells of two or three weeks of sparkling blue skies. Daytime temperatures range from 15°C to 25°C; but when the sun sets, it is decidedly cooler and cold winds can make the air feel chillier still. It is very much a climate of warm sun but cold air. As soon as the sun dips, the temperature drops dramatically. One minute you are comfortable in an open-necked shirt, the next you need to don a woolly. Heating of some sort is definitely necessary in the home, especially from late afternoon onward.

Only the masochistic swim in open-air pools; the water is far too cold. The precious rainfall has to be conserved and stored for summer irrigation.

That is just as Plato indicated. Other areas frequently suggested as sites for Atlantis—off the coast of West Africa, for example—are automatically ruled out, as winter temperatures there are far too high. The more temperate zones of northern Europe, where winter weather is foul and summers are seldom hot and dry, can also be dismissed. This idyllic Algarve climate is helped enormously by the 40-kilometer-deep tract of mountains immediately to the north. Thousands of years ago, in the era Plato alludes to, the range was even grander and would have played a vital role in protecting the area from the Ice Age and the five thousand years or so of thaw that followed it. In most places, the mountains are within 10 kilometers of the coast, in some areas they practically reach it, and—despite millennia of erosion, earthquake-induced landslides, and, most likely, some subsidence—they are still substantial. Numerous fertile valleys nestle in the folds, and many of the hillsides, particularly those farthest south and in river valleys, have been terraced in order to grow timber or orange trees.

There is, though, one doubt—especially relevant in view of the current uproar over global warming. Was the southwest Iberian climate in 9600 B.C. the same as it is today?

As the glaciers receded and the ice caps melted, from around 16,000 B.C., the earth warmed up. By approximately 11,000 B.C., the conditions were much like today's, and the sea level was about 120 meters higher than before.

Then, around 11,000 B.C., there was a sudden and dramatic reversal known as the Allerød or Younger Dyas period. Temperatures dropped, as did sea levels, since the water was again being trapped in ice.[53]

Then temperatures once more suddenly started to rise, quickly reaching the previous levels before 9600 B.C.

This muddies the water swirling around the current man-made global-warming theories. The temperature tap has repeatedly, and often suddenly, opened or closed during periods when humans could not have been responsible.

It indicates that at the time Atlantis disappeared, the climate would have been the same as it is today. A few thousand years before that, however, as the empire was growing, it would have been cooler, though far more agreeable than in northern Europe.

There is something else worth noting that was a by-product of these climate changes. The great agricultural plains of the Sahara were converted into desert, presumably by global warming.

As for comparing Plato's clues about climate, however, the inescapable conclusion is that he could just as well have been describing the conditions in southwest Iberia. They are identical.

Crops and Vegetation

One of the most intriguing aspects of Plato's description of Atlantis is that sophisticated agriculture existed thousands of years before it is thought to have been developed. It would have necessitated a long period of careful selection and propagation first—or, alternatively, people with the advanced biological knowledge that we possess today. It was not a case of just collecting wild seeds, sticking them into prepared ground, and then harvesting: high-yield versions had to be developed before the intensive labor involved in farming could be really worthwhile. Archaeological records show that around 8000 B.C., the so-called "eight founder crops" suddenly appeared out of the blue in the Levant, the countries bordering the eastern Mediterranean. There were two varieties of wheat, together with barley, peas, lentils, bitter vetch, chickpeas, and flax. Agriculture required settled communities and they, in turn, required the developed crops; they were interdependent. Only after these communities were successfully established could more complex societies develop, together with technical abilities and other occupations . . . civilization.

It is clear from what Plato wrote that Poseidon, the founder of Atlantis, and his fellow gods were well acquainted with this form of society and went about setting it up in each of their allotted territories. First, Poseidon *peopled* the land (clues 18 to 20), then organized an efficient irrigation system to maximize agriculture. Plato left no clue as to who this founder race was, where they came from, and how they acquired their knowledge, apart from telling us that they were gods.

Many have suggested that it was the survivors of this Atlantis ruling elite who brought their far superior culture and their crops to the Middle East's

Fertile Crescent, Egypt, and the Americas. This, it is proposed, explains the sudden appearance in each area of agriculture and more sophisticated societies, without any apparent evidence of prior development.

Don't get the wrong idea about these gods. Apart from what Plato wrote, references to these ruling elites from other cultures, such as Sumeria, Egypt, India, and South America, make it clear that they were not supernatural beings, but rather flesh and blood. They had the same appetites, requirements, pleasures, and lusts that we do. I will leave readers to ponder the implications.

Returning to the comparison with southwest Iberia, Plato specified that "Atlantis" provided most of what was required for *the uses of life* (clue 40). This included root crops, herbs and pulses, all manner of fruits, nuts such as chestnuts, and plenty of timber (clues 48 to 52). As you will see, that description fits the Algarve as tightly as a Victorian corset pinched a lady's waist.

The land yields two crops every year of fruits, wheat, maize, sunflowers, and animal fodder. Bountiful amounts of citrus, apples, pears, quince, plums, apricots, peaches, nectarines, pomegranates, figs, loquats, grapes, olives, avocados, and nuts are harvested—although these are not all necessarily indigenous. A huge variety of vegetables is produced at intervals throughout the year. Runner and broad beans are particularly beloved, and a wide range of dried pulses makes attractive, colorful displays on market stalls.

Plato particularly mentions chestnuts (clue 51): ". . . and a good store of chestnuts." It is the only crop or fruit he names individually, and that is an important indicator. Many of the Algarve's hills, close to the plain, have groves of them, coincidentally providing rewarding harvesting grounds for edible mushrooms like exquisite chanterelles. Yuletide shopping expeditions in Algarve towns and cities wouldn't be complete without the tempting aromas emanating from roast-chestnut stands.

It is usually assumed that Plato was referring to the sweet, edible chestnut variety, which is generically known as the Portuguese or Spanish chestnut. Where this originated is still debated. Eastern Spain is the favorite, but that is only to be expected as it is in the Mediterranean basin, in an area better documented than the little known far southwest of Iberia.

That Plato selected chestnuts for special mention indicates that they were spread across that area too.

They are not the only nuts that are prolific in the region. Most mature gardens have a walnut tree, and the Algarve is also famous for its almond blossom—so much so that the Tourist Board made it the region's official symbol. Kilometer after kilometer of the countryside is smothered in pink and white blossoms in January and February . . . a visual substitute for snow.

Like citrus fruit, it is suggested that almonds were introduced by invaders such as the Romans or the earlier Phoenician traders; but there appears to be little, if any, proof of this. The possibility of anything much ever having been native to the area, or introduced during a much earlier epoch, is not even entertained. It is a repetitive theme. For thousands of years, the Algarve was little known, regarded as insignificant: a forgotten land.

The hypothesis developed in this book supports the opposite view . . . that an ancient civilization flowered here, probably preceding all others known in Europe, the Mediterranean basin, and the Middle East.

One of Plato's clues that has been the subject of much debate is number 50, referring to a fruit with a hard rind, which the Atlanteans used for food, to make a drink, and to extract oil from (for ointments). The assumption perpetuated in many books is that this was the coconut. This led to a further assumption: that the Atlantis climate was tropical, thus leading to theories of all sorts of exotic locations for Atlantis. This is an excellent example of how the story is often twisted. The explicit clues provided by Plato most certainly do not indicate a tropical zone. Coconut palms would not have survived in an area where the seasonal chill factor made the water too cold for swimming in open-air pools during the winter.

More tellingly, as already discussed, Plato specifically referred to chestnuts, which simply do not grow in the same climatic zone as coconuts. The latter prefer tropical climes like that of Hawaii. They might just survive in lower temperatures, provided there were no frosts and provided they were planted in containers that could be brought under cover or indoors at night. In those circumstances, though, the palms would be unlikely to fruit.

Nevertheless, the puzzle remained: what on earth *was* Plato referring to? I kept returning to this problem for many months until one day, while walking the dog, I had a "Eureka" moment: as we reached the bottom of our drive, Coco paused to nuzzle and sniff in the leaf litter and fallen fruit of the carob tree. Suddenly the answer to the conundrum flashed before me. It had, literally, been under my nose all along—and was now under my dog's. The mystery fruit was the humble carob.

The carob tree produces three- to six-inch broad bean–like fruits in summer. They are black when ripe and have a hard, brittle skin with several beans inside. These beans were used in the ancient Middle East to weigh against gold, due to their incredibly uniform weight—hence the word "carat," used to define the quality of gold. During the Second World War years, when I was very young, almost the only sweets available to us were pieces of carob fruit. It softens as it is chewed, releasing a pleasant, faintly sweet, chocolaty taste. (SEE IMAGE 14 BELOW.)

(IMAGE 14) *The fruit of the carob tree.*

The carob tree is one of the most common in the Algarve, often seen alongside country roads. It needs little or no attention. In fact, it is more prevalent there than anywhere else in Europe or the Middle East, indicating that it could well be native to the area.

Carobs have become a valuable, much-sought-after crop. An extract from them is used for a diverse range of products, including white chocolate and a thickener for fruit drinks, as well as in the beauty and ointment industries.

Algarve country folk still make a kind of flour from them, used in baking certain types of breads and cakes. Carobs are also used to brew a potent alcoholic liquor. These products are found on sale at regional fairs, and restaurants offer cakes and puddings made with the flour for desserts.

Overall, that sounds pretty much as Plato described.

Finally, Plato specifies a good supply of timber (clue 43): "There was an abundance of wood for carpenters' work." The mountains mentioned earlier are known to have been originally covered in indigenous trees, much used for boatbuilding by the Carthaginians, Romans, and, later, the Moors and the Portuguese. Today's elderly Algarveans remember the rivers being used to float timber down to the shipyards for this very purpose. The museum on Portimão's quay has an area devoted to this industry and its traditions.

Animals

In clues 44 to 47, Plato indicates Atlantis had many tame and wild animals, particularly elephants. There was plenty of food for them, including those that lived in lakes, marshes, rivers, mountains, and plains. Note the word "tame." It implies that animals were domesticated on Atlantis long before their introduction has been generally acknowledged by historians. The control of herds of cattle would have required the prior taming of horses and dogs. Again, this is at odds with the established view; horses were thought to have been first tamed around 4500 B.C. on the steppes in central Asia. This, however, ignores such visual evidence as engravings on bone and antlers found in caves in southwest France depicting horses with straps and bridles. These have been carbon-dated to between 10,000 and 14,000 B.C. Drawings in another cave have been found in La Marche in France, also of horses with bridles and straps.[54] It would appear that Plato's comments stand up in the light of the most recent evidence and horses were being used by man well before the demise of Atlantis. Coincidentally, the Portuguese Lusitanian breed is recognized to be very old, and the animals are much sought after for their temperament and intelligence.

The story is the same for dogs. There is mounting evidence that they have been man's companion for a very long time. One touching example was an ancient grave, dated to a period long preceding the end of Atlantis, found to contain a human together with a puppy.[55]

Unfortunately, as a consequence of civilization and competition with man, many wild animals have now been eliminated in southwest Iberia. The process is still continuing; but 11,500 years ago, the area would have been rich in wildlife, including elephants. As elsewhere in southern Europe by that time, these would have been mainly of the pygmy variety.[56] They were also prevalent on the large Mediterranean islands. Like numerous other wild animals, they had been driven inexorably south seeking refuge from the Ice Age and the slowly encroaching glaciers. Plato would almost certainly have been aware that elephants between one and two meters tall were still to be found in Sicily in his era, as they were not extinct there until the first century A.D. Elephants were also known to roam northern Morocco, itself almost certainly part of Atlantis if my theory is correct. They would inevitably have crisscrossed the original land bridge between Gibraltar and Africa.

I know of an elephant's tusk in a private collection that was exposed on an Algarve beach after a particularly violent storm. It has not been tested to ascertain its age, so the following explanations are possible:

- It could be from the period when elephants roamed the area.
- The famous Carthaginian general Hannibal was noted for the elephants he trained and used in warfare to terrify the enemy. Imagine the horror of suddenly facing a herd of huge, rampaging beasts you had never encountered before while armed only with spears, tridents, or swords. It was an ingenious ploy and must have caused mayhem. An Algarve legend has it that, when recalled from a campaign in Africa to fight the Romans, Hannibal returned, complete with elephants, sailing via the Algarve and establishing a port at Alvor called Porto Hanibalis. It is said that he exercised the elephants and trained them for his famous epic trek across the Alps by walking them into the mountains to a spa called Caldas de Monchique, where they slaked their thirst before returning to

the coast. The beach where the tusk was found is next to Alvor; it could have been from one of his herd. Incidentally, Anibal is a not-uncommon boy's Christian name in the Algarve.

- It could have been from a Portuguese caravel, an oceangoing boat, returning from Africa a few hundred years ago with ivory as part of its cargo, shipwrecked in a storm.

We will never know unless the tusk is carbon-dated.

Interestingly, in 1967 an issue of *Science* magazine reported that a research ship had recovered mastodon and mammoth teeth two to three hundred miles off the Portuguese coast, indicating that the area could have sunk alarmingly. The earthquake in 1755 alone resulted in the seabed sinking over a three hundred–kilometer radius, well within range of the mammoth finds. The combined subsidence caused by the many other huge quakes in the last twelve thousand years could have been considerable.

One of the animals left that would still have been common up to a few centuries ago, the wild boar, was hunted to virtual extinction but has now been given the freedom to rapidly repopulate the mountains. It is increasingly foraging farther south and wreaking havoc overnight in holiday villa gardens. Deer have been reintroduced, and game birds such as the red-legged partridge are prevalent. Mixed herds of goats and sheep are still a common sight, complete with marshalling shepherds and foraging over wide areas.

The wild Iberian lynx, common in the mountains as recently as a hundred years ago, is now almost extinct.[57] It is the most threatened species of wild cat in the world. Sterling efforts are being made to save it at special breeding centers in Spain and the Algarve.

It is little appreciated that many of the African wild animals originated in Europe. They include, for example, rhinos, giraffes, and antelopes. They migrated south over land bridges that once existed between countries and continents—like Gibraltar and Morocco.

Clue 99 refers to sacred bulls roaming free in the temple and, as part of an alternate fifth- and sixth-year ceremony, one of them was captured by the ten rulers with only staves and nooses, then sacrificed. That sounds very much like a Plato adornment. The detail given is just too fanciful and it would have been unlikely that bulls would be permanently roaming free—with the inevitable excrement—amongst so much pristine adornment. No one would have been able to worship freely without being in fear for his life. Would you bend over, eyes closed, to pray to heaven, given a fair chance that a sharp horn would be planted in your backside, hoisting you there? Nevertheless, it does have echoes in parts of the current proceedings in Portugal's bull rings. The poor bull is tormented by a skilled toreador on horseback, who repeatedly pierces its neck with barbs. Eventually the bull, its neck running with blood and somewhat winded, is allowed a brief respite while a team of unarmed, colorfully attired men, the *Forcados,* enters the ring on foot. Their leader starts to goad the bull into charging him while the rest of the team members line up behind him. It is barbaric, but an incredibly brave and riveting spectacle, as the bloodied bull thunders into a full head-down charge. The *Forcado* stands his ground and literally throws himself on the bull's head, hands on his hips, letting the horns through the space between his arms and sides. The bull tries to toss him, but he usually clings on, limpetlike, often almost upside down with his legs flying in the air. All but one of the remaining team then pile in behind to support him, forcing the bull to a standstill. The last *Forcado* runs around the back and anchors the animal by pulling its tail. The men then disperse and the bull is finally released. (SEE IMAGES 15A, 15B, AND 15C IN THE PHOTO INSERT.)

It would not be beyond possibility for the man with his arms around the bull's horns to let go as the bull tosses its head. He would go somersaulting back as depicted in illustrations of Minoan ceremonies.

Unlike in Spain, in Portugal the bull is not killed in the ring but is put down after the fight if he is badly injured.

Plato also mentions marshes and their wild life. Repeating clue 46: ". . . for as there was provision for all other sorts of animals, both for those which live in lakes and marshes and rivers. . . ." Large areas north of Cádiz and east of Huelva, in Spain, are now national parks. Not swamps, they can more accurately be described as wetlands. Wild life—including a few lynx—is left in peace there. In the Algarve, huge areas around river estuaries and stretching well inland were once marshy or underwater. As in Spain, many of them are now protected sanctuaries, havens for wading birds. Others have been drained and reclaimed, one example being the famous Penina Golf Course, designed by legendary English golfer Sir Henry Cotton. Thousands of eucalyptus trees were planted there to help drain the land. The course is not far from the 3,500 B.C. necropolis at Alcalar mentioned in Chapter Three. In the days when the latter was constructed, the estuary from Alvor would have reached far inland, probably encompassing Penina.

Conclusion

So . . . more clues click into place.

The inescapable conclusion is that the conditions in southwest Iberia are exactly as Plato described. It's as though the ancient Greek philosopher were a modern-day travel writer. His descriptions match so well, it's as if he were filing a report on the region for a weekend color supplement.

The same climate now prevails and the fruits, pulses, and vegetables he writes about can all be found today in any Algarve or southern Spanish market, even down to the bountiful chestnuts.

They would, however, all—including those elephants—have needed water with efficient storage methods and an effective irrigation system. Plato was very specific about it. I need to investigate, look at water sources, and see if some tangible proof has survived more than 11,600 turbulent years.

CHAPTER ELEVEN

Refining the Target

In clues 93 to 96, Plato describes an incredibly large canal/reservoir that completely encircled the vast Atlantis plain. "The depth, and width and length of this ditch were incredible, and gave the impression that a work of such extent, in addition to so many others, could never have been artificial. Nevertheless I must say what I was told. It was excavated to a depth of a hundred feet and its breadth was a stadium [185 meters] everywhere. It was carried around the whole of the plain, and was ten thousand stadia in length. It received the streams which came down from the mountains and winding round the plain and meeting at the city, was there let off into the sea. Farther inland, likewise, straight canals of a hundred feet in width were cut from it through the plain and again let off into the ditch leading to the sea. The canals . . . brought down the wood from the mountains to the city, and conveyed the fruits of the earth in ships, cutting transverse passages from one canal to another, and to the city."

Standing on a road bridge, as I looked to either side, a shiver ran down my spine. To say I was skeptical about Plato's grand canal surrounding the plain was an understatement; but, confound it, here was proof that he might not have been embellishing that much after all. Stretching away on both sides was what must once have been a wide canal. It was now only a few meters deep, due presumably to the buildup of silt and earth. Its walls were reinforced on both sides and the base was now just fertile soil, used for agriculture. Westward, it continued until it would have joined the estuary of the river Arade and emptied into the sea. Eastward, it trundled on in front of Estômbar, a typical Algarve hill village dominated by a church at the top with houses spilling down steep, narrow streets, looking like a wedding-cake confection. Once past it, the "canal" disappeared into the countryside. The local school was built on part of its bed. (SEE IMAGE 16 IN THE PHOTO INSERT.)

As with all civilizations, water was essential to Atlantis. Over millennia, many cultures have waxed and waned depending on its availability. Plato refers to water in twelve of his clues. Those referring to the grand canal simply beggar belief, and many have suggested that they owe more to his vivid imagination than to fact. I had tended to agree, but the canal I was now standing over was forcing a reassessment. I will return to it later.

Canals apart, everything else Plato wrote about the water supply for Atlantis is completely practicable and mirrored in modern-day southwest Iberia.

One of the delights of the area is the number of large rivers. Many of them are dry in summer and only tidal for a few kilometers upstream, as rainfall is then zero. Some have been dammed to create substantial reservoirs. Over millennia, they have carved out large inlets in the coast and, as would be expected, many have sizeable ports at their mouths. Fishing has been one of the major industries for thousands of years.

Plato credits Poseidon with creating a supply of water from underground on the capitol hill (clue 27): "He himself, being a god, found no difficulty in making special arrangements for the center island, bringing up two springs of water from beneath the earth, one of warm and one of cold." Note that Plato hints here that Poseidon had special abilities and technology. It is one of the few times he ever does this.

Today a large percentage of the local water supply comes from underground lakes and aquifers. These underground layers of permeable rock yield water even in the driest years. In the foothills, just below the mountain town of Monchique, the small spa of Caldas de Monchique is built up around a prolific spring of hot water that runs at a constant 32°C. This is where Hannibal supposedly watered those elephants. There is now a hospital there, continuing the spa tradition, which dates back to at least Roman times. It sits alongside a bottling plant that markets the mineral water as a major brand in Portugal. Neither of these establishments spoils the atmosphere of the small village of whimsical buildings and delightful shaded walks through a hillside of massive granite boulders with springs and streams on every side.

There are two more hot springs in the area. One of them, Fonte Santa, is on the neighboring Picota mountain.

Natural springs, called *fontes*, also feature on most country roadsides. They are unmistakable, often framed in stone with a seat and a small collection basin where the weary, parched traveler can rest up and refresh. Some have a stronger flow than others, and they often have a queue of people waiting to fill numerous five-liter bottles for domestic use. They can help themselves to as much free mineral water as they want.

Apart from a few areas, it is possible, with the aid of a traditional dowser, to drill and find water, which is what most new villa owners in the countryside have done.

The countryside is dotted with large wells topped with huge wheeled mechanisms called *noras*. They consist of a large upright wheel that was turned by a mule to bring the water to the surface. Their introduction is attributed to the Moors, but there was extensive contact with North Africa long before they invaded.

Local councils all have large wells to tap into the underground supply, providing mains water for domestic and industrial consumption. This bountiful supply from beneath the ground is not sufficient, however, to meet the huge demand for summer irrigation and domestic use and is now supplemented by a supply from reservoirs in the hills.

Back in the 1970s, when the first Algarve tourist packages began to appear in the holiday brochures, each old farm and house had a large, circular water deposit, called a *cisterna*, dug out of the ground. Either level with the ground or slightly raised, the top sloped so that any rainfall drained into the tank below. The more sophisticated systems also collected water from the terraces. These were not small affairs. Many of them were the size of large swimming pools and held between sixty and a hundred thousand liters. Many country properties still have them, some having been converted into pools by second-home owners.

The reservoirs set back in the mountains make use of the natural valley contours. From some, a system of small concrete canals distributes water far and wide. The simple system operates by gravity, with gates opening to drain the water off to where it is needed.

Elsewhere, in much the same way as in Morocco's Atlas Mountains, smallholders and farmers cultivate a system of furrows and drills to gravity-feed plots from their own collected water. Often these are opened and closed by the simple removal or insertion of a bung of earth.

All this is far less ambitious than what Plato described—that huge hundred-foot-deep canal, more than six hundred feet wide, circumventing the entire plain for around eighteen hundred kilometers with all those crisscrossing interlocking canals. If such a system existed today, it would be one of the wonders of the world, and I suppose it could be argued that that would also have been a valid reason for the Egyptians to have bothered to record it in the first place.

Putting its length into perspective, the distance from the top of northwest Spain to the bottom of the Algarve is only around seven hundred kilometers, less than half of the distance given by Plato for the canal. Granted, it would have been a perfect low-technology system for irrigation and transport, but it would have been a mind-boggling project to construct using only manual labor. As mentioned earlier, the popular consensus has been that it was more a figment of Plato's imagination than grounded in fact.

Would it have been possible? Perhaps, given a sufficiently long time span and enough available hands, but there would have been considerable obstacles hindering both construction and the operation of the system. Apart from the immense size of the project, there could well have been the problem of getting through the rock. Much of the existing Algarve land contains, or used to, considerable quantities of rock, both in large outcroppings and huge boulders. It is often seen piled on the edges of fields, where farmers are zealously claiming land from nature—but they have the advantage of JCB earthmovers to assist them. No matter where it was situated, in whatever country, excavating to a depth of a hundred feet along a width of six hundred feet with only pickaxes and spades seems far-fetched.

If Atlantis was southwestern Iberia and the cultivated plain described by Plato was the part that is now submerged, it would possibly have been easier if the soil was similar to the sand-based variety that is currently found along the coastal strip. Even then, a hundred feet is a huge depth, and the likelihood of hitting rock would have been high.

Plato does not enlighten us as to how the system operated. Ideally, it would have had to have been almost on one level; otherwise, a considerable number of locks would have been needed. There is no mention of building materials like cement, so locks would have to have been constructed in stone. Cast metal would have been needed to operate them, unless another system had been devised.

Nevertheless, some sort of organized storage and supply would have been needed to support the large agricultural society that Plato described—though not necessarily on the scale he indicated. It is far more likely that the excess winter water was trapped in separate reservoirs in the foothills as required. It could then be used to gravity-feed the great agricultural area to the south when required. The very gentle slope of the large submerged plain forming the current seabed would have made this possible. That canal at Estômbar could have been servicing one such reservoir and providing an outlet to the river estuary. It would have been essential to reduce the water level in periods of excessive rainfall to avoid flooding. It would have needed to have been of the proportions Plato indicated in order to siphon off sufficient volume in an emergency. In fact, there are vestiges of what could have been such a storage area in the vicinity. Close examination of the area inland between Albufeira and Portimão revealed this very possibility. Running more or less parallel to the coast, there are several interlinking, long, wide, fertile valleys that were once floodplains. An example can be clearly seen from the A22 motorway that runs east to west, between the mountains and the coast. Just east of a town called Lagoa, a few kilometers south of Silves, a long viaduct stretches across and above one of them. Continuing eastward, other small bridges carry the road over narrow, dry river valleys running roughly south. They could once have taken water from the floodplain if it was used as a reservoir to the existing coast and the submerged plain.

These appear to be completely natural—inevitably so, after 11,500 years. It is perfectly feasible that the Atlanteans made use of the natural topography to create vast inland storage areas like these floodplains, bordered on both sides by low hills and ridges. This particular plain has some of the most fertile soil in the Algarve. It could easily be the product of thousands of years of silt and was originally at a much lower level. Incidentally, Lagoa town, which sits at the western end of it, is derived from the Portuguese word for "lake." Part of these plains still floods after heavy rain, and an area is artificially flooded each summer to grow rice. (SEE IMAGE 17 IN THE PHOTO INSERT.)

The width of the canal mentioned at the beginning of this chapter, at Estômbar, is between 130 and 180 meters, which is close to that claimed by Plato. It also approaches Estômbar from the direction of Lagoa. Interestingly, it and the floodplain are at the most northerly point of the existing coastal plain and, therefore, likewise of any submerged plain. That is where Plato said the northern part of his grand canal was. He also said that at one point the excess water was released into the sea. This channel at Estômbar heads straight to the estuary and so to sea. It would have to have been higher than the sea to prevent tidal salt water entering the canal, unless there was a system of gates to let the water out at low tide. If it was only for releasing water in an emergency, the flow might have been strong enough to prevent the sea entering. Eastward, the canal heads back toward Lagoa and the floodplain. Could there have been a connection?

To summarize, supplies of water—both hot and cold—exist in southwest Iberia, exactly as Plato describes, whether from beneath the ground, from rainfall, or from rivers in winter spate. Some of the rivers dry up in summer, so a collection and irrigation system is needed, just as Plato indicated it was 11,600 years ago.

As far as that huge canal system is concerned, most serious Atlantis researchers dismiss it as pure make-believe, or at least exaggerated to a marked degree. To put it into context again, the length was supposedly about the same as the distance from the south coast of Portugal to the south coast of Britain—six hundred feet wide and a hundred feet deep all the way. That is just the main canal. There were also many thousands of kilometers of interconnecting waterways.

After nine thousand years it was also most unlikely to have been recorded by the Egyptians to the level of detail Plato expresses. There would have been no real point.

More probably, he was told that there was an amazing, extensive, and efficient water storage and irrigation system and then embellished the facts he had been given to make it sound more impressive. (He was, to say the least, cavalier with his use of mensuration statistics.) It would certainly have been in keeping with his ideas of a wonderfully simple system fit for his perfect state.

It is far more likely that the Atlanteans made use of a combination of man-made and natural land features to produce adequate water supplies when and where needed.

The many rivers, tidal up to a good penetration of the hinterland, were used for the transportation of goods and people. As they do today, boats traveled upstream with the tide and back as it ebbed. Very large rivers—the Guadiana and the Guadalquivir, for example—flow all the year around. Large boats still travel the many kilometers inland to Seville, and during the last century the Guadiana was still used in the export of copper from the mine at São Domingos, which is way up the river. The river Tinto has been used for thousands of years for transport of ore via Niebla from the Rio Tinto mine.

The system I have outlined could have broadly fulfilled the functions Plato described, but on a simpler, less ambitious scale. Alternatively, the search for vestiges of the canal system might be completely pointless, as it could have all disappeared under the sea with the plain.

So, my search was over. There were enough comparisons, most identical, to now be certain that southwest Iberia was the area Plato was referring to. It was Atlantis. But there was still one thing left. I wanted to try to find where one of its cities might have been. What a prize it would be if I could even find the fabled ancient capital. Now that I had established that Atlantis was not an island and some land survived, the site might just still exist.

CHAPTER TWELVE

Quest for the Citadel

Plato's clues about the capital give incredibly detailed information including its size, its geology, and the terrain relative to the surrounding area, even down to exacting details for the materials it was built from. Taken with the other clues discussed in the preceding chapters about the geographical location, they specify an utterly unique location. Surely it would be impossible for there to be more than one site on the whole planet that matched all of them. If there is one, that is.

Following is a summary of some of the details I used to help narrow the search.

"The hill, on which the capital was built, not very high on any side, was near the main plain in the center of the 'island.' It was fifty stadia [9¼ kilometers] from the sea." It must have already been connected to the sea when Poseidon first settled there, probably by a tidal river, as clue 25 states that he enclosed the hill by alternate circles of land and sea.

"The Kingdom was divided into ten portions shared among Poseidon's ten sons. As Atlas was the first born son, he received the most important area, around the citadel. Gadeirus, his twin brother, received the eastern extremity as far as the region around Cádiz."

"The island had a diameter of 5 stadia [925 meters]. The capital and the plain were surrounded by mountains descending to the sea, leaving the southern side of the plain bordering the sea."

If my hypothesis was correct, considerable amounts of the north part of the land forming the original Atlantis homeland survived. There was a chance that close examination might just reveal something startling in relation to that ancient capital, or at least about other cities.

The biggest obstacle to discovering the capital's site was that Plato was specific about its distance from the sea: just 9¼ kilometers. His clues also indicate that Poseidon was first able to surround the citadel with sea, before later opening a canal to the sea. This could only mean that the small plain around the hill was already connected to the coast by a tidal river.

With the help and advantage of my local knowledge, I decided to explore the whole region, focusing particularly on the major existing cities. Throughout history, there has been an overwhelming tendency to build on sites where old cities had been destroyed. I started from Gibraltar and worked west.

Cádiz

It has frequently been suggested that this city might have been the capital of Atlantis. I analyzed its credentials earlier but must reiterate that Plato said Cádiz was in the region given to the second son and at the eastern extremity of Atlantis. It was obviously not the capital, since that was given to Atlas.

It was also once indisputably situated farther out on what is now submerged land—remains have been identified on the seabed, testimony to its being ancient and possibly even an Atlantean city. This is credible, as Plato seems to indicate that the city was named after the second son, Gadeirus, and the name has been perpetuated throughout the ages. Its location on the river mouth makes it an obvious choice for a port. The position of the submerged remains is known, and further archaeological investigation there would be more worthwhile than uncovering yet another Mayan pyramid or pharaoh's tomb.

Jerez

This is the famous Andalucía "Sherry City," undoubtedly an ancient and fascinating place but only just up the road from Cádiz and, therefore, ruled out by the same criteria.

It has also been subject to considerable archaeological investigation by those who seriously believed it could have been the Atlantis capital, but with no results. It's a pity those investigators didn't study Plato properly first.

The same applies to the 2011 National Geographic TV documentary that claimed, with the help of satellite images, that the Atlantis capital had been discovered buried in the marshes north of Jerez. The site was already being investigated by Spanish archaeologists before the American professor who fronted the program latched on to it. It is doubtful it could consist of remains dating back to the era of Atlantis, as the archaeologists involved think they are far more recent, more likely from Tartessos.

Seville

This city is connected to the coast by a large river, the Guadalquivir; but it's about 85 kilometers away, which is a lot farther than the 9¼ that Plato gave. Neither is it any closer to the center of the kingdom than Cádiz. Elena Wishaw was convinced, however, that it was of a great age. Before moving to Niebla, she had investigated Seville and had been fascinated by a couple of ancient sites.

One of them was well known: the temple of Hercules.[58] Three of the six huge columns had been excavated *in situ* early in the twentieth century, to find that their bases were 6 meters below the then-current level of Seville. This could only mean that they were indeed ancient.

The other monument was, at the time, less well known, and Elena made overtures to the authorities to excavate it properly. She was given provisional permission—but, sadly, this was in 1914; the First World War intervened, and she transferred her attention to Niebla. She thought the site was that of a sun temple and tomb that had been looted long ago.

Known locally as the *El Laberinto* ("The Labyrinth"), it was discovered in the sixteenth century by workmen who were cleaning a well.[59] On descending into the well, they were surprised to find that at a depth of 6½ meters, the wall suddenly widened. A staircase was constructed so that visitors could descend to what the locals apprehensively regarded as a very mysterious place, thinking it was an old "School of Magic of the Moors."

At the time, Elena thought that no other sun temple in such good condition had been found anywhere else in western Europe. Off one of the lateral galleries on the right was what she regarded as the most sensational part of the monument, dubbed locally *La Capella* ("The Chapel"). It had a barrel roof supported by beautifully worked brick ribs. She was convinced that it was originally a tomb intended for a great ruler, which had been rifled by looters thousands of years ago. On the opposite side, down a left-hand gallery, was another unopened tomb—and this is what she had sought permission to investigate. An eminent archaeologist, together with other experts whom she had persuaded to descend into the bowels of the earth to assess the complex, thought it to have been built in the Neolithic—perhaps even the Megalithic—period, certainly before the Roman era.

She became convinced that Seville had once been Tharsis, capital of Tartessos. Local myths associated the founding of the town with Hercules and Atlas; but the official version is that it was originally a small trading settlement in a lagoon on the banks of the river, built on piles, probably established by Phoenician traders and called Ispal. The Romans were later responsible for developing the town into a major center, calling it Hispalis.

There does not seem to be any evidence for Elena Wishaw's assertions that this was Tharsis or, as she also speculated, that it was the seat of the fabled King Arganthonius—other than her intuition and the age attributed to the sun temple. She also maintained that the columns of the Temple of Hercules were archaic in shape and dated to long before the Roman period.

Like Cádiz, Seville was in such a logical strategic position, at the head of the navigable stretch of the Guadalquivir River, that it was most probably an Atlantean settlement.

It is, though, too far to the east and too far inland to conform with Plato's clues, so it must be discounted as a capital contender.

Huelva

This area figured prominently in the export of metals from the Rio Tinto mine, but most of this was probably from the old ports of nearby Palos and Moguer.[60] Huelva seems most likely to have been established by the Phoenicians as their trading base. Its position between two rivers, the Odiel—then called the Luxis—and the Tinto, was absolutely typical of the type of site they preferred. The Phoenicians called it *Onoba* and, again, the Romans developed it. This would appear to nullify claims made by some that it was the old capital of Tartessos.

Considerable remains of Phoenician and Carthaginian pottery have recently been found there, which has again reinforced the archaeologists' theory about its connection to Tartessos. It seems a tad too optimistic, based on such flimsy evidence. The Phoenicians could well have established a factory there to supply their other Iberian bases, and the Carthaginians then found it convenient to continue.

Niebla

This is not far north of Huelva, so also too far east to be considered for the Atlantis capital. Nevertheless, Elena Wishaw was convinced that her discoveries, particularly the ancient hydraulic system and the *desembarcadero*, proved that the city was exceptionally old. It was known as a city of great importance when the Carthaginians laid siege to it in A.D. 560. They exacted an awful revenge on its inhabitants for their resistance. Later, it became an important Roman city; they rebuilt large parts of it to protect their exploitation of the metal trade. Even its current distance from the sea—around thirty kilometers—rules it out as the Atlantis capital. If, however, Gadeirus was given this area by his father, Poseidon, because of the huge importance of the metal deposits, it would have been as logical a position as any to establish his regional capital. Plato made it clear that this was not Cádiz, which he said was opposite.

Faro

I was way into my research and had already reached the broad conclusions of this book when a local newspaper report alerted me to Dr. Roger Coghill. He seemed to hold views similar to mine. I obtained the telephone number of his home in South Wales, and we had an interesting conversation, swapping ideas.

We agreed on many points but differed on others. One of the most significant divergent issues was that he believed the site of the Atlantis capital to be at Faro. In 2001 he had produced a CD called *The Atlantis Effect* suggesting this.[61]

He is a well-known expert on electromagnetism and has achieved national prominence in the UK, speaking on the effects of electricity pylons and mobile telephone masts, et cetera, and acting as an adviser to the government.

His arguments for Faro being the Atlantis capital emanated from several facts: evidence, for example, that the water that once existed behind the town and the sandbanks offshore are in a rough semicircle resembling the embankments surrounding the capital, as described by Plato. In fact, it would appear likely that the sea once occupied a huge inland lagoon behind Faro, as far back as a town now known as Estoi.

There is no red rock, from which Plato stated the capital was partly built, in Faro or its immediate surroundings. Neither is there any evidence that in 9500 B.C. it was only 9¼ kilometers from the sea.

The seabed chart shows the first submerged cliff beyond 9¼ kilometers and, interestingly, the final one much farther out to sea in front of Faro than in any other part of the Algarve. It must have formed a cape and is also much higher at the extremity of that cape than on any other part of the plain. Topped by a substantial hill with a rocky peak, it would have been a noticeable landmark from the sea. There is an old legend of a famous lighthouse off Faro, but I suspect that this rocky headland was submerged too long ago for that to have persisted, and too distant from Faro to have been associated with it. Intriguingly, though, *faro* is also the Portuguese word for "lighthouse."

Again, it was the Romans who established a town there—known as Ossonoba—probably because the original lagoon behind it had silted or dried up as a result of earthquakes, rendering Estoi landlocked. Alternatively, Faro may again have been an earlier Phoenician settlement. The Romans knew Estoi as "Milreu"; it is a most interesting site.

On his CD, Roger Coghill relates that an Arab chronicler, Rasis, originally uncovered the remains of an extensive Roman villa there in the tenth century. He was not constrained by the current painstaking approach to archaeology and promptly set about lifting the Roman remains. What he found was astonishing. He was amazed at the magnificence of the pre-Roman buildings. In order to avoid completely destroying the Roman remains, he covered the site up again, saying he had uncovered the "most wonderful city in the world."

In the closing few decades of the last century, the Milreu villa was seriously investigated by several archaeological teams, particularly from

Germany. The present state of the site is mainly due to those teams; but many remains are in museums and, probably, private collections, since the site was open to looting for a long period. The impressive mosaic floor is on display in the Faro museum. The house was probably very large, most likely for an extremely wealthy nobleman or merchant. In its prime, it would have been magnificent.

As far as I can ascertain, no one has tried to explore to a significant depth beneath the current remains. In March 1999, a resistivity survey was carried out to assess whether any other remains were buried in the proximity. Outlines of significant buildings were detected in several areas around the site.

The villa is on the perimeter of the current town of Estoi, conveniently located by a river. Indeed, the locals relate that remains—Roman or otherwise—extend unexplored for kilometers across the nearby terrain. Local archaeology seems to be interested only in the Algarve's more recent Moorish past, perhaps because it is regarded as part of the current population's ancestry. The rural Moorish inhabitants were allowed to remain after the ruling class finally fled.

Milreu would not have been 9¼ kilometers from the sea, as it would appear to have been lapping on its doorstep at one stage and to be between 25 and 60 kilometers away in earlier eras. Its name may have some significance: *mil* means "a thousand" and, replacing "u" with "i," *rei* means "king." Today's Estoi is on the side of a hill and does not in any way conform to Plato's description of a low hill completely surrounded by water. It is, however, around 9 kilometers from Faro.

I mentioned earlier that when the Romans invaded Lusitania (modern-day Portugal), the local Conii tribe diplomatically agreed to cooperate rather than be decimated and subjugated. This infuriated other tribes in the north, who were implacably hostile to the Romans. They descended on the Algarve and exacted dreadful retribution on the Conii, reputedly totally destroying the tribe's royal capital.[62] Its site has never been identified; but a Roman description and map show it inland, somewhere behind Faro. The town was called Conistorgis, and Milreu/Estoi would seem to have the perfect footprint for the Conii city of "A Thousand Kings."

Please, will someone take a serious look at it?

It would originally have been an ideal, tempting site for establishing a town, situated at the northern end of a lagoon and with the shelter of the mountain range immediately behind. It is unlikely that it would have been established any farther north. With the Roman indication that Conistorgis was directly inland from Faro there are few, if any, other places where it could have been. As an interesting exercise, extracting the central letters from Conistorgis reveals *istor,* which is not wildly different from *Estoi.* The prefix *Coni* obviously reflects the indigenous people, the Conii.

If it was the Conii capital, the chances are that it was built on the site of another Atlantis town possibly overlooking a lake, inland lagoon, or reservoir . . . but not, I suggest, the capital.

One of Poseidon's sons who was given dominion over an area of Atlantis was Mestor. If the "M" was dropped and the "E" replaced with an "I"— which would not have been unusual—this again gives "Istor." In the same vein, another son was named Evaemon. One of the most famous ancient towns in the Alentejo region just north of the Algarve, a Unesco Heritage protected site, is Evora.

So, had I exhausted all the possibilities? All the obvious ones, yes— but, incredibly, there is another Algarve site that matches so many of the exacting clues left by Plato that it is quite impossible to be mere coincidence.

Prepare to be amazed. . . .

CHAPTER THIRTEEN

The Capital Revealed

For those sighting it for the first time, this city exudes a strange fascination. The main roads from the south and east approach it from an elevated level; and when it first comes into view around a bend, there is invariably a sharp intake of breath. Tourists inevitably pull the car over and reach for a camera. Despite the urban sprawl now fanning out from its base over the plain, it is still very impressive, and coaches disgorge hundreds of sightseers there every day. But to be able to examine this town's credentials, I first had to gather together all of Plato's clues, including those used in the last chapter:

"Close to the plain in the center of the 'island/peninsula' was a mountain, not very high on any side." In the next clue, Plato describes it as a hill: "It had a diameter of 925 meters [5 stadia]"—although as a natural hill, it is highly unlikely to have been exactly circular. "The hill was on flat land surrounded by mountains which descended in height toward the sea. It was close to the large coastal plain. Poseidon 'broke the ground' to completely encircle it with separate different width zones of land embankments and sea water. The first zone of sea closest to the hill was 185 meters [1 stadium] wide, followed by ones of land and sea, each of 370 meters [2 stadia], then a land zone of 555 meters [3 stadia] and, finally, a sea zone of the same width where the towns harbor and docks were situated. This harbor was always heaving with activity, day and night. It was connected to the sea by 9.25 kilometers [50 stadia] of waterway." Plato claims that these zones were so precisely spaced, they could have been turned with a lathe. "The land zones were faced in stone with towers and gates on the bridges where the sea passed from one zone to another."

"They obtained three different colors of rock: white, black, and, unusually, red. All three colors were quarried from the center hill/island itself or from the encircling land zones. As they quarried, they hollowed out double docks, the roofs formed from the natural rock."

"They built a variety of buildings, the grandest from all three colors of stone in a manner to please the eye."

"The stone face of the outer zone embankment was overlaid with brass, the next with tin, and the one closest to the citadel in orichalcum"—a metal no longer available from mining and till now generally assumed to be a naturally formed alloy of copper and another metal. You will recall that an earlier chapter identified this as an alloy of gold and copper.

In the center—and one would presume on the highest part of the hill—was a holy temple dedicated to Poseidon and his wife. It was inaccessible to the public and encircled with gold.

Poseidon's own temple palace was also here, and Plato implies that it included the above. It was 92.5 meters (half a stadium) wide and 185 meters (one stadium) long and covered on the outside in silver, with pinnacles in gold.

"In the next place, presumably immediately below, were two plentiful fountains, one of cold water, the other hot."

"They also built cisterns, some of them open to the heavens, others roofed over for winter bathing."

There was sufficient run-off water to irrigate the "grove of Poseidon" (on the central island), which was full of "all manner of trees of wonderful height and beauty, owing to the excellence of the soil," and also to provide a supply to the outer zones.

"The docks were full of naval stores and triremes" (a type of Greek ship powered by rows of oarsmen; his reference to these vessels illustrates my earlier point that Plato colors the story for his Greek audience).

"There was yet another stone wall starting at the sea, forming a circle of 9.25 kilometers' radius from the harbor, encircling the whole complex and countryside."

"The entire area was densely crowded with houses, and the canal and harbor were also full of vessels and merchants from all parts." (This implies that Atlantis wasn't the only advanced civilization at that time, unless he meant to imply "from all parts of the empire".)

By now, readers will have appreciated that we have been given much definitive information here: distances, measurements, topography, and geology. If I found a site to comply with half a dozen of these points, it would be considered acceptable and regarded as beyond coincidence. Many theories have been built on less, such as that for the Greek island of Santorini. The city mentioned at the beginning of this chapter, however, complies with eighteen of them! The chances of that being a coincidence would have to be expressed as many millions to one.

If there remains any doubt about my theory that southwest Iberia was the Atlantis described by Plato, then this chapter offers conclusive evidence.

The town is Silves, the once-opulent Moorish capital of the Algarve and the one the Crusaders laid siege to (Chapter Six). It is a five-minute drive from where I have been living for twenty-seven years—and, I must confess, when I was first assembling the complete list of Plato's clues I immediately saw a remarkable number of similarities with Silves. But I determined that I should verify all the other clues about Atlantis first: to not jump ahead of myself based only on what I saw here. If the clues *all* stacked up, then the astounding revelation about Silves could be the equivalent of the final dazzle and explosion at the end of a pyrotechnic display.

Surprisingly, Plato gave more precise clues relating to the Atlantis capital than anything else. The account is so detailed that it could almost be firsthand, rather than a record preserved for nine thousand years. So why has no one recognized it before? It is as though there has been a collective amnesia about the role of the Algarve in Europe's ancient past, almost as if it didn't even exist.

So why me? Why now? The answer could simply be because I had bought a house just down the road from Silves and was fascinated by Atlantis and with ancient civilizations in general. The right place at the right time—luck, or fate. Or, if you are inclined to conspiracy theories, and higher or sinister forces, it could be that, until now, mankind had not reached the level to appreciate what we could now be about to discover from archaeological research on the seabed in front of the region.

Back to Plato's clues. The first similarity to strike me was the distance from the sea. Silves is connected to the coast by the River Arade. It rises in the wilds of the mountains and eventually runs through a small but fertile plain before shouldering right up against Silves and then flowing on down to the sea.

Today, despite being only a vestige of its former self, the section from Silves to the coast is still a substantial river. Significantly, it is tidal right up to Silves. On fine days, a flotilla of boats takes tourists upstream on the tide from Portimão, the port at the mouth of the river. They stroll about and wonder at ancient Silves and its monuments, then return on the ebb tide.

Before reaching the coast, the river flows into a large estuary, its water swollen by the confluence with the Odelouca River just west of Silves and yet more water from a river descending from Monchique pouring into the same estuary. Years ago, other rivers joined the Arade on either side of Silves, but today these flow only after heavy rain.

Depending on where it is measured from, the coast or somewhere in the estuary, the distance from Silves could be 9.25 kilometers. From the coast to Silves city, it is a little farther; but Plato gave the measurement of 9.25 kilometers from the harbor on the outer ring of water surrounding the town. That is pretty well the distance it is today, from what will presently be shown to have been the harbor area.

Silves is built on a small hill, only a couple of kilometers from the remaining narrow coastal plain, and is itself on a separate small plain, all exactly as Plato described in clues 24 and 26. The hill is not particularly high; but when you puff your way up to the castle from any side, it is easy to appreciate that it was sufficiently steep to make laying siege to it difficult.

In clue 62, Plato gives the hill's diameter as five stadia; that's 925 meters. It is difficult to arrive at a current measurement for comparative purposes because of the inevitable changes due to rising sea levels and the effects of earthquakes and tsunamis. Measured from what would have been the water level if the surroundings were flooded, it would be 800 to 850 meters east to west, and 600 to 650 meters north to south. The Silves hill is not exactly circular, and this is exaggerated by a park of trees that extends from the hill on the west side. If this park is included, the measurement would be nearer a thousand meters. I think it should be, and will explain why later.

There are, however, many other variables. The high-tide level of the river is, for instance, lower than the current land levels around the hill. These land levels will have risen over thousands of years, so diminishing the width of the hill. Infuriatingly, Plato made a habit of giving measurements in round stadia rather than as a precise fraction. I suppose that should not be surprising, given the huge time span involved. That he was a little cavalier with his figures is, however, illustrated by the fact that he had to convert them from the Egyptian—or Solon did. The chances of them all equaling exact Greek stadium lengths must be extremely remote. Just for example, 4.6 stadia would have been 851 meters. (SEE IMAGES 19, 20, AND 21 IN THE PHOTO INSERT.)

Allowing for all of this, I was amazed at how remarkably similar the size is.

Clue 25 states that Poseidon, "breaking the ground, enclosed the hill all round, making alternate zones of sea and land, larger and smaller encircling one another. . . ." Note that he said "sea." That Silves was once surrounded by water looks obvious when the topography and vegetation are studied—but I wanted certainty. I arranged a meeting with Ricardo Tomé, head of the Geographic Department of the local authority. A knowledgeable geologist, he has made a study of the whole area around Silves in the course of his work as well as researching the geographical and seismic events that have folded and shaped the landscape of his native land over millennia. He confirmed my suspicions. His survey had shown clear evidence from sedimentary deposits that the hill had once been surrounded by water.

Ricardo and other local Portuguese people I have spoken to also remember large areas of land, in front of and to the west of Silves, being reclaimed from the water. In their youth, they recollect seeing men laboring there to build up the riverbank and depositing or redistributing soil to raise the overall level so it would not be subject to future flooding. Part of this land is now the town's main car park, together with a new recreational park complete with hundreds of trees.

The existence of the 9.25-kilometer tidal river would explain how Poseidon was able to surround the hill with the "sea."

Further on in *Critias,* Plato writes that the Atlanteans later dug out a huge canal linking the city to the coast, also three hundred feet wide and a hundred feet deep, seemingly ignoring the existing river (clue 56). Plato was obsessed with canals and, over the years, many people have scoffed at the sheer size of this one. Why so deep and wide? Were ocean liners navigating it daily, with passengers gaily waving as their vessels passed each other? The depth is extraordinary. By comparison, the Panama Canal, regularly used by ocean liners, is only forty-two feet deep.

The existing river has silted up considerably, affecting its depth and width, particularly after it was dammed upstream from Silves during the last century. As recently as fifty years ago, large boats regularly traversed it, collecting such produce as cork from Silves. Even today it is still expansive in places, and plans have existed for more than a decade to dredge huge amounts of silt from it to make it navigable for large tourist boats and leisure craft at all times, instead of just at high tide. Given that Plato indicated that the hill was already connected to the sea by what must have been a substantial river for it to have provided enough water to surround the hill to widths of 185, 370, and 555 meters, why go to the enormous trouble of digging out another sea access? It just does not make sense and smacks of unnecessary embroidering by Plato—or at least an unfortunate misunderstanding of the original information given by the old Egyptian priest. Most likely, Solon was only told that the capital was connected to the sea by a wide waterway. That Plato was confused is highlighted by his telling us that the hill was surrounded by seawater before the canal was supposedly built. More conceivable is that Poseidon dug out parts of the river that may not have been of adequate depth and effected a little widening and straightening here and there.

During more recent episodes in the history of Silves, notably the Moorish and Roman eras, accounts indicate that even during those periods there was extensive water, at least to the west of Silves. One part of it was used for curing timber destined for boatbuilding, and it is thought that the Romans had a harbor there.

The account of the siege by the "anonymous Crusader" quoted in Jonathan Wilson's book discussed in Chapter Six also mentions ditches surrounding the fortress, which the besiegers had to negotiate. Today we usually understand a "ditch" to be small and narrow, but in those days it meant a substantial water hazard.

So, I had already ticked off seven of the clues as a match to Silves:

1. It already had a connection to the sea.
2. This was fifty stadia long (9.25 kilometers).
3. It was on a small hill.
4. The actual size of the hill is still very similar today.
5. It was on a flat plain.
6. It was once surrounded by water.
7. It was close to the great agricultural plain.

I now switched my focus to several crucial clues relating to detail about the capital.

Today Silves is topped by an imposing castle, not unlike to the one that confronted the Crusaders. Just below it stands the town's cathedral, although the Crusaders would have seen a mosque. In clue 70, the area given by Plato as being occupied by the temple was 185 meters by 92.5 meters (one stadium by half a stadium). That closely matches the current quadrant of space taken by the castle and cathedral . . . about 200 meters by 100 meters. As mentioned earlier, successive civilizations tend to build like over like.

Poseidon arranged for the town's water supply to flow from two fountains he created just below the palace (clue 73). Today, not far below the castle, is the town's museum. It was constructed in the 1990s around a huge, unusual well—dating back to the Moorish period—that had recently been uncovered. Apart from being surprisingly wide, it has a staircase winding down around its outer circumference. It is not known whether the Moors built it on the site of an earlier one. (SEE IMAGE 22 IN THE PHOTO INSERT.)

The earlier chapter on water detailed the frequency with which it naturally pops out of the ground or rock as springs. Most of the houses in the Algarve countryside today have a borehole to tap into the underground supply. Interestingly, in most cases the spot to drill is still pinpointed by a traditional dowser. Hot or warm water is, even now, still flowing profusely in places like Caldas de Monchique.

Quite large *cisternas* for storing water have been found in Silves. One of them is in the castle grounds, and another was recently discovered between the castle and the cathedral. It was excavated and mapped, then recovered.

"Of the water which ran off, they carried some to the Grove of Poseidon, where were growing all manner of trees of wonderful height and beauty, owing to the excellence of the soil . . . while the remainder was conveyed by aqueduct bridges to the outer circles" (clues 76 and 77). On the west side of Silves, there are a park and gardens at the bottom of the hill. It well could once have been wider, as it is bounded by houses and tennis courts to the south and a technical college to the north. At its western extremity, it is bordered by a small river flowing north to south. Its current soil level is a little higher than the plain surrounding the town, particularly to the south, and it would have been even more so before the plain was reclaimed from water. This park has tall, handsome trees and shaded, fertile flower beds. We do not have exact information from Plato for the position of the *grove,* but this area fulfills his description. It could not have been on the steep sides of the hill, so it would have also distorted the size and the shape of the land imprint of the capital, making it more egg-shaped. That is exactly what the Silves hill is today.

Like everyone else, I don't care to visit the local tax office more than absolutely necessary, but I have to admit that there is something there that fascinates me. One day while standing in line to pay our local council tax, I noticed a large painted tile panel on the back wall near the counter. It was obviously copied from an old print depicting Silves a good few centuries ago, and it was more or less what you would expect the town to have looked like, apart from one intriguing detail: emerging sideways from the town's ramparts on the west side is what looks like a tall aqueduct. Unfortunately, it is chopped off by the end of the panel and only three arches are visible. Nothing remains of it today, so I turned to my historian friend, Jonathan Wilson, for more information. He said the archaeologists' view was that it had been a defensive emplacement and had a tower on the end to enable the town's defenders to fire arrows and hurl rocks and/or flaming fat at any enemy trying to scale or damage the town walls. It may well have been used for that purpose eventually, but it is where Plato indicated that an aqueduct existed to take water out to the embankments in the direction of the grove. The arches and pillars supporting it are very slender, so demolishing one or two to bring it crashing down would not have been a difficult task for a besieging army. If it was going to serve that purpose, it would have needed to be more robust. Consequently, I doubt it was built originally as a defensive ploy; but, in later life after the outer reaches had been damaged by earthquakes, the remaining part abutting the town wall had been adapted for that purpose. It would be impossible for it to have survived ten or eleven thousand years, but it is quite feasible that later occupants, such as the Romans or the Conii, redeveloped it on the remnants and foundations of an original aqueduct.

In view of the many changes in the intervening millennia, it might seem presumptuous to claim the grove and aqueduct as exact clue "hits," but they definitely demonstrate that there is an area and structure that could have fulfilled this purpose. They are both more likely to have been on this west side as fresh water from "upstream" would have been available for the other side, so water from the fountains would not have been necessary for irrigation.

So, four more clues measure up:

8. The size given for the palace equates to the current space occupied by the castle and cathedral.
9. There is freely available water.
10. An area within the confines of the city that could have been Poseidon's Grove.
11. Vestiges of an aqueduct.

Silves was looking very promising indeed, but I still had to tackle both the most telling and most difficult facts. They would be very hard to comply with.

"The stone which was used in the work was quarried from underneath the central island, and from zones on the outer as well as the inner side . . . one kind was white, another black, and a third red" (clues 64 and 65). This refers to the buildings in the city and on the embankments.

This is astonishingly precise information, and the chances of meeting it seemed daunting. The first two colors are prominently visible in most Portuguese towns, if not in buildings, then most certainly to be spotted in the traditional cobbled pavements and squares. The Portuguese call these paving stones *calçadas*, and white and black are often combined in intricate, attractive patterns or simple pictures such as boats, anchors, or birds. Silves is no exception.

Much less common is red stone.

Except, that is, in Silves, where you simply cannot get away from it. The mighty castle and town walls were built from it, as were many other buildings. Ricardo Tomé, the town's geologist, informed me that a narrow stratum of this unusual lode runs from the western Algarve, near Lagos, through and behind Silves, then eastward in an arc through the foothills, before petering out in the region of the town of Tavira. It is red sandstone and was formed by the compression of an ancient beach. Nowhere, however, is it more prominent than in the Silves area—and nowhere else is it used so prolifically for building. (SEE IMAGES 23 AND 24 IN THE PHOTO INSERT.)

Before meeting Ricardo, I had mentally wrestled with Plato's other assertion, that the three colors were all hewn from the small hill and some from the outer embankments. It would be unique and highly unlikely within such a small, closely defined area: that the red stone was available in Silves was indisputable, but the white and black were more problematic.

A short way downstream from Silves is a spot called Rocha Branca, which translates as "White Rock." It is significant for another reason, which will be divulged later. Not far away, but not in the immediate vicinity, is the dark gray granite of the Foia and Picota Mountains.

About thirty kilometers west, along the coast at Praia da Luz, there is a visible remnant of the Algarve's volcanic past. The tall, dramatic, honey-colored cliffs abruptly give way to rock formed from a black volcanic outflow, not surprisingly known as Rocha Negra or "Black Rock." It would have been quarried, I reasoned, and brought by boat back along the coast to the Arade River and on up to Silves.

But this did not accord with the precise details of Plato's clue. Had I hit a wall? The combination was so unusual, so specific. He obviously considered it significant in identifying the capital.

On several occasions, I have recounted my elation at discoveries that supported my theory. None of them compared with the thrill I experienced at Ricardo's answer when I put the conundrum to him. His reply: "Simple. They were, indeed, all available on the hill!"

Apart from the red stone, the top of the hill consisted of white limestone, and down the eastern flank, there was a substantial outcropping of black volcanic rock.

In addition, Ricardo said that the elevated southern land encircling the town consisted of white limestone and that there were two other substantial outcroppings of the same lode a few hundred meters from the base of the hill—one to the east, the other to the west. These are perfectly positioned for the embankments Plato wrote about. Farther to the west was the Rocha Branca area. It was all as Plato recounted: all three colors of rock could have come from under the hill, with some from the inner embankments and the outer surrounding areas.

If confirmation was still needed that Silves undeniably complied with Plato's clues, this was it. It felt like winning the lottery, except that I wanted to tell the world, not keep it secret. How many small hills of that size can there be on the planet, on a flat plain, surrounded by water, just over nine kilometers by water from the sea, and containing white, black, and red rock?

In total, thirteen clues had now been ticked off.

12. A town built of white, black, and red rock.
13. All three colors available on the hill or the surrounding embankments.

Ricardo also confirmed that many storage areas had been found all over the town and inside the castle. These would have been essential for storing food or water in case the town was besieged but could originally have been the result of earlier quarrying and put to good use as Plato had suggested. The original roofed docks adapted from the quarrying, mentioned in clue 66, would have been at great risk of collapsing during serious earthquakes.

Most of the other clues are impossible to check or verify due to the passage of time. The metal facings of the walls would long since have disappeared as plunder. The watchtowers, walls, guardhouses, and embankments detailed in clues 25, 26, and 63 would not only have been seriously damaged by earthquakes during the destruction of Atlantis, but also demolished by later inhabitants to use the stone for building. Any remains would have crumbled long ago from more quakes and tsunamis sweeping up the river.

But what of those encircling embankments, I asked myself? They were supposed to loom large. Could any remnants have survived the successive disasters?

Surprisingly, the answer is yes.

Toward the end of the last century, a company owning land on what appeared to be a low, oblong hill about one kilometer west of Silves started to remodel it for agriculture.

It transpired that there was an order on the land, forbidding any work on it pending a thorough investigation by archaeologists. Phoenician, Carthaginian, and some Roman artifacts had been found there, and it was presumed to have been occupied from at least Phoenician times.

The local authority was slow to react, despite the land being right beside a main road. Many days passed before officials belatedly stopped the vandalism. By then, the evidence had been destroyed. I drove past the site almost daily and had always thought it was a curious situation. I had reasoned that a Phoenician base there was an anomaly. Why would they pick that spot, way upriver, where they could easily be trapped—and when they almost certainly had a coastal base nearby at Alvor—as well, it is thought, as another at the Arade River mouth around Portimão. They were not settlers, only maintaining bases for trading purposes. They also had a distinct preference for river mouths.

The only logical explanation is that there was another place close to that upriver base that was of overwhelming importance during the period when the Phoenicians were active, yet thousands of years after the date given by Plato for the demise of Atlantis.

If you look at the Phoenician site from a distance, it is clearly more like the remnant of a large embankment, sideways on to the town, with what might have been a small stepped pyramid-shaped mound on part of it and with water once lapping at its base. (SEE IMAGE 25 IN THE PHOTO INSERT.)

The main N124 road has cut through it, and vestiges of it continue on the other (north) side, swinging around toward Silves. I walked up this part to investigate and was amazed that after the ridge along the top, there is a steep face on the other side, down to what is now a flat, fertile, cultivated area.

The distance given by Plato from the outer embankment back to the base of the hill was 925 meters (five stadia).

To arrive at precise comparative measurements is problematic. Thousands of years have passed and erosion has taken its toll, as have earthquakes and the resulting tsunamis surging up the river. I was surprised then that, calculated from the local authority's own map, the current measurement from the east face of this embankment facing the town, back to what I thought would have been the approximate end of the grove at the base of the hill, was, incredibly, between 900 and 950 meters.

Plato said the area of water on the west side after this outer embankment was the city's harbor. The current area to the west of the embankment remnant matches that description and is perfectly situated for a large harbor. Shelter is provided from the prevailing southwesterly winds by the high Rocha Branca headland and other hills. It also directly adjoins the river, and that it was once underwater is self-evident. After coming to this conclusion, the Silves archaeology department confirmed that it is believed that the area housed the Roman harbor. (SEE IMAGE 26 IN THE PHOTO INSERT.)

If the Phoenicians had established a base on the top part of the remains of the old embankment, it would have overlooked this harbor. As already suggested, this implies that it was positioned there for an important trading partner, almost certainly a rich city a short distance upstream.

The River Falacho also flows into the same large harbor basin from the north but now only contains an appreciable volume of water after seasonal rains. Thousands of years ago it would certainly have been more prolific and contributed to this whole area being permanently underwater.

So we have the remains of the outer embankment and harbor area exactly as described by Plato.

What, then, of the other inner embankment?

Logically, it was constructed linking in to those two limestone outcroppings on each side of the central hill. Both now have a property sitting on the highest point, but a lower, sheer face is still clearly visible where they had been cut away to allow the N124 road to pass. Plato intimates that Poseidon built the embankments using the earth and rock from the excavation of the beds for the rings of seawater. There is no sign of this embankment continuing on the other side of the road, but that is hardly surprising after nine thousand years of being shaken by successive earthquakes, battered by tsunami surges, and the soil spread to help reclaim the land. (SEE IMAGE 27 IN THE PHOTO INSERT.)

Today the remaining cutaway face on the west side of Silves is about 130 meters wide. This limestone rock and the one to the east of the town would have protruded above the flooded plain and been the obvious keys on which to base this inner embankment. As these outcroppings are of white limestone, it would also explain Plato's assertion that there was some quarrying on the first embankment. The rock outcroppings could originally have been much higher. They may also have extended farther sideways but then been quarried away by the succession of different cultures as they were conveniently situated for supplying rock to town builders.

The existing distance from the west side of the western outcropping, across it, and back to the the hill is approximately 550 meters. In clue 61, Plato said it was 555 meters (that is, one stadium of water plus two stadia of land). Then there was supposedly a further 370 meters of water (two stadia) from the west side of that embankment to the final outer one already discussed. Give or take a few meters, that is the same as it is today. I think you will agree that these measurements are quite an astonishing match. Even now, the remnant of the outer embankment is of quite a height, indicating that the banks were "raised considerably above the water" (clue 60).

We have a problem, however, with Plato's contention that these embankments were at all times equidistant from the hill as though "turned with a lathe" (clue 26).

Again, it is extraordinary detail. Plato was obsessed with mathematical precision. Others have pointed out that he may have copied the idea from cities with rings of encircling land, which were fashionable around Plato's time. The famous harbor at Carthage has often been cited as an example.

Unless there have been considerable upheavals in the terrain surrounding Silves (more of that later), the embankments and water channels could not have been uniformly equidistant from the hill, apart from the first one of water closest to the city. The other embankment and water channels, if they continued unobstructed all around, would have had to be elliptical, much closer together and narrower to the north and south due to the natural contours of the land. (SEE IMAGE 28, OPPOSITE PAGE.)

Plato's circular description could then be explained by the view that any visitors would have had from the Phoenician base on that far western embankment. They didn't have Google Earth to consult, or bird's-eye views from helicopters. Looking toward the city, they would have seen the next stretch of water glistening in the bright sun, then the next embankment looming over it and circling around away from them, backed by the city. With the diminishing perspective, they would not have been able to ascertain exactly what happened with the embankments and water north and south of the city—and certainly not what happened to the east.

Most likely, they would not have been allowed to venture any farther than the harbor, as that was the principal purpose of the whole layout: privacy, to keep out anyone other than those specifically invited.

All trade would have been kept to the harbor area to avoid impinging on the daily routine of the city. They could have gained a better indication of the layout had they been allowed to climb the high land to the south of the city, but were more likely to have spent their time carousing and enjoying the delights of the harbor front.

So we have evidence that embankments could have existed, separated by water, and measurements taken westward from the city correlate amazingly accurately with those quoted by Plato. That is quite remarkable in light of the huge timespan. The fact that it could not have been exactly as Plato indicated could again be credited to a misunderstanding, or to his attempting to make the story more impressive—or to the distorted view obtained from the outer embankment.

Also, it cannot be discounted that the terrain to the north and south of Silves could have changed at the time Atlantis was originally destroyed. The convulsions that engulfed the area were obviously profound, and it is not unheard of for contours to dramatically change. In 1692, for instance, Port Royal, the infamous pirate den in the Caribbean, was destroyed by an earthquake. The town sank below the waves, and two mountains moved a quarter of a mile. The enormous pressures caused by two continents in collision are suddenly released as the plates move. It is how mountains were originally formed.

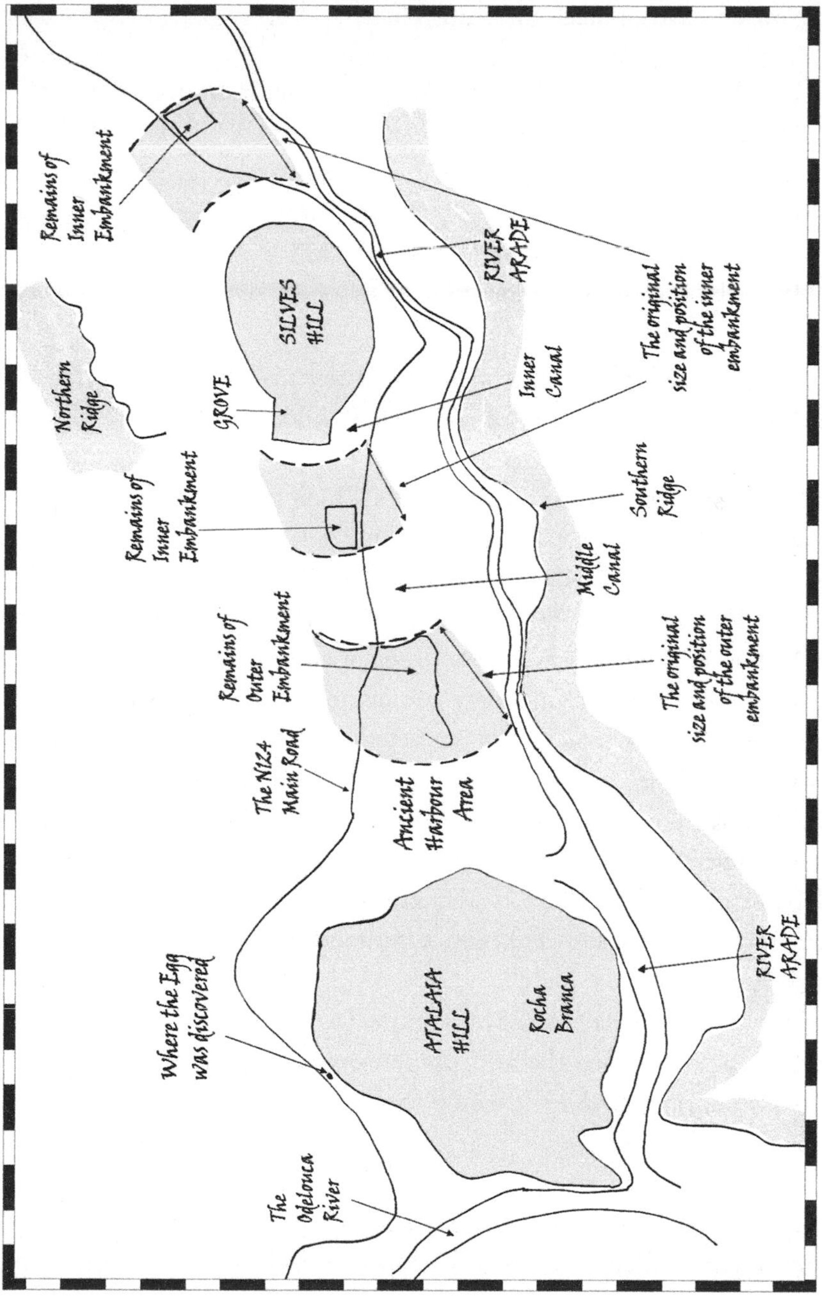
Remains of Inner Embankment
RIVER ARADE
SILVES HILL
GROVE
Northern Ridge
Inner Canal
The original size and position of the inner embankment
Remains of Inner Embankment
Southern Ridge
Middle Canal
Remains of Outer Embankment
The original size and position of the outer embankment
The N124 Main Road
Ancient Harbour Area
RIVER ARADE
ATALAIA HILL
Rocha Branca
Where the Egg was discovered
The Odelouca River

(IMAGE 28) *Chart depicting the remnants of the embankments around Silves, their relationship with the original larger ones, and how these would have compared with Plato's measurements.*

Now we have eighteen matching clues:

14. The outer embankment in the correct position from the west.
15. It was of considerable height.
16. The large sheltered harbor area in the correct position.
17. The points used to key the inner embankment, again in the correct position to the east and west of the hill.
18. The surrounding mountains.

One clue that cannot be reconciled with Silves is the stone wall that Plato said encircled the capital at a radius of 9.25 kilometers (clue 81). It would have been yet another huge construction project almost 100 kilometers long, but, considering the Great Wall of China and the Roman Hadrian's Wall from coast to coast across northern England, possibly achievable.

The problem is the 40-kilometer-deep tract of mountains immediately behind Silves and to a lesser degree to the sides. They are not massively high, but the majority of the hundreds of conical/pyramid-shaped hills have sides sloping at around forty-five degrees. Although I haven't walked the supposed perimeter, to my knowledge there are no vestiges of such a walled structure to be seen anywhere. Plato also said these mountains had originally been higher than still existed in his day, indicating that they had been subjected to a massive shakedown at the time the southern plain disappeared. There is also the possibility that the whole area remaining above water had been simultaneously lowered in height just as the seabed was.

Why would the Atlanteans have wanted to build this extraordinary extra defense anyway, when the area immediately around the citadel sounded pretty well impregnable? It would be like deploying an anchor on a car with modern ABS brakes.

What were they afraid of? In the case of Hadrian's Wall, it was to counter a definite threat, the constant niggling of raiding parties from the fiercely independent and resentful Scottish to the north. Atlantis would not appear to have had problems like that; the province ruled by Atlas was surrounded by others ruled by his brothers. Surely he did not need defenses against them—they were part of a family alliance.

The only threat could have come from the sea, but, given the high cliffs on the immediate coast, any invasion would have to have approached via a river mouth. These would have had towns and ports and would have been fortified with defensive emplacements if there was any hint of danger. Even today, the mouth of the Arade River flowing down from Silves has an old fortress on one side and a small castle on the other, very picturesque for the passengers on the cruise liners that now regularly dock there.

Plato's account contains no indication of invaders; it was, in fact, the Atlanteans who are ultimately painted by him as the aggressors, but even that has been suggested as an embellishment by many researchers.

What would happen to the wall where that wide encircling canal/reservoir had to pass through it twice, not to mention numerous substantial rivers? There would have been a breach of some sort at many points, as well as at the 700-meter-wide river mouth that gave access to the city upstream.

Given the immense time scale (around 11,600 years), however, together with the violent seismic upheavals and the usefulness of the hewn rock for subsequent building, it is hardly surprising that no vestiges remain. If, that is, it ever existed.

Finally, clues 24 and 25 do not, at first sight, support the case for Silves: "Near the plain again, and also in the center of the island at a distance of about fifty stadia, there was a mountain not very high on any side." Over the years, the precise meaning of this clue has been much debated. Did Plato mean in the center literally, from east to west? Or in the center from the sea? Just before mentioning that, in clue 23, he indicated that the plain was bordering the sea to the south but in the center of the kingdom. If he had meant in the center of the *island* from the coast, the plain could not have been bordering the sea. He obviously meant from east to west. It seems reasonable, therefore, to adopt the same interpretation about the city, although it would be easier to present a case for Silves complying with the alternative. He was indicating that it was in the middle from side to side, but fifty stadia (9.25 kilometers) by water to the coast.

When referring to the center, he would only have been giving an approximation, not meaning absolute dead center; that is, nearer the middle rather than closer to the west or east. Indeed, it has been suggested that the wording Plato used translates as "around the center."

Today Silves would fall outside these parameters. It could have been 9.25 kilometers from the sea, as it still is, but be in the western segment of the entire homeland. But, I reasoned, if a large area of land had sunk or been submerged by rapidly rising sea levels, the original distances would have been affected. The sea chart indicates that the land originally extended way west from Cape St. Vincent. I drew a horizontal line across from the western limit of the now-submerged land to a line level with Cádiz. It indicated a distance of about 280 kilometers.

From the same point at the western edge, Silves would have been around 100 kilometers distant, making it nearer the center (140 kilometers) than to the eastern or western limits. Plato said that the kingdom was divided into areas to give to Poseidon's various sons to rule. If Silves was the capital, it would have been part of the central region, not the eastern or western. There is also the near certainty that the southwestern tip of the Algarve once extended much farther toward the Gorringe Bank. That could have been enough to even up the discrepancy.

I still had one last obstacle to overcome, however, one that may well have already occurred to you. Silves is 9.25 kilometers from the sea today; but what of 11,600 years ago? If a large area of land to the south of it that existed then is now submerged, it must surely have been farther away from the coast.

Not necessarily so.

Earlier, I mentioned that on the seabed chart, the original Arade riverbed is clearly seen stretching far out to sea. It gets increasingly deeper and wider where it took over a natural canyon until, at the furthest point on what would have been the original coastline, it is 7 kilometers wide and four thousand feet deep. From the sea, this would have appeared as a wide indentation in the Algarve coast. Even today, the mouth of the estuary is nearly 700 meters wide where it finally meets the coast. Up to that point, the indentation would have appeared as coastline, leaving Silves 9.25 kilometers upriver from the sea.

Further proof that this is correct can be deduced from careful analysis of Plato's information. He recorded that the southern coastal plain was more than 100 kilometers deep and bordered the sea. The capital was said to be close to this plain, so that could only mean at the back (north) of it. How then could it possibly be 9.25 kilometers from the sea unless it was on a wide, deep inlet? It would also explain why Plato did not indicate that the site of the capital had survived. He had not thought through the implications of the information he inherited. Because the capital was only 9.25 kilometers from the sea, he assumed it must have sunk with the plain.

In Chapter Eight, I put forward the theory that the great plain could have been on an island that was separated from the mainland by narrow straits, though possibly only as far as Portimão and the Arade River. This would also have meant that Silves was 9.25 kilometers from the sea.

So, to sum up, Silves offers practically identical matches to clue after precise clue, eighteen in all. The odds of its being coincidental are too enormous to bother calculating. If the equivalent body of evidence was presented by the prosecution at a murder trial, the jury would barely take time for a quick coffee break before returning to consign the accused to life behind bars. The fact that its geographical location coincides with that given by Plato for the Atlantis homeland must also be considered; this could even be counted as the nineteenth clue match.

More than two thousand years of speculation and argument can at last be put to rest. There is overwhelming proof that Plato's Atlantis has been found. It is extremely doubtful whether another site exists anywhere in the world with the same geographical and geological template as Silves.

Unfortunately, it is unlikely that any remains from the Atlantis era could be found in Silves itself. The hill is now extensively developed, and the original bedrock is not far below the surface. There would have been little topsoil there originally, and parts of the bedrock have been quarried away. For millennia following the Atlantis period, each time the city was destroyed by earthquakes, or by enemies such as the Carthaginians, there would have followed a period when looting and carting away of building materials would have been rife. When the town was eventually rebuilt, the new structures would have made use of any remains. Most of the housing for the population outside the citadel would most likely have been built from wood.

Archaeologists have systematically examined large areas of the city and found that only remnants of the Moorish era still exist. A richer vein for

Atlantis archaeological investigation is more likely to be the harbor and the seabed, an undersea world that is ripe for exploration today.

I can't wait for someone to start. To see the first dateable evidence hauled to the surface. To see the faces of all those experts who have so resolutely denied the possibility of a great earlier culture. To witness the complete reevaluation of how civilization developed. But above all, to discover what secrets the Atlanteans took with them when their homeland plunged beneath their feet and the raging sea stole their last breath.

PART TWO

Further Mysteries Resolved

I was exhilarated to have finally nailed Atlantis, but still bursting with questions. What had really destroyed it? What was Silves when the Phoenicians set up a base there to trade with it? How far had the Atlanteans spread throughout the world? Where was their great empire that Plato alluded to? What were the people like, and could you or I even be related to them? What more could be discovered about that ancient alphabet? Perhaps most interesting of all, what about that great white egg that helped prompt the whole quest in the first place? Tall orders all; but the more I delved, the more fascinating were the discoveries.

CHAPTER FOURTEEN

The Destruction . . .
and What Remained

Her long, plaited golden hair trailed over one shoulder as she knelt on the rush mat outside her house. Each of the precious figs from the final harvest had to be delicately placed, ready for drying in the hot autumn sun. They would be especially enjoyed at the midwinter festival at the end of the year, together with the walnuts from the tree that shaded her two toddlers as they played with their new puppy. The children were fascinated by its big pointed ears, and their squeals of pleasure could be heard above the chattering of the birds.

She was happy; life was good. Much earlier that morning, her man had left in his boat to fish from the little bay and beach beyond the high sand dunes sheltering their home. They had enough to eat, and the gods from the glittering citadel, close to the mountains inland, ensured that the kingdom ran in an orderly manner. Everybody had a role to play and a job with a contribution to make to the overall well-being of the community.

The previous evening, her man had told her a strange tale he had heard. Apparently, during the day the river inland had welled up without any obvious reason, and there was general concern as to what could have caused it.

She had almost finished sorting the figs when suddenly she realized that the birds had gone quiet. Apprehensively, she slowly stood to look around. Suddenly, the deathly hush and stillness was broken by a loud, awful groaning-and-grinding noise. It seemed to be emanating from the very bowels of the earth beneath her feet.

A split second later, there was a huge jolt and she was thrown to the ground, squashing the figs. Suddenly, the earth took on a life of its own—it was moving and writhing like a huge serpent. Instinctively, she looked to her children, but her attention was drawn to the house just beyond them. Like the others in the village, it was sturdily constructed from timber, but it was now swaying drunkenly. She watched, hypnotized, as each movement became more exaggerated than the last, until it collapsed with a final shudder. She screamed and, with difficulty, rushed to gather the children into her arms. The tremors persisted for about six terrifying minutes, as did the horrible noise now mingling with the screams of her neighbors and the crashing of buildings.

When it finally subsided, she crouched with the children, stunned, too frightened to move. After what seemed an age, her eyes weakly began to focus on odd things around her. The children were agape as they pointed to the dunes that had once towered high above them but were now reduced to such an extent that parts of the sea could be seen. Gradually it dawned on her that her parents had been inside the house. An inner strength surmounted her terror and fear for her own safety, and she began to frantically claw at the rubble, momentarily oblivious of the bawling babes.

Twenty minutes later, she was still agitatedly digging in the debris, trying to pull clear some of the timbers, when another noise impinged on her consciousness. It was a strange whooshing noise, growing stronger by the second and coming from the direction of the beach. Then a curtain of gray dramatically rose over the dunes, rapidly gaining height to at least ten times that of a house, obliterating the blue sky. In the instant when it dawned on her that it was water, it was upon her. She did not drown. The impact killed her.

The terrible sequence of events that overwhelmed and obliterated the Atlantis homeland and its civilization in southwest Iberia had begun. The foregoing is my fictional account of what it would have been like for one of the victims.

Was it that dangerous fault line close to the southern coast that caused the sinking and destruction, or was something else responsible? Of one thing I am sure: a cataclysmic event of the size indicated by Plato could well have occurred there. (SEE IMAGE 29 BELOW.)

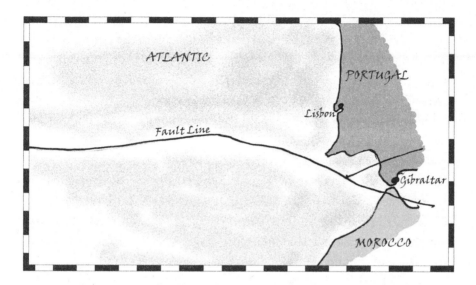

(IMAGE 29) *Chart of the tectonic fault line running in front of the Algarve and the Costa de la Luz.*

We can get some idea of how and why it may have happened from the clues and information available from the great 1755 quake detailed in Chapter Four. Geological seabed research has also demonstrated that there was one such event around the very time frame given by Plato: 9600 B.C.

The great southern plain that now lies off the Algarve coast, beneath the waves, may not have subsided immediately. Like that fateful quay that sank in Lisbon in 1755, the subsidence could have coincided with after-tremors. It would not have needed to sink to great depths. Plato's account of "mud and low bottoms obstructing passage in the region" confirms this as a fact. In some places, as far as 30 kilometers out to sea, the seabed is still only 130 meters deep, and we have to factor in rising sea levels and subsequent quakes.

The next chapter on the Atlantis Empire details just some of the geological research that indicates areas of land in the mid-Atlantic that had sunk to incredible depths—as deep as six thousand feet. Chunks of the seabed plummeting that distance would have caused mayhem, not the least consequence being towering tsunamis circling the globe. It is, therefore, not beyond the realm of possibility that the land off southwest Iberia has sunk a significant amount. Some of the chasms around the Gorringe Bank are testament to tremendous geological activity in the area. It has been estimated that an area of three hundred kilometers' radius around the epicenter sank thirty meters in the 1755 event alone.

The initial violent tremors would have killed much of the population, burying bodies under demolished buildings. Any homes left standing would have been devastated by further tremors over the next few hours. If you survived the first tremor, imagine then being in the path of a gigantic wall of water, up to a hundred feet high, traveling at hundreds of miles per hour. Time for horror and panic would have been brief. The first tsunami would have battered and vaulted the Algarve cliffs, torn up the estuaries, and, farther east along the coast, swept over sand dunes as far as Cádiz. Debris, rocks, and soil would have been carried inland, quite possibly as far as the mountains in places. Trees and vegetation would have been ripped up and intermingled with the general detritus, dead animals, and human bodies.

An inferno would have raged through the mountains. It would have started in the villages as a result of the quake, and quickly spread to the wooded hills. It would have devoured everything in its path. Nothing would have stopped it until it reached the flooded coast—or until there was no more left for it to engulf. I have experienced and witnessed such an event, when our house was saved with literally seconds to spare. My neighbors had evacuated with my wife, and I had stayed to try to dampen down the garden. I was preparing to escape by jumping into the river, as I helplessly watched the huge flames tear down the mountain behind the house at an incredible speed I had not bargained for. Thankfully, two helicopters arrived to swiftly scoop water out of the river on their approach, then swooped low to dump it over our garden and surrounding woodland to frustrate the fire. As quickly as they had arrived, they disappeared into the swirling smoke to save someone else. Brave men. In all, the fire burned for more than two days and devastated fourteen thousand hectares.

In 1755 and all earlier similar massive upheavals, the River Arade and its valley would have acted as a funnel for the tsunami, directing the full force toward Silves. The harbor would have felt the first impact. The multitude of boats would have been flung around, with many pounded to matchwood and others left broken and marooned on high ground. However, surprisingly, the city itself might have escaped the full force—and maybe it had been deliberately planned that way.

On reading the accounts of the 1755 quake, I was struck by the statement that Faro, the current Algarve capital situated in the center of the coast, was spared the worst of the tsunami, as it was protected to a degree by offshore sandbanks and Faro Island. A good deal of the impact was absorbed and dissipated. This sparked a train of thought. Perhaps those two huge embankments and wide water channels protecting ancient Silves were not designed just to keep people out, but also to break the surge of any tsunami cascading up the river. If Atlantis had been in existence for a few thousand years, the ruling elite would certainly have been aware of the danger and its frightening, destructive potential.

The access channel from the outer embankment by the harbor to the next inner ring of water could have been positioned where the river still runs today—that is, to the south, up against the surrounding ridge. The next channel into the inner ring of water could have then been considerably offset farther north, or even on the other side of the city altogether. This would have had the effect of forcing the surge of water to largely bypass the town to the south, pouring on around the high embankment and on up the river. The embankments themselves would have broken a lot of the impact, and the wide rings of water between each one would have helped dissipate it. Repeated tsunamis since then might also explain why only the parts of the embankments now remaining are those embedded in rock. If the rest had been artificially heaped up, using earth and rock cut out to form the deep channels for the rings of water, they would have been battered and devastated over the years.

Remember that, according to Plato, the area depended on a vast irrigation system. Without one, agriculture certainly would not have flourished.

The effect of the flooding would have been disastrous for such an elaborate scheme if any of it had survived above the sea. Salt water would have polluted it, and the complete emptying and flushing of what was left of the whole system would have been required before it could have served its purpose again. Some points would also have been breached by the earthquakes, and others blocked by the debris dumped by the receding sea. Its use for transport would have been nullified. Life for any lucky survivors would have been virtually impossible.

The capital itself may have been capable of supporting life, as it had an abundance of fresh water, not least from that flowing down the River Arade as well as springs within the city. If the ruling elite had not had forewarning of the looming disaster and not fled in advance, they could well have survived the quakes in their stone homes built in the ancient polygonal style to absorb the tremors. However, with most of their homeland now forming the seabed and what was left uninhabitable and unproductive, they would eventually have been forced to seek new pastures.

Apart from this local scenario, the possibility cannot be ignored that the destruction of Atlantis could have been linked to a global disaster. In his groundbreaking book *Fingerprints of the Gods*, originally published in 1995, Graham Hancock chronicles how there are accounts from many parts of the world of a truly immense disaster occurring around twelve thousand years ago. The legends invariably recount huge floods, often reaching mountaintops, and indescribable shaking of the land, with mountains collapsing and new ones thrust skyward. The sun took fright and disappeared behind darkened skies for long periods. Temperatures plummeted, crops would not grow, and livestock died.

Our school history books neglected to teach us about catastrophism, as the establishment had set its face firmly against it, embracing uniformitism instead. Big words for simple concepts. Uniformitism is the theory that the world has slowly developed in a uniform way and has not been affected by worldwide catastrophes that have stop-started or drastically changed the environment and the development of man. This dogma is ingrained, despite many scientists' drawing attention to geological discoveries indicating a combination of the two. The discoveries last century in Alaska and Siberia of whole ice fields of frozen mud full of remains of thousands of horses, bears, bison, mammoths, lions, and wolves are apt examples. In the 1940s, Dr. Frank C. Hibben, professor of archaeology at the University of New Mexico, dramatically recounted the unbelievable sight of bulldozers heaving around the remains. He described tusks and bones being rolled up in front of the blades "like shavings before a giant plane."[63] The carcasses were a terrible mangled sight, most of them pulled apart by what must have been a catastrophic but unexplainable disaster. Other remains, particularly mammoths, recovered from the permafrost in Siberia have undigested vegetation—such as buttercups, bluebells, and wild beans—in their mouths and stomachs.[64] Clearly, they were not grazing in a cold climate at the time the catastrophe befell them, but, like those in Alaska, they were washed there by a huge flood of global and apocalyptic proportions. For further evidence, look at R. Cedric Leonard's web site.[65]

That all sounds even more serious than the major quakes affecting southwest Iberia. Various explanatory scenarios have been suggested. One of the most plausible, prompted by accounts and legends of a fiery dragon traversing the sky and falling to earth, is an asteroid strike. Even a small asteroid of tens of meters in diameter can have disastrous results.

Exactly *how* dramatic can be gauged from the Tunguska incident that some readers may have heard of. It occurred at around 8 A.M. on June 30, 1908.[66] Tunguska is a remote, inhospitable, and fortunately uninhabited region of Siberia. Eyewitness reports from a long way away spoke of a kind of fire that produced an unbearable heat, then brief darkness, followed by an explosion that threw people to the ground. In northern Europe, the sky was illuminated for nine days. In England, people were able to play cricket and read the papers at midnight. The explosion has been estimated to have been the equivalent of a forty- to fifty-megaton bomb.

It was a full nineteen years before Russian scientists were finally able to visit, as the site was so remote. What they found was awesome. The area of the forest affected was between twenty-four and thirty-two kilometers in diameter. The landscape was badly scorched, and all the trees were flattened—but side by side, the tops facing outward, fanning out from the center. And, where they had expected to find a meteorite crater, there stood an area of denuded trees. The scientists concluded that an object had exploded in the air.

If this had happened over any large city, it would have been mostly flattened—and there would have been no survivors.

The object in question was almost certainly not large. If one of, say, a mile in diameter collided with the earth (there are plenty of those whirling around in the asteroid belt), it could be good-bye for all of us.

Another strong suspect for a worldwide disaster is a significant, sudden movement of the earth's crust. It has been argued that Antarctica once occupied latitudes much farther north, in a more temperate climate zone— and that it was Atlantis. Its swift movement south, together with simultaneous shifting of the earth's crust elsewhere, gave rise to the disaster story.[67]

I briefly dealt with the Atlantis part of this theory in Chapter Three, excluding Antarctica as a possibility based on Plato's clues. That does not, however, preclude an event such as described here having happened in Antarctica or elsewhere. The effects would have been truly worldwide, and few would have survived such a trauma.

In another more recent epic book, published in 2002 and titled *Underworld . . . Flooded Kingdoms of the Ice Age*,[68] Graham Hancock details the tremendous forces at work during the melting of the great glaciers. He pulls together the work of many scientists and academics to demonstrate that the thaw was not at a slow, more or less uniform rate—as has generally been believed—but that three massively accelerated events took place around fifteen thousand, eleven or twelve thousand, and seven or eight thousand years ago. Each resulted in the flooding and rapid submergence of huge coastal areas all around the globe. One cause for these events was the catastrophic breaking of ice dams that had been holding back immense reserves of melted water built up during the thaw. The breaking of these dams released massive floods cascading and descending over the ice, sweeping in front of it other substantial lakes and, eventually, assuming gigantic proportions by the time it was ejected into the sea.

Another cause was immense sheets of ice that had been destabilized, also plunging into the sea. At one stage, this happened to a sheet a third of the size of Canada. Another significant factor was that the incredible weight of the ice caps was enough to force the earth's crust beneath them into huge, basinlike depressions. Conversely, the weight of less water in the oceans (the water being locked up in glaciers) decreased the pressure on the seabed, causing it to rise. The opposite happened when the glaciers melted: the fall in the level of the seabed from the beginning of the melt to its end has been estimated to have been around fifty meters.

Geologists have long suggested that these gigantic swings in pressure on the earth's crust, particularly in the area of serious fault lines like the one in front of southwest Iberia, could also trigger monumental seismic upheavals.

It is clear from the various sources marshaled so well by Graham Hancock that "a devastating global flood occurred around 11,600 years ago . . . and was accompanied by enormous earthquakes."

This again supports Plato in that he had his basic facts correct, as that is exactly the date he gave for the destruction of Atlantis. It also highlights the pointlessness of perpetuating the suggestion that Santorini, with its Minoan civilization, inspired the Atlantis legend.

Perhaps it was a combination of events that actually overwhelmed Atlantis. The sudden accelerated melting of the ice caps around 11,600 years ago, apart from causing huge tsunamis and the subsequent drowning of the immediate, sodden coastal areas by rising sea levels, also triggered the dramatic seismic event and tsunami that the seabed research indicated happened around the same time in front of southwest Iberia. The result was a substantial lowering of the land combined with a rapid rise in the sea levels, resulting in its being swallowed by the sea.

Some researchers have postulated that Atlantis did not sink in just one episode, but that remnants lingered and were destroyed in subsequent disasters. The frequency of the seismic events recorded by the geological research off southwest Iberia certainly makes this a possibility, but I know of no direct evidence to support this hypothesis—apart from the fact that there are what would appear to be three distinct levels of the seabed in front of the current coastline.

Subsequent to the major Atlantis disaster of around 9600 B.C., further quakes could each have resulted in more subsidence of the seabed. This would explain the many chronicled claims (detailed in Chapter Eight) that around 2,000 to 2,500 years ago, the sea immediately outside the Straits of Gibraltar and off the southwest coast was still not navigable in parts because of the low depths and mud. The ancient accounts of these difficulties, mostly written more than nine thousand years after Atlantis sank, and the fact that sea trade continued from the Mediterranean with southwest Iberia during the last millennium B.C., indicate that the blockage was not necessarily universal. Only some areas had more recently sunk prior to the accounts; others probably remained as islands or sandbanks.

Each event stirred up the mud anew and submerged other areas. More recent quakes could have caused the seabed to have dropped sufficiently to improve the clearance to current levels.

Unless some ancient records are discovered, we will never know precisely what happened. We do, however, now understand that the extraordinary destructive power embedded in the fault running in front of southwest Iberia is more than capable of causing the type of disaster detailed by Plato. If it could have happened anywhere in the world, it was here.

There is a general misconception of how the Richter scale used to express the strength of earthquakes actually works: 2.0 on the scale represents *ten* times 1.0, not just twice, which is what many people think. Then 3.0 is ten times 2.0, and so on, so an earthquake of 7.0 is 100 times the strength of 5.0. Most quakes that cause widespread damage are in the region of 6.5 to 7.0. The Algarve's 1755 quake has been estimated to have been at least 8.9 or 9.0. That means it was at least a hundred times as strong as the one that devastated Haiti in 2010. Frightening, isn't it?

But what exactly sank—and what was left? Did all of that great plain, the one Plato was so keen on, sink? If you accept the hypothesis of this book, certainly a major part of it is now underwater, but enough remains to give a flavor of what it would have been like. You can visit it, stroll through the citrus groves, and admire the orderly rows of the vineyards and, in the spring, discover the best show of wild orchids in Europe.

The current Algarve coastline, west from Faro, still echoes Plato's description of Atlantis being "lofty and precipitous." Beautiful, high, honey-colored sandstone cliffs, mostly backing golden beaches, make this one of the most stunning and memorable stretches of coast in the world. These cliffs have been sculpted and weathered into fascinating shapes by wind, rain, and sea. An undulating plain runs behind the entire coast, punctuated by pretty villages and ports, where rivers flow—or used to—out to sea. In places it is relatively narrow, only a few kilometers wide, but elsewhere it's as much as fifteen kilometers north to south.

This plain continues on the Spanish side of the border, over the Guadiana River, and broadens considerably toward the eastern end. The area close to the border makes good use of the fertile soil, cornering a considerable share of the European strawberry market. Plastic tunnels shimmer in the sun like huge lakes, for kilometer after kilometer.

Over time, large parts closer to the coast past Huelva have become wetlands: the famous Dõna Ana National Park. At some stage it has been invaded by the sea, almost certainly as the result of one or another of the huge quakes, and was a lagoon in Roman times. Northeast of this area, the gently undulating, fertile plain continues for around 70 kilometers to Seville and beyond.

When combined, the plains of the Algarve, southwest Andalucía, and the vast submerged area out to sea present a significant size. The total area is not as big as that described by Plato, but it is certainly large enough to have been noted as part of the history of Atlantis. Plato said it was rectangular, but on the other hand that translation has been questioned. It has been suggested that the original Plato script only indicated that it had four corners, which were not necessarily ninety-degree angles. Image 30 on the next page shows the existing area combined with the sunken area, and illustrates how they formed a wedge, narrower in the northeast but broadening out considerably as it reached the coast and out to sea. The measurements could have been around 300 by 200 kilometers. Plato cites a larger area, about 555 by 370 kilometers, but the proportions are similar.

At this point, it is worth noting again that Plato only writes in round figures, albeit in stadia, the ancient Greek measurement—always, for example, "100" or "500"—never precise lower numbers like "86" or "468." It would have been true to his nature to have exaggerated by rounding everything up. There is also still some disagreement about the length of one stadium. I have taken the generally accepted figure of 185 meters, but it has been suggested that it could have been less than that. Another theory is that the priest gave his information in the Egyptian unit of length, the *khet*, of only 52.4 meters. Solon could have noted that figure and later forgotten to convert his numbers into stadia. This, however, hardly sounds plausible for someone of Solon's intellect.

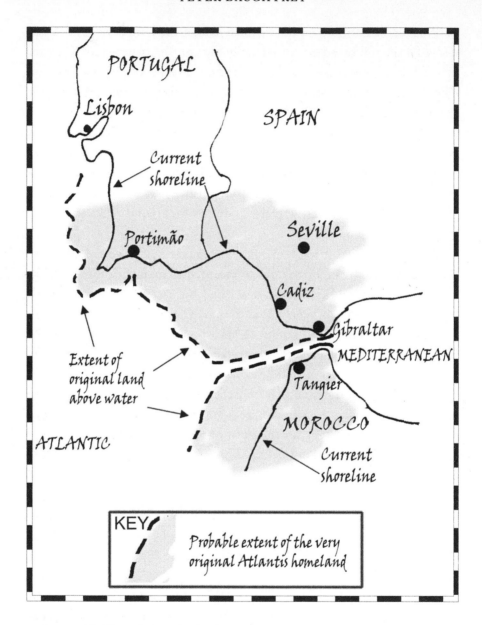

(IMAGE 30) *The probable Atlantis original homeland before flooding and submergence.*

Masses of unusual, small, pyramid/conical-shaped mountains exist inland, immediately behind the existing Algarve coastal plain, particularly around Silves. The early morning and evening lights produce pronounced shadows that, eerily, make many of those mountains that have been terraced resemble earth-covered "step" pyramids.

As the mountains roll farther inland, they initially get larger. They are densely crammed together but punctuated by some fertile valleys, rivers, and lakes. In the west they are dominated by two sizeable mountains, with the town of Monchique between them. The tallest, Foia, is partnered by the slightly smaller Picota. They are unique in the whole mountain range in that they are formed of a type of granite: all the others are schist. Foia is almost three thousand feet high, just short of the height of the celebrated Mount Snowdon in Wales. It is possible to drive all the way to the top and gaze down at the awesome view over the foothills and the narrow coastal strip, imagining what Atlantis was once like, with the plain rolling out uninterrupted for mile after mile, where now there is sparkling sea. (SEE IMAGE 13 IN THE PHOTO INSERT.)

Imagine also the towns and ports dotting it, together with the roads and canals that linked them all up. The seabed charts show many areas marked as rocks, and perhaps some of these could have been the remains of Atlantean settlements. Apart from a few recent wrecks, nothing has been explored. The whole area is fairly flat and shallow, sloping gradually from the beaches to around 100 to 120 meters before the first submerged sea cliffs—all easily investigated using modern techniques. I know the approximate position of at least one unexplored, submerged settlement. Just think what archaeological riches await.

The existing mountains continue north for about 40 kilometers, providing the shelter that contributes immensely to the Algarve's sublime climate. As Plato indicates, the mountains are not as grand as they once were—but, significantly and crucially, they survived the sinking. (SEE IMAGES 12A, 12B, 12C, AND 12D IN THE PHOTO INSERT.) The same chain continues across into Spain, angling slightly northward, all the way past Seville to Granada. Other mountains drop south to the coast at Gibraltar and to the east of Jerez. They are famous for the incredibly pretty "White Villages" that pepper them.

With the destruction of Atlantis, it is of little surprise that any survivors could see no future there and took off in all directions, some of them to surviving parts of the empire. But what, exactly, was that empire?

CHAPTER FIFTEEN

The Empire

He was up at dawn; the captain had promised they would sight the island around that time. From his stance in the prow of the boat, he could just make out something smudged on the horizon, but the sun had not yet revealed itself. Suddenly, as he swept away his long red hair swirling over his eyes, the first rays burst over the edge of the ocean; he gasped. The island was there, all right, with buildings barely discernible around the bay. Hanging above the settlement was a long, horizontal pillow of cloud. Emerging skyward from the cloud was the great volcano, its snow-capped peak glowing salmon pink in the dawn sunlight. He had heard stories about this vision, but the reality was still breathtaking. His excitement and anticipation rose; he had been looking forward to this next year for so long. All had been arranged when his nine uncles from the four corners of the Kingdom had visited his father in the citadel last year for their periodic conference. He had just turned eighteen, and it was time to start familiarizing him with the great empire.

This is an imaginary account of a young Atlantean prince starting out on a tour of the empire he would one day rule. The island is now known as Tenerife, the volcano Mount Teide. Many tourists from Europe will be familiar with it as a popular holiday haunt, particularly in the winter when the climate is warmer and more reliable than in the Mediterranean. Like the other islands in the Canaries group, however, at the time the prince went calling, it would have differed considerably from how it is today.

There is no doubt that Atlantis had an empire, with a healthy mercantile trade (clues 11, 35, and 39). Plato said that on leaving the Mediterranean, you immediately came across Atlantis, then . . .

"From there you could pass westward to other islands, and from those to the vast opposite continent that bordered the Atlantic Ocean."

"Atlantis had a great and wonderful empire which had ruled over several other islands in the Ocean and parts of that great continent."

It should be noted that he said "several" islands, not "many." There are numerous islands in the Atlantic, particularly off the eastern seaboard of Central America, and he seems to indicate that Atlantis may have annexed only the important, or larger, ones. On the other hand, 11,600 years ago, many of these groups of islands would have been joined together, forming much larger, but fewer, islands.

According to Plato, it was the main Atlantis homeland that disappeared under the sea, not the rest of the empire. I reasoned that it was worth trying to identify the islands on which they ruled, then search for any remains or hints of earlier civilizations that may have existed there.

The Canary, Azores, and Caribbean islands all fit Plato's description. Even today they are much used as ports of call for taking on fresh water and supplies, as well as carrying out repairs and minimizing the number of continuous days at sea. In the past, with slower boats—employing sail or manpower—and poor storage facilities, they were crucial for Atlantic crossings. Christopher Columbus on his first epic voyage of discovery, for instance, stopped in to the island of Gomera in the Canaries to take on fresh water. Some ports in the Azores Islands are regarded with great affection by transatlantic sailors because of their historic role. Calling there is almost a pilgrimage. (SEE IMAGE 31, NEXT PAGE.)

It has been suggested at various times that each of these island groups might be the remains of Atlantis. Some of the evidence is certainly intriguing and links with Atlantis, as will be revealed, but not one of them fits the clues for the Atlantis capital and homeland. They do not support many of Plato's pointers, particularly those regarding position and the potential for huge wealth from metal mining.

(IMAGE 31) *The current islands in the eastern part of the Atlantic.*

So let's imagine that, like the fictional prince, we are setting out from an Algarve port on an Atlantean boat, following a well-charted route, hopping from island to island and eventually stepping ashore in America.

As they were for Columbus, the Canary Islands would have been the first port of call—unless there were other, closer islands that have since sunk. In fact, that is certainly a possibility, as the now submerged Gorringe Bank, mentioned in the previous chapter, could certainly have once been above water. It is a substantial size and has two volcanoes. It cozies right up against that notorious fault line which then runs in front of the Algarve and would have been subject to the full force of seismic upheavals, such as that in 1755.

One of the peaks of the Gorringe Bank is only about thirty meters below the surface, and the bank itself is now thought to be slowly rising; but that doesn't necessarily preclude it from once having sunk. At its current depth, at least a part of it would have been well above the surface before the great glacier melt, in which case it would certainly have been part of the Atlantean Empire. Its sinking could not have been the cause of the mud blockage that Plato refers to, as it was too far away from the Straits of Gibraltar.

There are seven islands in the Canary group, all formed from upwelling magma from a depth of three thousand feet. Apart from their popularity as holiday venues due to the particularly equable climate, they are most famous for the inhabitants who occupied them when they were rediscovered by the Spanish. Called Guanches, they astonished the Spaniards with their fair or red waist-length hair, blue or gray eyes, and the men's height—generally six feet or more.

I called it the *rediscovery* of the islands, since they were undoubtedly already known to the Phoenicians, Carthaginians, Greeks, and Romans. It is claimed that the Guanches strongly resembled Cro-Magnon man, like the remains, from 8000 B.C., found at Muges in Portugal.[69] This is the race that has frequently been associated with Atlantis. Equally important for this book's hypothesis, it is thought that the Guanches shared a common origin with the Berbers from the Atlas Mountains of northwest Africa.

This ancient race from the Canaries has long been regarded as a fascinating enigma, with practices and customs that, incredibly, linked them to other ancient civilizations, such as those in Egypt and South America. They embalmed their nobility, for example. A few of the resulting mummies are still in existence in museums today, notably with well-preserved red hair and incisions made by the embalmers almost identical to the Egyptian ones. Interestingly, a three thousand-year-old Egyptian mummy in London's British Museum has red hair.

Perhaps the most astounding but little-known fact is that six small step pyramids were recently discovered in the Canary Islands, precisely aligned east to west. Similar to well-known examples in Egypt, Mesopotamia, and South America, they are at Guimar on the island of Tenerife and were identified by the famous explorer Thor Heyerdahl in 1998.[70] Experts originally scoffed at the notion that they were pyramids, suggesting that they were terraces or simply heaps of stones piled up by the Spanish when clearing the land. Heyerdahl, together with an archaeologist he had brought in to investigate, was able to refute this. They found that each stone had been purposely stacked "flat side out" and that the corner stones had been carefully shaped.

The stairways on each of the main complex of three were precisely aligned with the rise and fall of the sun on the summer solstice. Like the Egyptians, Guanches were sun worshippers. The archaeologist carried out test excavations on a ceremonial platform between two of them and confirmed that it had been built from stone blocks, gravel, and earth. The platforms on the tops of the pyramids were perfectly flat and consisted of gravel.

Heyerdahl was convinced they were the work of pre-European explorers, constructed in the same way as those found in South America and Mesopotamia.

No one knows for how long the Guanches inhabited the Canaries, but the popular theory is that they came from North Africa. Strangely, though, it is recorded that when the Spanish arrived, the locals did not possess boats. As a result, the various islands existed autonomously. Unless they had been dumped on the island by others, they must once have been capable of sea travel, but they had regressed and/or forgotten how to build boats. Maybe this was the result of the horrors of being stricken by huge tsunamis—resulting from the Algarve quakes—that had destroyed any boats they had and devastated low-lying areas? Perhaps they were just too terrified to put out to sea afterward?

If they were part of the Atlantis Empire, in the wake of the disaster striking their homeland they could suddenly have been left to fend for themselves without their knowledgeable ruling mentors. They were, however, intelligent; it would be surprising if they had not been able to work out how to build some sort of primitive seagoing vessel. Before the rise in sea levels, the islands would have been larger, and it has been postulated that some of them could have been joined together at some point in history. Any sudden sinking of land and rise in sea levels could also have contributed to the surviving inhabitants' trepidation about venturing forth and braving the waves.

Sadly, as in South America, the Spaniards were not concerned with preserving the history of conquered lands, and the Guanches' early history remains a mystery. Who knows what was destroyed by the religious

TOP (IMAGE 6): A small section of the ancient massive walls of Niebla. BOTTOM (IMAGE 7): The Rock of Gibraltar seen from inside the Mediterranean. (*Courtesy of the Costa de Sol Golf Guide*)

Reflecting the description given by Plato, some of the typical high golden cliffs and beaches of the Algarve. OPPOSITE (IMAGE 9): Praia da Marinha. LEFT (IMAGE 10): The soft sandstone is often weathered into peculiar shapes. ABOVE (IMAGE 11): Praia do Camilo.

ALL OPPOSITE AND ABOVE LEFT AND RIGHT (IMAGES 12A-12D): Mountains and river valleys, typical of the range that stretches back 40 kilometers to the north of the Algarve. Note the small pyramid-shaped hill in the center of the top right photograph. BOTTOM (IMAGE 13): Part of the existing plain and the sea viewed from Foia, the highest point of the Algarve.

ALL (IMAGES 15A-15C):
The *Forcados* bringing a
charging bull to a standstill
in a Portuguese bullfight.
(Bull-fight blogspot.com.
Arteeemocao blogspot.com.
Facouruche.blogspot.com)

TOP (IMAGE 16): The remains of an old canal in front of Estombar, only a few kilometers west from the flood plain. It continues a short distance to the west until it meets the River Arade estuary. BOTTOM (IMAGE 17): A small section of the old floodplain adjacent to the town of Lagoa. Photographed when part was flooded to grow rice.

ABOVE (IMAGE 18): The entrance to the River Arade estuary. OPPOSITE (IMAGE 21): Silves from the river as it meanders up to the town from the south.

Various aspects of Silves: THIS PAGE (IMAGE 19): Silves seen across the plain from the east. OPPOSITE TOP (IMAGE 20): Silves from the north. OPPOSITE BOTTOM (IMAGE 22): The ancient well in Silves that dates from the Moorish occupation, in the position indicated by Plato for a water supply created by Poseidon. The town's museum has been constructed around it, just below the castle and the cathedral.

OPPOSITE AND TOP (IMAGES 23-24): Silves' ancient town gate in red sandstone with black, white, and red stone paving in front of it. MIDDLE (IMAGE 25): The remnants of the outer embankment seen from the position of the inner one (ie., closer to Silves). The area between was filled with seawater and the ancient harbor was the other side of this outer embankment. RIGHT (IMAGE 27): The remains of the inner embankment.

LEFT (IMAGE 26): At the point downstream where the River Arade would have entered the old harbor area on the left, with the outer embankment just beyond it. Silves is visible about two kilometers in the distance. BOTTOM LEFT (IMAGE 37): A stone originally erected in memory of a warrior, engraved in the local "southwestern script." Note the unusual depiction of the deceased with a crude indication of the Libyan side lock. (Museu da Escrita do Sudoeste, Almodôvar, Portugal.) BOTTOM RIGHT (IMAGE 38): A section of a stone engraved with the "southwestern script" in Silves Museum.

ABOVE (IMAGE 44): The egg in the Lagos museum. RIGHT (IMAGE 45): Close-up of the symbol sculpted on the outside of the egg. BELOW (IMAGE 46): A mock-up using a mirror image of the top half of the egg placed underneath to show how it would have been a perfect egg shape. The outside is discolored due to its being buried in the local red earth for thousands of years, but the white of the limestone is evident from where it has been scratched.

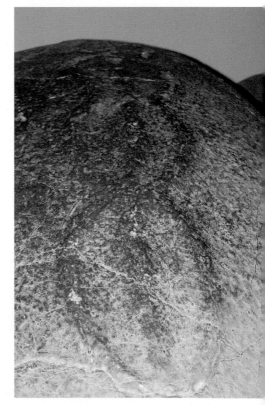

ABOVE (IMAGE 47): One of the many natural round pyramids in the vicinity of Silves. This one overlooks the ancient harbor site. RIGHT (IMAGE 48): Another round pyramid hill immediately behind Silves. BELOW (IMAGE 49): A view looking over Silves from the southwest. Note the pyramid-shaped hill, which is circled.

zealots amongst the Spaniards? A few examples of a long-forgotten script have survived and, significantly, a good percentage of the symbols are the same as those found in the Algarve, such as on the gravestone mentioned in Chapter One.

The Guanches resisted the Spanish for decades before succumbing. Those not put to the sword eventually intermarried with Spaniards, who were much taken by the extremely attractive Guanche women; but the odd throwback to the original gene pool can still be seen.

Leaving the Canaries, we may have charted a course north to Madeira, or possibly taken the Canary current, like Columbus, direct to the Caribbean.

The island of Madeira was uninhabited when discovered by the Portuguese around 1418 A.D. Some people believe it was alluded to in various earlier Greek tales; but, apart from the following story about the Carthaginians, my researches suggest that no signs of earlier habitation have ever been found. It is an extremely precipitous island, with high mountains. One of the surprises for tourists is the ingenuity of the current Portuguese inhabitants in constructing terraces for cultivation on slopes steep enough to panic a mountain goat.

Classical writers have often described journeys by individuals to various legendary isles in the Atlantic Ocean. One account, generally associated with Madeira, is that by Pseudo-Aristotle. An impostor of the famous Aristotle, he was possibly one of his pupils. In one work, *On Marvelous Things Heard*, he refers to a "desert island" in the Atlantic outside the "Pillars of Hercules," a few days' voyage away.[71] According to him, it was discovered by Carthaginians, who established a colony there. They were so taken by it that they adopted the same tactics against any other nationality venturing too close as for those trying to navigate the Straits of Gibraltar: their boats were sunk and the occupants caught and summarily killed.

Interestingly, Pseudo-Aristotle reported that the island did have inhabitants but the Carthaginians had massacred them. He also said, however, that the island had large rivers but, despite reasonable rainfall, the mountainous landscape means that these are noticeably absent on Madeira today.

It was subject to volcanic activity up to around 6,500 years ago (4500 B.C.).[72] If Plato's figures were correct, that is 5,000 years after Atlantis was destroyed. When the sea levels were 100 to 120 meters lower, part of

Madeira from the Ponta de Sao Lourenço extended a significant distance above water toward another small group of uninhabited islands called Islas Desertas. So we appear to have at least one submerged area, much flatter than the rest of the island and perhaps more suited to habitation and cultivation.

Another ancient account was brought to my attention by Roger Coghill.[73] He had found it in the writings of the Sicilian Diodorus Siculus, who is probably better known for his account of the legendary Amazons, which also contains some illuminating comments referring to possible survivors from Atlantis. "There was once in the western parts of Libya, on the bounds of the inhabited world, a race ruled by women who practiced the arts of war." He goes on to relate how the Amazons conquered a race called the Atlantoi, described by him as "most civilized men," living in a prosperous country with great cities—and much given to astrology. He continues that in mythology, that country, along the shores of the ocean, was the birthplace of the gods. Does that sound familiar?

About a decade ago, a stone-lined grave was uncovered in the Algarve while a country road close to Silves was being repaired. It contained the skeleton of a woman warrior complete with spear. Elena Wishaw had a small cup in her museum in Niebla that was decorated with a picture of a woman warrior fighting two male warriors. All very intriguing, but, that aside, Diodorus talks of an island a number of days' voyage to the west of the Libyan coast. For readers familiar with Madeira, his description of part of the island and its climate will strike a chord. "Its land is fruitful, much of it mountainous and not a little being a level plain of surpassing beauty. Through it flow navigable rivers which are used for irrigation, and the island contains many parks planted with trees of every variety and gardens in great multitudes which are traversed by sweet water; on it also are private villas of costly construction, and throughout the gardens banqueting houses have been constructed in a setting of flowers, and in them the inhabitants pass their time during the summer season. . . . There is excellent hunting of every manner of beast and wild animal. . . . And speaking generally, the climate of this island is so altogether mild that it produces in abundance the fruits of the trees and the other seasonal fruits of the year, so that it would appear that the island, because of its exceptional felicity, were a dwelling place of gods and not of men."

Today, Madeira is justifiably promoted as "The Garden Isle," and "hotels" could be substituted for "banqueting houses" in the above account. The diversity of the trees, shrubs, and flowers that currently grow there is partly the result of the Portuguese discoverers, who dropped seeds off on their way back from the New World. There would not, however, be such a huge variety flourishing there without the extremely equable climate. The rivers allegedly encountered by the Carthaginians and described by Diodorus may have flowed on the now-submerged area; there is plenty of water on the island, but the land is too precipitous for many rivers to flow. When touring there a few years ago, to leave a small road tunnel we had to drive under a cascade of water. No need to find coins for a car wash there.

Strabo, the Greek writer already mentioned in an earlier chapter, quotes an earlier account from Poseidonius, another ancient chronicler, of practically the same legend Diodorus detailed, and says that the land was known to have changed its level there.

There is another, much smaller island a few hours' boat trip away: Porto Santo. Its claim to fame is that a few years before Columbus sailed to discover America, he married the daughter of its Portuguese governor and lived there for a while. Intriguingly, his father-in-law was head of the "Order of Christ" in Portugal—a society previously called the Knights Templar, which changed its name in a ploy to be spared by the Portuguese king when the pope decreed that all members of the order be simultaneously murdered throughout Europe.

At the time, toward the end of the fifteenth century, the Order of Christ specialized in navigation. Henry the Navigator, the famous Portuguese (he was, in fact, half English) prince who instigated the great "Age of Discoveries," was also a head of the order. It has long been speculated that Columbus obtained old maps from the order that showed the Atlantic and the Americas. Henry's brother was also a cartographer and dealer in maps in Portugal's capital, Lisbon.

The Turkish admiral Piri Reis added handwritten notes to his famous map discussed in the last chapter. One such note asserted that Columbus had obtained a book indicating that the Atlantic ended in a coast with islands in front. Columbus's own journal covering the first epic voyage indicates that he and Martin Pinzón, the captain of the caravel *Pinta* and his second-in-command, regularly consulted a chart passed back and forth between the boats. Apparently, the chart had islands marked on it.

Taking leave of his uncle, the young prince in the tale at the beginning of this chapter would have left Madeira and headed for the group of islands known as the Azores. These approach the halfway point between Europe and the Americas. It is thought that in ancient times they comprised more islands and that the existing ones were much larger. Today there are nine major islands.

The Piri Reis map shows sixteen islands, plus another one conveniently located midway between them and Madeira. The remnants of this could, perhaps, be the deserted Ilhas (islands) Selvagens. The current Azores islands were claimed for the Portuguese in 1427 when they were discovered by Diogo da Silves. None of them is of any great size. The largest, São Miguel, is about forty by ten miles and has boiling-hot springs. When we visited some twenty years ago, in the area around the springs a tourist attraction had been provided in the form of regularly lowering a large pot full of meat and vegetables into a narrow silo in the ground. On its removal a few hours later . . . dinner was ready, cooked by the intense underground heat.

There is no real evidence of previous habitation, but a hoard of Carthaginian coins was discovered in a black pot near the foundations of a destroyed building. More intriguingly, a stone statue of a horse and rider pointing to the west was found on the island of Corvo. Unfortunately, it was inadvertently broken by the men sent by the Portuguese king to retrieve it.

This statue was reported to have had an indecipherable inscription on the base. Confusion reigns over a statement in the same report that the inhabitants called the statue "Catés." It does not clarify whether these inhabitants were on the island when it was discovered or were the recent new immigrants from Portugal. "Catés" resembles the Inca-Quechua word "Cati," meaning "go that way" or "follow." It is not a Portuguese word. Either the statue was imported there, or a civilization had developed a sophisticated culture with artisan skills. Sculpting such a statue would have required metal tools, and that meant mining, smelting, and casting. And what of the development of an alphabet for that inscription on the base?

This is the most volatile area of the entire Atlantic seabed, unique in that it is the meeting point of three continental plates: the North American, the European, and the African. It is from here that the fault line extends across to, and in front of, southwest Iberia.

Evidence from numerous geological expeditions indicates that areas of it had at some stage risen by as much as a thousand meters, exposing it above sea level. Then, many thousands of years later, it subsided by an incredible *six* thousand meters. Dr. René Malaise of the Riks Museum in Stockholm commented in 1957 that a colleague—Dr. R. W. Kolbe—had found evidence from a Swedish deep-sea expedition ten years earlier that indicated recent subsidence in the mid-Atlantic Ridge area; samples taken showed fossilized land plants and freshwater organisms. Earlier evidence was revealed in the U.S. Geological Survey of Deep Core Soundings in 1936, undertaken by Charles S. Piggot. It found heavy deposits of ash on underwater slopes dated to twelve thousand years ago. Commenting on this in 1944, Swedish oceanographer Hans Petterson wrote: "The topmost of the two volcanic strata is found above the topmost glacial stratum, which indicates that this volcanic catastrophe or catastrophes occurred in post-glacial times. . . . It can, therefore, not be ruled out that the mid-Atlantic Ridge, where the samples originated, was above sea level up to about ten thousand years ago and did not subside to its present depth until later." That at least parts of this area were above water for a considerable time seems incontrovertible. It could have been as one island or separate islands of which the Azores are remnants.

One possibility that cannot be discounted is that the Phoenicians and, later, the Carthaginians developed a port or base there to assist their trade with South America, as suggested in Chapter Three. Even earlier, the Minoans may have exploited the islands as a stopover point. It is obvious that, like Madeira and the homeland back in Iberia, any earlier civilization would have been subjected to particularly violent seismic activity. Habitation would inevitably have centered on the low-lying agricultural areas and the coast, the very regions that would have been inundated. Fierce fires, landslides, and volcanoes would have obliterated any settlements in the mountains. It is not surprising that when rediscovered by the Portuguese, the land was empty of humans.

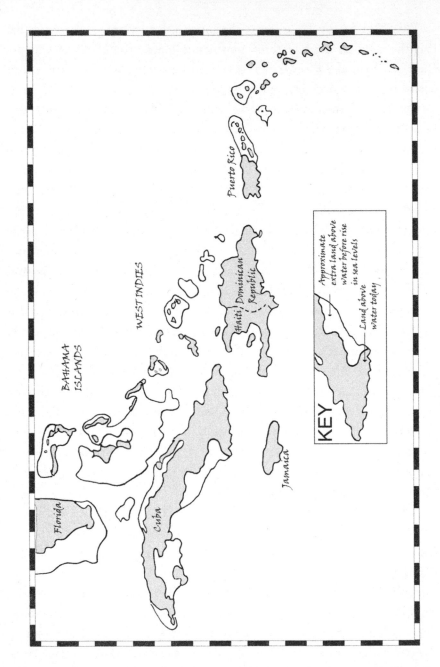

(IMAGE 32) *The Bahamas group of western Atlantic islands today and what they would probably have looked like twelve thousand years ago, when they would have been much larger but fewer in number.*

That "Catés" statue pointed west to the Caribbean, which would have been the prince's next destination. Here we are entering an area where there has been intense speculation and controversy over finds that could relate to Atlantis. Edgar Cayce predicted that parts of "Posedia" would be found slowly rising from the seabed in the vicinity of Bimini in the 1960s.

It is apparent that much more land was once above water in this region, and that it had either sunk or been immersed by rising sea levels. (SEE IMAGE 32, PREVIOUS PAGE.) The Edgar Cayce Foundation, run by his family, has been very active in exploration and has made controversial discoveries of ancient ruins not far below the sea's surface. Some of these ruins are thought to have been breakwaters and harbors, indicating that they were from a maritime civilization. These finds may be "old news," but it is worthwhile examining them here because of their relevance to the Atlantis Empire.[74]

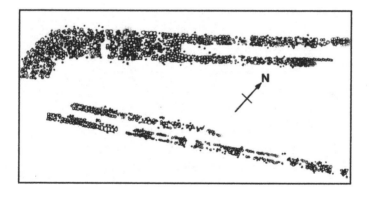

(IMAGE 33) *A drawing of the "Bimini Road" discovery.*
(Courtesy of Drs. Greg & Lora Little, "Edgar Cayce's Atlantis" © 2006.)

One of the earliest finds, which has received a lot of publicity, was of a large extended underwater construction dubbed "The Bimini Road," only fifteen or twenty feet below the surface. It is a massive formation of huge stones consistently placed, with the extremities of the formation extending under the sand. (SEE IMAGE 33 ABOVE.) One end curves smoothly around like a hockey stick. Part of the "handle" has a cut-out center. The site was originally discovered by a Miami-based biologist, Dr. J. Manson Valentine, after two local fishing guides had shown him its position, about a mile off north Bimini. It is more than sixteen hundred feet long.

Geologists were immediately skeptical, and one of them, Wyman Harrison, after examining a couple of blocks, said they were limestone that had simply fractured *in situ*. In a 1971 edition of *Nature* magazine, he asserted that the site was completely natural, stating "at no place are blocks found to be resting on a similar set beneath."

The Edgar Cayce Foundation was convinced that the site was the remains of a huge harbor installation. Their belief had to be balanced with the fact that Edgar Cayce had predicted that remains of Atlantis would be found in this area, so they had a corner to fight from. The foundation claims, however, that they were vindicated when three of the organization's researchers—Drs. Greg and Lora Little and John Van Auken—returned to the site in May 2005 to conduct a detailed underwater examination.[75] Their findings enabled them to emphatically refute the debunkers. The evidence was clear-cut. The Bimini site had ancient artifacts that included stone anchors. It was built from multiple tiers of stone blocks, many supported by leveling prop stones.

The ancient stone anchors had holes bored in their centers and grooves cut for ropes. The Littles claim that they are almost identical to ancient Greek examples found near Santorini (Thera) and those used by other civilizations—the Phoenicians, for example.

Graham Hancock had also examined the site and, prior to diving, had been skeptical of the claims that it was a man-made structure. After many hours of close-up underwater examination, however, he had to admit that the evidence was very convincing.[76] He noted that some large blocks were even supported by smaller stones, like little pillars, so that you could see under them from one side to the other. He also drew attention to some stone circles close by. As a result of Graham's observations, the 2005 expedition searched for, found, and closely examined the circles. Some were constructed from large rectangular blocks arranged in a circle, with the center consisting simply of seabed. The circles are at fairly evenly spaced intervals, and the seabed between them is covered by small, flat stones. Other circles are of large blocks of stone piled into heaps. The Littles point out that several ancient Mediterranean harbors utilized "mooring circles." Like these at Bimini, they were usually built outside the main harbor as brief holding stations for boats not permitted to enter.

(IMAGE 34) *Artist's impression of how the "Bimini Road" would have looked when in use as a harbor.* (Courtesy of Drs. Greg & Lora Little, "Edgar Cayce's Atlantis" © 2006.)

Many old harbors in the Mediterranean and Aegean Seas were constructed in a similar way to the "Bimini Road."

When all the evidence was combined—the 1,600-foot-long breakwater, the mooring circles, and the anchors—it persuasively indicates that the installation off Bimini was built as a harbor. (SEE IMAGE 34 ABOVE.)

Allowing for various factors, the Littles came to the conclusion that the complex was in use as far back as between 8000 and 6000 B.C. By 5000 B.C., rising sea levels would have made it obsolete. This last date precludes its being of Minoan or Phoenician origin; it ceased being of any practical use long before their civilizations existed.

There have been other similar discoveries off Andros, the largest island in the Bahamas. Some, thought originally to be the remains of large buildings, have been identified as recent sponge pens; but one other, dubbed the "Andros Platform," is similar to the "Bimini Road." For more information, read *Edgar Cayce's Atlantis* by the Littles and Van Auken[77] and Graham Hancock's *Underworld*.[78] (SEE IMAGE 35 BELOW.)

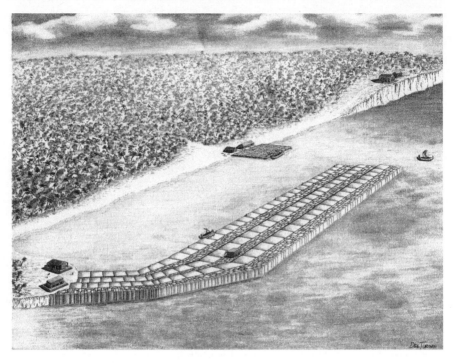

(IMAGE 35) *Artist's impression of the "Andros Platform" when in use as a harbor.* (Courtesy of Drs. Greg & Lora Little, "Edgar Cayce's Atlantis" © 2006.)

In 2007, an expedition was mounted by the foundation specifically to explore Andros. It discovered a stone wall in shallow water near a small offshore island. It consisted of limestone blocks, clearly hewn and dressed with tool marks still visible.

The Caribbean is on the other side of the vast Atlantic Ocean from Iberia, and the possibility of the Atlanteans and their lifestyle continuing there long after the tragic sinking of the homeland must be considered. Plato makes it clear that the various constituent parts of the empire were ruled autonomously by the heirs of Poseidon's sons and did not have to rely on the original Atlantis, except for trade.

This would explain the evidence of contacts with South America by tall, blond, bearded individuals, which contacts could have been more recent than dates given by Plato for the demise of Atlantis. Graham Hancock's *Fingerprints of the Gods* details the many stories of these superior beings who suddenly appeared in boats from the east, landed in various parts of South America, and proceeded to civilize the indigenous population.

There are dozens of islands in the Caribbean, the most easterly being the Lesser Antilles group, the most northerly the Bahamas, and, below them, the largest: the Greater Antilles group of Cuba, Hispaniola, and Jamaica. Most of them would have been considerably bigger before the Ice Age thaw. Andros Island is the best example. Much of the seabed surrounding it, including the Grand Bahamas Bank, is thought to have once been land that was submerged. It is still very shallow. During the Atlantis epoch, it would have been a considerable landmass.

Bimini also sits on part of the Grand Bahamas Bank. The Little Bahamas Bank to the north would once also have been above water and would have linked up several islands, including the Grand Bahamas. Cuba, to the south, has several such archipelagos off its north and south coasts, all of which would have once been part of a much larger Cuba.

It has been suggested by author Andrew Collins that Cuba was Atlantis and that, from there, the Atlanteans influenced the development of the great civilizations in South America.[79] That could be correct, except in one respect: Cuba was quite likely one of the biggest islands in the Atlantean Empire and, therefore, important—but it wasn't the homeland. I am sure that was back in southwest Iberia.

Interestingly, Edgar Cayce, in his famous reading about the rediscovery of Atlantis off Bimini, said that Posedia would be amongst the first *portions* of Atlantis to rise. This seems to indicate that Posedia was part of the Atlantis Empire, but not necessarily the main part.

The fabled island of Antilia, shown on many early nautical charts in the area of the Caribbean, has long been associated with Atlantis, if for nothing else than the similarity of names.

It first appeared on a map by a Venetian cartographer, Zuane Pizzigano. Elena Wishaw pointed out that Columbus was having great difficulty in assembling a crew at Palos until the return from a voyage by the renowned local navigator Martin Alonso Pinzón. He threw his weight behind Columbus, as he believed the proposed expedition would rediscover Antilia, and the local seamen rallied to him. The area had a wealth of sailing experience going back to at least the Phoenician era, and had passionately preserved the memory of a great island of that name that existed way across the western ocean. Pinzón captained one of the two caravels that sailed out of Palos with Columbus's *Santa Maria*. It has been suggested that the name of the island derived from *ante* (originally Latin), meaning "before" or "in front of," together with *ilha*, meaning "island." This temptingly led to the conclusion that it was in front of a large continent.

In *Underworld*, Graham Hancock speculates that Antilia was quite possibly the large island originally formed by the Grand Bahamas Bank. It appears to be shown on the Piri Reis map and has been dubbed the map's "Ghost Island." Certainly, by the time Columbus reached the Caribbean, Andros was nowhere near that large, so it could not have been recorded or mapped as that size by him. It could, however, have already featured large on the chart he showed to Martin Pinzón. This could explain Pinzón's assertion to potential crew that they hoped to rediscover the fabled Antilia. That this island existed at least earlier than twelve thousand years ago, together with the other enlarged islands in the Caribbean, is really beyond dispute. Plato appears to indicate that islands in the Atlantis Kingdom existed in that area. Their close proximity to each other would make it likely that they were all part of the empire.

The case for the Atlantis Empire stretching even farther into colonies on the North American mainland seems strong. Certainly this was indicated by Plato. The various possibilities are covered elaborately by other authors and web sites. Many unexplained archaeological finds have been discovered, including a controversial one from West Virginia in North America, known as the "Grave Creek Tablet." It is engraved with three rows of letters that are undisputedly akin to ancient Iberian ones. Each row is separated by ruled lines in the manner that is more or less exclusive to those found in the Algarve.[80]

Apart from the growing number of archaeological finds, the native North Americans have numerous legends about their own ancestors or of immigrant peoples they have come into contact with. Typical is one from the Algonquian Indian tribe. They have preserved a legend of a disastrous great flood that was engulfing their original homeland. As they made their escape in more than a hundred boats, they watched their land being consumed by fire before it sank. The survivors made landfall on the eastern seaboard of America and were the tribe's ancestors. These and many other tribal myths may refer to more recent catastrophes rather than organized settlement by Atlanteans.

In writing this book, I have deliberately avoided mind-numbing amounts of detail and made it broad-brush, in an endeavor to provide enjoyable reading. There are plenty of signposts highlighting the detailed work of many specialists engaged in the Atlantis search. Anyone thirsting for more supporting information will find it in many books speculating on ancient civilizations in North America. It is sufficient here to note that it seems highly likely that, if there were active communities of Atlanteans on the Caribbean Islands, then there would inevitably have been colonies in America.

Recent research into the genetic DNA of Native Americans carried out by several prominent American universities has also resulted in some very interesting findings. Details of this are summarized in a recent newsletter on the ARE web site.[81] The researchers found that a small percentage of Native Americans have an unusual DNA marker only found in a few places elsewhere in Europe, the Middle East—and a small pocket in the Gobi Desert. The researchers claim to have proved that it was not the result of genetic mixing after Columbus, as the same DNA was found in a bone from an ancient American grave.

Scientifically, this DNA marker is known as Haplogroup X, and is particularly prevalent in Europe in the Basques. The main time of entry into America was between 12,000 and 10,000 B.C., and this matches the epoch given in some of Cayce's own readings on the migration of groups to America from Atlantis.

At the time of the ARE article, the research was ongoing and not all of the native tribes had been tested, along with only a limited number of ancient remains. It did, however, appear to confirm that America was settled early and by many different racial groups, with waves of immigration at different times.

Reverting back to Europe, Plato said: "They held sway in our direction over the country within the Pillars as far as Egypt and Tyrrhenia" (clue 36).

If the Mediterranean basin was eventually annexed for the Atlantis Empire, it is a certainty that the civilization would also have spread to other parts of Portugal, particularly the Atlantic seaboard and so to Galicia, the current home of the Basques in northern Spain. There are several theories about the origin of Olisippo, the ancient name for Lisbon, the current capital of Portugal. Intriguingly, one of Poseidon's other sons was named Elasippo. If Cádiz (Gades) was named after its ruler—Gadeirus, Poseidon's second-born son—maybe Elasippo was given the region around Lisbon (Lisboa in Portuguese). It provides yet another link with Plato's clues.

Apart from the islands, the empire would have included North Africa from a very early stage. Given that Gadeirus ruled down to the Straits of Gibraltar, and the crossing from there to Morocco was very short, contact would have been inevitable.

Before 9500 B.C., the straits would have also been longer, due to the additional dry land stretching out into the Atlantic on both shores. Up to around that time, northwest Africa would also have been much more verdant. At the end of the ice age and global warming, the landscape dried out and agriculture would have become increasingly concentrated, some in the highlands of the Atlas Mountains, much as it is today—where the blond Berbers live.

Anyone visiting this latter region will still find inhabitants in some villages with distinctly Nordic features, similar to the Guanches. I have already mentioned Elena Wishaw's belief that the Libyans, as these people were called in ancient times, were part of the population of southwest Iberia at some stage. She cited a town in the mountains behind Niebla where she was astonished to see so many tall blonds, men and women, with blue or gray eyes and distinctive features. I once regularly traveled the highway from Huelva to Seville, passing close to Niebla, always stopping at the same service station and café. Inevitably there was at least one tall, attractive Spanish girl who precisely fitted that description serving behind the counter. There is much more of this later, in the chapter on the people of Atlantis.

To sum up, the initial Atlantis territories would have been southwest Iberia, north Morocco, and, probably soon afterward, the Canary Islands. As they developed into a fully fledged maritime civilization, they spread across the Atlantic islands to the Caribbean, where they may only have had representation in the ruling class. From there, the tentacles would have spread into the Americas.

At some stage, as indicated by Plato, they also extended their supremacy eastward into the lands bordering the Mediterranean and at least some of its islands, but did not necessarily replace the indigenous populations. I have a strong suspicion that the Minoans could well have represented a link from the original Atlanteans. If their Aegean islands had been once ruled by Atlanteans, then the kernel of their culture and maritime skills could have been preserved to blossom again thousands of years later. Don't get excited, though: this is only a hunch prompted by the latest evidence suggesting the Minoans were a great trading power, sailing as far as the east coast of America and Canada. As in Atlantis, bulls also figured strongly in their culture.

It is difficult to make as strong a case for the empire as for the homeland, since Plato left us so little to base it on, just a few sentences. The circumstantial evidence does, however, indicate that he could have been correct. There seems little doubt that there was once an earlier, more sophisticated civilization on the Canary Islands. They had a form of writing and built pyramids, and the Spaniards attested to their intelligence. They embalmed their dead in much the same way as the Egyptians and, as you will read later, the Egyptians would appear to owe the very early founding of their culture to the Atlanteans.

In the teeth of initial fierce opposition, it is becoming increasingly apparent that there was once a significant maritime civilization in the Caribbean. Because the area did not conform to all of Plato's clues, many people have been rightly skeptical about theories that it was the Atlantis homeland.

In researching and writing this chapter, I have attempted to connect the dots: from southwest Iberia, to the Gorringe Bank, to the Canary Islands, Madeira, and Azores, across to the Caribbean and so to America. My hypothesis complements other researchers' work at different sites and Plato's assertion of a vast empire stretching from the Straits of Gibraltar to a huge continent across the Atlantic. Are there enough tantalizing clues and discoveries for us to consider that Plato was right? I think so; how about you? The fact that, more than twenty-four hundred years ago, his information about the Atlantic islands and a great continent on the other side of the ocean was correct is, on its own, a powerful argument. He knew what he was writing about.

I was now confident that I had once and for all solved where Atlantis and the reaches of its empire had been, but there was still another mystery nagging at me. I felt sure that Silves must have been a great important city when the Phoenicians were trading with it from a base on the remnants of the outer embankment.

What was it?

CHAPTER SIXTEEN

The Silver City

Carlos Castelo, an expert on the ancient language of the Algarve region, provided the vital clue that I thought might solve the mystery of what the current site of Silves had been, circa twenty-six hundred years ago. In an interview with a Portuguese newspaper in 1996, he stated that he was convinced that Silves was known during the last millennium B.C. as "The Silver City." He was not aware of the connection speculated on in this chapter, and his conclusion was based entirely on an exhaustive research of the forgotten script over many decades.

The current Portuguese word for silver is *prata*, but it was not always so. In old Irish, it is *zilver;* in Basque, *zila;* and in the Bible, *zilah.* Among the ancient names for Silves used at various periods by the mysterious Conii (Konii) people were Cilbe or Cilbes and, most significantly, Zilb, which meant "silver" in the old script. This throws open fascinating areas of speculation:

- The exact location of the capital of the legendary King Arganthonius has never been established.
- Arganthonius was fêted for being incredibly wealthy, with huge hoards of silver.

- He was known as "The Silver King."
- His name was thought to have derived from the Greek word *argan*, meaning silver.
- His fabulous capital was visited by Greek mariners, who were famously befriended by him.
- A century or so before Plato wrote his Dialogues, the city that Plato described as being the Atlantis capital was known locally as "The Silver City" or "The City of Silver."

What do you think? It is certainly another remarkable series of coincidences, and we could conclude that Arganthonius's capital and Silves were, quite possibly, one and the same place.

Anyone harboring doubts should consider this: another of Plato's clues, number 71, now assumes major significance. It indicates that the outside wall of the temple at the top of the Atlanteans' citadel was covered in silver.

It was the highest visible wall and, as it encompassed or stood in front of the golden temple, it couldn't be missed, reflecting the brilliance of the Algarve sun. As the sun traversed the sky from east to west, it was in front of the city for most of the day. Imagine the spectacular and unforgettable sight it would have presented. What an awe-inspiring effect it would have had on visitors seeing it for the first time—the silver-faced wall, topped by gold-tipped pinnacles, reflecting the sun like a giant mirror. There could hardly have been a better reason for it being known, even then, as "The Silver City."

Perhaps the reason Arganthonius's capital has yet to be identified is because, as in the search for Atlantis, the Algarve region of the southern Iberian coast has never been given the consideration it deserves. It was an extremity of Europe about which little was known or recorded, yet the answers that authors of more than two thousand books on Atlantis have strived to find have been sitting under our noses all the time. Could the same be true for Arganthonius's capital city?

In earlier chapters, I have already presented some detailed arguments as to why this was way to the west of Cádiz and, in Chapter Twelve, why Seville could be ruled out.

There has been recent speculation that Huelva could have been the elusive capital, but it is close to Cádiz and, although King Arganthonius eventually conquered Cádiz, for them to have existed so close together for any length of time is inconceivable. In recent years, archaeologists have unearthed a large number of pottery fragments from a site in Huelva. They are a mixture of Phoenician and Greek and are thought to date from the first half of the last millennium B.C. This resulted in claims that Huelva existed as a city at that time and is, therefore, one of the oldest cities in Europe—perhaps even the capital of Tartessos.

This seems a rather extravagant claim based on the evidence. It was already thought to have been a Phoenician trading base and could well have housed a ceramic factory and distribution point for imports, supplying their other bases in the area; then the Greeks could have continued using it after their demise. This would have made a lot more sense than transporting all the pots and storage jars needed for the considerable trade all the way from the eastern Mediterranean. Substantial remnants of pottery would, therefore, hardly be surprising and are not evidence for the existence of a grand city. As explained in the earlier chapter on metals, the area would have been of great importance in the sale and export of the products from the mines back up the Rio Tinto. Elena Wishaw, however, thought the evidence pointed to the ancient ports close to Huelva—Moguer and Palos—as being the center of export activity. This would have left Huelva relatively free for the Phoenicians and, maybe earlier, the Minoans to set up a trading post.

A more likely contender for Arganthonius's capital could have been Niebla: but Kolaios, the Greek mariner mentioned earlier who was blown off course and ended up at the capital, would have made port at Palos at the mouth of the Rio Tinto—not Niebla, which was much farther upriver.

Estoi, or Conistorgis, as it was probably known then, could be considered as a possibility, but that would not correspond with the silver clues from Carlos Castelo and Plato. The fact that Arganthonius's capital was never recorded by ancient chroniclers implies that it was hidden and in a region that was not so well visited by merchants and sailors as the Atlantic coast closer to Gibraltar.

If the capital was Silves, where did the old king obtain such vast quantities of silver? From the same place as the old Atlantean kings, of course: some from Portugal, but the majority from mines he controlled a short distance away in the Sierra Morena mountains, north of Huelva. Shipped down to Palos or Moguer via Niebla, it would only have taken a day at sea to reach the Arade River mouth en route to Silves, or it could conveniently have been exported directly to the Middle East and the Mediterranean.

This would also explain how Arganthonius came into conflict with Cádiz, which at that stage was an autonomous city-state, largely peopled by Semites of Phoenician stock. Traders, they were inevitably meddling in the metals business from the far eastern corner of his kingdom. They were constantly needling Arganthonius, and he successfully moved to shut them up, ending up defeating them in a sea battle.[82] He proceeded to throw the city open to Greek immigrants and traders.

After much research, an archaeological organization in Tavira, an old town on the Algarve's coast, produced a map that shows the dispersal of the various peoples existing in the Algarve and across into Spain at around 200 B.C., at the beginning of the Roman period. It shows the Conii (Kunii) and Turdetani (Tartessians) peoples overlapping and merging into one culture from Lagos, in the far western Algarve, right across to beyond Cádiz at the eastern extremity. It encompasses the whole surviving area of Atlantis.

It is not a big step to assume that it had been melded into one kingdom, with one king and one capital—Silves, just as it was more than a thousand years later by the Moors. The Tartessos country has generally been thought to have been a relatively small triangle, extending from Huelva to Cádiz and then northeast to Seville—another reason why Arganthonius's capital has not been considered to have been farther west. This is a very small area for such a famous and enigmatic civilization, one important enough to have been frequently mentioned in the Bible and one that wielded control over such vast wealth. It would have been too small to stop a more powerful expanding empire from invading. This did eventually happen with the Carthaginians; but, before that, the region had retained its independence for several thousand years. A few brave voices have already suggested that Tartessos extended into Portugal's Algarve. The evidence would seem to prove them right.

It is thought that there were influxes of other races into the region, like the Celts and perhaps the Libyans, but no strong evidence of warlike invasions and conquests exists. They appear to have been largely absorbed, or coexisted amicably—maybe after a little local hostility.

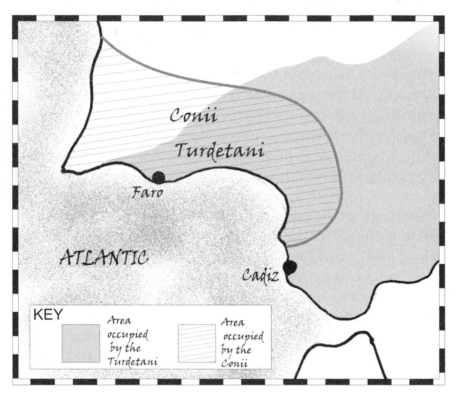

(IMAGE 36) *A map depicting what is thought to have been the disposition of the tribal groups inhabiting the Algarve and the Costa de la Luz in 200 B.C.*

Consider this hypothesis: Tartessos could have been a kingdom stretching from the far west of the Algarve to Cádiz in Spain, one big enough to have had clout, in fact occupying the remnants of Atlantis. (SEE IMAGE 36 ABOVE.) At one stage, its ruler was King Arganthonius, who probably had some Greek blood from earlier settlers. He was known to be exceptionally well disposed to the Greeks, even imploring them to come and settle in his kingdom. Had the latter been a small triangle of land between Cádiz, Huelva, and Seville, he would hardly have been so forthcoming.

He has been recorded in history as "The Silver King" partly, perhaps, because of his name (*argan* means "silver"), but principally for the vast amounts of silver he possessed.

Silves, which was known as "The Silver City," could have been his capital. It could have been given that title because of his name, his wealth, and the amount of silver used for basic city adornments like horse troughs.

According to Strabo, records had already existed in the region for more than six thousand years. He said the Tartessians were a "refined, cultivated, civilized, ingenious, and laborious society, to have poetry, laws, and a written alphabet." That certainly sounds more like a substantial organized state than a small primitive tribe. Did their records include the legend of Atlantis? Had he recreated his kingdom on the land that remained from Atlantis and rebuilt Silves in its image as the capital, complete with the topmost wall covered in silver?

He was reputed to have lived to the age of 120, but what happened to him, how he died, and what became of his city is not known. He lived too early to have witnessed the Carthaginian invasion, despite having foreseen it. Perhaps he died a natural death, since anything more remarkable would probably have been recorded. Soon after his death, the ruthless, merciless Carthaginians would have swept through, laid waste to the citadel, looted it of its silver and other precious metals, and destroyed those ancient records.

Eventually, it was probably reoccupied and rebuilt by the indigenous Conii/Tartessians and called Cilbes by the time the Romans arrived a few centuries later, but it was by then but a shadow of its former glory. Local archaeologists are inclined to the opinion that ancient Cilbes was on the same site as the earlier Phoenician post on the embankment, but it appears too small for anything other than a very modest settlement such as a trading post. The Conii would have had many settlements larger than this, so why would the Romans single out Cilbes for special mention? It must have been substantial. Roman artifacts were also found on the old embankment site, but that is not surprising if they maintained the harbor there. The Conii had probably developed Conistorgis (Estoi, Milreu) as the new main capital instead. Later still, the Moors appreciated the unique position of Silves—and maybe also had an inkling of its history—and set about reestablishing it as the capital of the region. Toward the end of the Moorish era in Silves, its occupants and rulers were Berbers from the Atlas Mountains, an area quite likely to have once been part of the Atlantean Empire.

This theory ticks all the boxes and would explain why, for centuries before the rise of the Carthaginians, the Phoenicians had considered it important enough to have a trading base next door. It is certainly a plausible scenario and would solve another of history's enduring mysteries.

It emboldens me to present yet another fascinating hypothesis, one that would explain many of the questions and uncertainties that have haunted Plato's accounts for centuries. What if Plato did not get all his information via the Egyptians, but most of it from Greeks who knew southwest Iberia well, from either living there or trading with it? It would appear they had been involved there for a good few decades before Plato wrote his Dialogues. Strabo has told us that ancient records also existed there and the people were cultured and civilized.

This would explain the amount of detail in Plato's accounts. If some of the information was also from firsthand observation, it would explain the extraordinarily accurate measurements, such as the distance from the sea and those from the embankments on the harbor side back to the hill, as well as the specification about the three colored stones. It would also explain his knowledge about the Atlantic, its islands, and America—as, apart from any written records the Tartessians may have possessed, local ports like Cádiz had played host to Phoenician fleets for a good few centuries. These ships sailed forth to trade with the Atlantic islands, the tin mines in Britain, and, if author Andrew Collins is correct, South America. Inevitably some residual knowledge about the great ocean and the great continent on the other side would have been left embedded in local lore. Elena Wishaw thought so and that it helped Pinzón hire crew for Columbus's boats.

Plato passed his information on in two separate Dialogues, produced some time apart. The first, *Timaeus,* gives only the barest outline of the Atlantis legend (clues 1 to 17). A considerable amount of this is concerned with the unprovoked attack launched against Egypt and Greece and the Atlanteans' subsequent defeat by the brave Greek Hellenes. It contains very few facts about Atlantis. It occurred to me that these sparse details could more logically equate to those preserved by the Egyptians for nine thousand years. Even then, many researchers and academics have queried some of this first account, specifically the part recording the role played by the Hellenes. It has been argued that this smacks of embellishment, of Plato playing to his local audience to get their attention. Could the second account in *Critias*, with all its amazing detail, be the result of information that came into Plato's possession after his publication of *Timaeus* and, therefore, the reason he decided to produce a second, more detailed account of the legend?

I must stress, however, that this theory—as well as that about The Silver City—is only that: just a theory. We will have to be patient and wait to see if archaeology produces any supporting evidence.

I have frequently referred to those written records preserved in southwest Iberia that Strabo told us about. Ever since I saw that broken stone in the museum with its mystifying alphabet, mentioned in the first chapter, I had yearned to discover more about it. Did those records and the stone use the same alphabet?

Now, having pinpointed the fabled lost land, I felt justified in also asking if, perhaps, the script could even be a relic from Atlantis.

CHAPTER SEVENTEEN

A Lost Alphabet

The old man rubbed at his tears with his sleeve as he watched the priest labor over the stone. It was huge, about three feet by five, and it had taken the help of several of his friends to lift it onto the cart and bring it to the priest. It was evident that this cleric was no artisan and wasn't used to wielding a wooden mallet and iron chisel. The words he was crudely carving into the stone had been agreed on the night before. They paid tribute to the old man's son and spoke of a great warrior who had been killed defending the village from the Northern Tribe who constantly troubled them. The father could not read the words in the strange alphabet the priest was using, but he knew that his wishes had been translated faithfully into the ancient tongue. Legends told of how, at one time, many people had known this age-old script but, sadly, only the priests had perpetuated it, passing it down from old to young.

The priest stood, stretched his aching limbs, and, with a nod to the grieving father, indicated that the work was finished. It did not look particularly grand with the crude, misshapen letters spiraling inward from right to left, but it made the old man's breast swell. Very few went to this trouble these days, but, oh, how he had loved that son.

The priest had worked on-site by the grave, and now they all struggled to erect the stone upright and secure it in position. When the old man was satisfied, the priest mumbled a few words over the grave; then it was over, and they shuffled away.

T his sad, poignant event, or something similar, probably took place during the Iron Age, six or seven centuries before Christ. You can see and feel the evidence; it is not a figment of my imagination. The stone, recently discovered, can be examined in the museum at Almodôvar, a small town in southern Portugal. (SEE IMAGE 37 IN THE PHOTO INSERT.) It is just one part of a growing body of evidence that suggests that the history of the Western world's alphabet needs reassessing. That may appear to be a bold, revolutionary, even an impertinent statement—but see what you think after reading this chapter.

In clue 100, Plato wrote: ". . . these [laws] were inscribed by the first king on a pillar of orichalcum at the temple of Poseidon." So it is clear, then, that the rulers of Atlantis possessed an alphabet and a form of writing.

It has long been taken for granted that the Western alphabet evolved from the Phoenician, with a little help from its later Greek nephew. That is not in dispute, but there is now overwhelming evidence that the Phoenicians did not invent their alphabet but adapted, and added to, a much older one.

The evidence points to this ancient script having originated in southwest Iberia, but it was also in use over a much wider area for many thousands of years before the Phoenicians. Samples have been discovered from more than twenty different cultures, including Minoan Crete, predynastic Egypt (before the pharaohs, that is), France, Spain, the Canary Islands, Morocco, Palestine, Pakistan, and Romania—with the greatest number of finds in southern Portugal. Some of these indicate that the characters were in use thousands of years before the Phoenician era. My interest was first aroused when, in the late 1980s, I came across that sample of the script in Lagos. Since then, I have inspected dozens of examples in other Algarve museums. They were all crudely engraved on large, flat stones or broken fragments, believed to be gravestones or monuments—known in Portuguese as *herouns*— dedicated to illustrious dead personages. The inscriptions are usually between drawn lines, spiraling inward from right to left. (SEE IMAGE 38 IN THE PHOTO INSERT.)

Academics refer to it as the "southwestern" script, acknowledging that it emanated from southwest Iberia where the most finds have been made and where it appears to have been perpetuated the longest. Samples of a similar script called the "northeastern" exist elsewhere in Spain.

The dates originally attributed to some of these earliest discovered Algarve specimens go as far back as 2300 B.C. Archaeological and academic circles have wrestled with the enigma these inscriptions present, and for a while have put forward a unified front. Because the script shares some characters with the Phoenician and Greek alphabets, rather than face the traumatic possibility that it might represent a source of writing that predated them—with the consequent need to completely redraft the history of the Western alphabet—academics have shoehorned it into accepted dogma: that the Algarve script must have developed from Phoenician and Greek influences in the region from about 900 B.C. The samples unearthed must, they reason, therefore date from the late Iron Age, around 500 to 900 B.C. (The Phoenician alphabet is thought to have emerged around 1050 B.C. and the Greek to have developed from it sometime afterward.) On analysis, this date for the southwest script is clearly nonsense. Consider the following evidence.

First, there are several references by ancient Greek writers indicating that the Phoenicians did not invent their alphabet. The Greek historian Diodorus Siculus, who flourished between 60 and 30 B.C., wrote: "Men tell us . . . that the Phoenicians were not the first to make the discovery of letters; but that they did no more than change the form of the letters, whereupon the majority of mankind made use of the way of writing them as the Phoenicians devised."[83]

Tacitus, a Roman historian (A.D. 56–117), wrote: "The Phoenicians gained the reputation of inventing a form of writing, which they merely received."[84]

The writings of the famous Greek Strabo (64 B.C.–A.D. 34)—known as "the Geographer"—which I have referred to in earlier chapters, are relevant. He said that the Turdetani peoples of southwest Iberia had a written script as long as six thousand years previously—an inconvenient and unwelcome statement dismissed by the establishment. "They are the most cultured of all the Iberians; they employ the art of writing and have written books containing memorials of ancient times, and also poems and laws set in verse, for which they claim an antiquity of six thousand years."[85]

If the script existed in 6500 B.C. in a form that was in regular use, it would have taken some considerable time to develop. It may even have been inherited from an earlier epoch. We do not know where Strabo obtained his information, but it smacks of the truth. What did he have to gain by inventing it? His most likely source was Greek merchantmen trading with the Turdetani region along the southern Algarve and Spanish coasts and, like Plato and Solon before him, the Egyptians. Why have none of the books to which he refers survived? The most likely culprits were the merciless Carthaginians. If anything survived, then other Lusitanian tribes from north of the Algarve destroyed cities and their contents in the south in retribution for the Conii cooperation with the Romans. Other villains could have been the Romans themselves. Then, of course, we have to take into account the periodic disastrous quakes, followed by fires and tsunamis.

Fortunately, solid examples have survived: the *herouns*. The samples were mostly found in the mountains, in their foothills, or just north of them, well away from any coastal inundations and the destruction of cities. They were monuments, erected in private places for personal reasons.

A number of Portuguese historians have published books on the subject since 1983, but the expert is a local Algarve man: Carlos Alberto Basilio Castelo, an amateur epigrapher. He has spent decades and devoted much of his life to solving this enigma. He is now able to translate the script and can even trace its subtle evolution over millennia. This enables him to attribute an approximate date for each find, according to the engraving displayed. In his opinion, many of them definitely predate 1050 B.C. and the Phoenicians. He may not be a professional academic, but his research is impeccable.

From the evidence Carlos has amassed, he is convinced that the script represents the remnants of a root language that, in the very ancient past, was taken to other countries, particularly to the Middle East, the Atlantic seaboard of Europe, and Morocco. Over the ages, it was developed by different peoples and changed, eventually finding its way back from the Middle East to the Algarve in an adapted form, via the Phoenicians. This explains why some of the characters remained the same.

Although I was familiar with Carlos Alberto's work, having saved newspaper articles detailing it from before the turn of the millennium, I did not meet him until 2009, having already mapped out this book. When he courteously showed me into the study at his home, I was stunned. It was reminiscent of a set from such movies as *Raiders of the Lost Ark,* and I half expected Harrison Ford to stride through the door. The walls were covered in charts, made by Carlos, of the script and its derivatives. There were also crammed files as well as eclectic artifacts, including a bust of an Egyptian pharaoh. Carlos's breadwinning career as a gifted graphic artist was evident from the general bric-a-brac.

He is currently working with other experts in northern Spain on a project tracing the history and spread of "The Royal People": the ancient Kunii/ Conii. There is much confusion and uncertainty about the various names given to these ancient people who lived in southwest Iberia, and many are probably interchangeable; the Conii, the Kunii, and the Turdetani are but a few. Carlos believes it was the Conii who perpetuated the script for many thousands of years. They were highly cultured and even had a religion worshipping just one god. They called him Elel or Eliel on some *herouns,* and the Old Testament's "Eloim" uncannily echoes this. Which came first?

Like other investigators of ancient civilizations, he theorizes that those we regard as "previously uncivilized man" existing, say, five thousand years ago, were the result of the degeneration of a great civilization from many thousands of years earlier, which had been annihilated in a huge disaster. Those who survived had migrated far and wide to different parts of the world. I believe this is partially correct, but also that other parts of the globe—India and Southeast Asia, for example—had parallel civilizations existing at the same time as Atlantis. The old Egyptian priest had prefaced his words to Solon: "There have been, and will be again, many destructions of mankind arising out of many causes: the greatest have been brought about by agencies of fire and water and other lesser ones by innumerable other causes."

Also, Plato comments in *Critias*: "In the days of old, the gods had the whole earth distributed among them by allotment."

The following examples are from those meticulously filed in Carlos's study, along with others I have been able to research.

Pre-10,600 B.C.

Carlos showed me an illustration of an engraving on a bone dagger dating way back to French prehistory.[86] I had seen it before. It is a celebrated archaeological find, but I had not realized its significance: it shows a pregnant wolf and the word *Laol* in the archaic alphabet. He maintains that this spelling was perpetuated by the Conii as *Laoba* or *Loba* and *Laobi* or *Lobo*. *Lobo* is still the Portuguese word for "wolf." One of the Algarve's most famous tourist and golfing developments is called *Vale de Lobo* ("Valley of the Wolf"). (SEE IMAGE 39 BELOW.)

(IMAGE 39) *The bone dagger from the Stone Age, engraved with letters from the ancient alphabet and the depiction of a wolf (circled). Carlos Castelo maintains that the word shown meant "wolf" in the ancient Conii script and has evolved into the word used for wolf today in the Portuguese language: lobo.*
(Courtesy of Carlos Castelo.)

4000 B.C.

One of Carlos's charts shows characters from a famous dolmen at Alvão in central Portugal. This has been dated to around 4000 B.C. Some of the characters on it again match the more recent Algarve examples.

4000 B.C.

In 1916, a piece of engraved stag bone was discovered at a place called Bancal Deta, near Coruna in the Galicia region of northern Spain, to the north of Portugal.[87] Archaeologists have scientifically dated it to between 3800 and 4000 B.C. They described the engraved letters as belonging to an unknown Iberian pre-Indo-European language. I dug out the chart given to me by Carlos Alberto showing the Algarve letters and those used in predynastic Egypt. Most match the ones on the bone.

Using the Iberian script as a reference, experts have recently claimed to have translated the engraving as spelling "A TA LA TA R TE."[88] If this is correct, it opens up a fascinating area for speculation. The name Tartessos, the ancient kingdom referred to in the Bible and possibly once ruled by King Arganthonius, could have been formed from a combination of TARTE and the Greek suffix ESSOS, or even NESSOS, meaning "peninsula." ATALA is the ancient civilization referred to in a Moroccan Berber legend about a fabulous, verdant land to their north, which was destroyed a long time ago in a terrible catastrophe (see last chapter).

Could this piece of stag bone have been carved by refugees to assert their identity and as a reminder of their sunken homeland far to the south?

Pre-3000 B.C.

Way before 3000 B.C., the Egyptians had an alphabet script similar to the Algarvean one, prior to their development of hieroglyphics. Mummies have been found in Egypt with inscriptions formed using Iberian characters. In 1890, the famous Scottish archaeologist and ancient Egyptian historian William Flinders Petrie found examples on stone splinters dating from between 3000 and 12,000 B.C.[89] Apart from the timescale, preceding the great dynasties and way before the Phoenicians, this has another important significance relating to the Atlantis legend that will be covered later in this book. In support of the Egyptian connection, it should be mentioned that Manetho (250 B.C.) wrote that the Egyptian script could be attributed to a western island and particularly their god Thoth, who had once ruled a "Western Domain."[90] The Turin Papyrus (1700 B.C.) has Thoth listed as one of the ten kings from the "reign of the gods" around twelve thousand years earlier.[91] (SEE IMAGES 40A AND 40B ON THE FOLLOWING PAGES.)

PORTUGAL	Luso-Iberian Pre-historic 2,344 B.C.	SPAIN	FRANCE Glozel 2,314 B.C.	EGYPT Pre-historic	EGYPT 1st to 18th Dynasties	CRETE Pre-historic
A	ΛΛΛ≢ΛΛΛ	▷Ρ	Λ∀ΚΓΚ	ΛΛ	⋉⋊Λ	Λ
Γ	ΙΧΓΡΒ	ΛΙ꒳	Δ ϛ ꒳	ℸℾℐ	ℾℬℾ	ℙℂ
	ℸϽϹ< Gↄ	<Ϝ◈	↖ ↗	<<	)ϹϹϹ	
Λ	Λ Δ Δ	ΔΛ	Δ ◁	◿Λ	ΔΛΔ	△
≢	ℓ⨼ℲℲℲ	≢ℓ	ℲℇℲ	Ⅎ⨼	≢ℲℶℲ	⨼ℇⱯ
ⴹ	Ⴤ ⴹ V	↑	Ⴤ Ⴤ	ⴹℲ	ⴹℲℲℸ	ჄℲ
↖	↊		ℸⱵⰍ	≢≢ℐ	≡≢ℐ	≢≢ℸ
ⴲ	ⴹⴹ⨼ⴲ		ℍℍℍℍ	ℍⴲℍ	ⴲⴲℍ	ⴲℍ
ⵙℬ	◆◆⨂ℬ⵰	◆◆	ⵙ ⊕	⊞	⊞⊕⨂	⊞⊙
↴	↴⊬↴↴	ℕ	⌐↊↊↴	Υℐℚ	↱↱Υ	Χↄ
ⴿ	ⴽↄⴿ⟋	Κ	ΥΧV	✳Υ⌿	✳↷ⴿ	ℋℋ
ℸↄ	↱Λↄ↴	ℾΛ	Ⳑ V	ℾⳑⱱ	ℳℾↄ	Λↄ
℥	ⵘⵘↆⵘ	ⵘ	ⵘ ꒳	◿◿	◿⋈ⵘⴺ	◿◿⋈
↴↴	↴↴↴ℕ	ℕ	⌐ Ⴠ	↱	⅄ℕⵘℕ	ℕℕ
≢	≢	ↆⴹ	꒳꒳↔	≢	≢ℇ≡	
ℿℴ	ℿℿℴ◇ⴿ	ⴹ	ℴ⁊⁊	ℿℴ	ℿℴ	ℴℴ⊙
	⌐ ℾ		⌐ ℝ	ℿℾ	ℿ	
			Υ ⴠ			
ℙ	ℙ ℙ		ℙ	ℙℚ	ℙℚ	ℚ
↋	◁⌐◁↋↋ℛ	◁ℙ◇	ℝ Υ	⅄⅄	ℙↃↃⅴ	ℚ
ℳⵟ	ℇℨℳⵑↆⵟ		ⵑⵑ	ⵟℇⵟ	ⵑℇℳ	ⵟⵟ
Χ	↥ ⊹ Χ	Χ	Χ ⊹	⊹ↅↅ	ℸⵟℸ	⊹ℾ↥
↥	Υ V ⴹ	↥	Υ ⴹ	ⴹⴹⵘ	ⴹⴹⵘ	
ℋ				℘	℘℘	℘⊙
ⴲ				✳✳	✳✳↧	Χ
ℍ		ⵘⵘⵟ		℘⅄		
ℊ				ℿ		

(IMAGE 40A)

Pre-1600 B.C.

Yet another of Carlos's charts demonstrates the startling similarity between the ancient Iberian characters and those found from the Minoan civilization on Crete. I suggested earlier that the Minoan civilization could have sprung from resurgent remnants of Atlantis. The presence on Crete of remnants of this ancient alphabet, which seems to have originated in the area of the Atlantis homeland, would certainly support this theory and might explain why the Minoans were so adept at maritime activities. Plato said that Atlantis ruled through the whole of the Mediterranean as far as Egypt. It would therefore have included Crete and Santorini.

Samples with some characters matching those from the Algarve and Moroccan script (ancient Libyan) have been discovered on the Canary Islands of Hierro and Grand Canary by Dr. René Verneau.[92]

Elena Wishaw pointed out the similarity of ancient letters she had found in and around Niebla and Seville to ancient Libyan and Viking runes. When she was conducting her research in the 1920s, the Algarve specimens had not yet come to light, but many of the letters tabulated in her book are the same as, or similar to, the Algarve script.

Scandinavian and German Runes

An assistant in an Algarve museum told me how a visitor from Ireland, confronted by an example on display there, exclaimed in astonishment that at first he thought he was looking at ancient Irish. I have not been able to trace any old Irish script that is sufficiently similar, but Dublin became a Viking city and he may well have been confusing the characters with Viking runes.

Dr. Roger Coghill, who devotes a chapter to the script on his CD "The Atlantis Effect," points out that Viking runes, known as "the younger Futharc," comprise sixteen characters, four of which are the same as the Algarve script.[93] He also perceptively observes that the runes are less sophisticated, probably so they can all be created by chiseling straight lines; there are no curves or circles. The Viking script was preceded by "the German Futharc," which had twenty-four characters. Perhaps the Germans and Scandinavians were reinventing remnants or memories of the original in a form that could easily be carved.

950 B.C.

Over the years, I have put together several vital pieces of exclusive evidence. Unless you were interested in—and familiar with—the Algarve script, you would not have noticed their significance. The first appeared in a news item in the world press in November 2005. I saved a half-page editorial from the English *Daily Mail* dated November 12, written by Julie Wheldon, the newspaper's science correspondent. The headline was GOLIATH, THE PROOF. The article was accompanied by a photograph of a seven-character inscription on a shard of pottery found by Israeli archaeologists at a site in southern Israel. The site is thought to have been a Philistine city named Gath. According to the Bible, this was the home of Goliath, the Philistine giant, famously slain by David using just a stone propelled from a slingshot. After extensive research, the excavation director, Professor Aren Maeir, concluded that the letters related to the name Aylattes, which is thought to be the Philistine name for Goliath. The latter is an Israeli version. The find was in the right place and dated back to the correct period: 950 B.C. Maeir consequently claimed it was the first real evidence proving that there was a "historic kernel to the biblical tale."

It was a fascinating story, and it is easy to appreciate why the *Daily Mail* devoted half a page to it. What particularly intrigued me, though, was that I immediately recognized the letters as being identical to those in the old Algarve script.

The article pointed out that the Philistines are believed to have ended up in Israel about 1200 B.C., complete with their own language and culture.

On analysis, I discovered that several of the letters on the pottery shard are not in the Phoenician alphabet, yet they are in the Algarve script. So the extra Iberian characters already existed. What were they doing in Israel? How did the Philistines come by the script? This is critical, indisputable evidence and supports Carlos Castelo's conclusions. (SEE IMAGE 41, NEXT PAGE.)

As the inscription has been identified by the archaeologists as being of an older Proto-Canaanite script predating Phoenician, logically the identical Algarve script is older too. Interestingly, the Phoenician alphabet is also thought to have developed from an old Proto-Canaanite language—in existence around 1050 B.C.

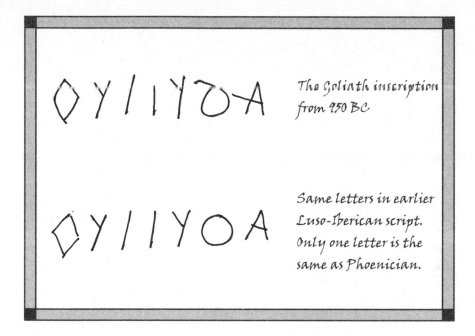

(IMAGE 41) *The characters on the "Goliath" shard, compared with the ancient Algarve "Southwestern Script."*

3500 B.C.

The other example is from a piece of broken pottery collected from a site in Pakistan or India. I originally spotted it on the BBC web site, where it was used to illustrate broken pottery brought up from the remains of an approximately 10,000 B.C. submerged city off the coast of India in the Gulf of Cambay (as discussed in an earlier chapter). The discovery was made while surveying the area where an ancient large river mouth would have been above water before the final inundation at the end of the glacial period. (SEE IMAGE 42, NEXT PAGE.)

The piece of pottery had a form of decoration that is too random to be artistic but strongly resembles the ancient Algarve script, the samples found by Mrs. Wishaw around Niebla, and ancient Libyan. Three of the five characters are the same, and the others are similar.

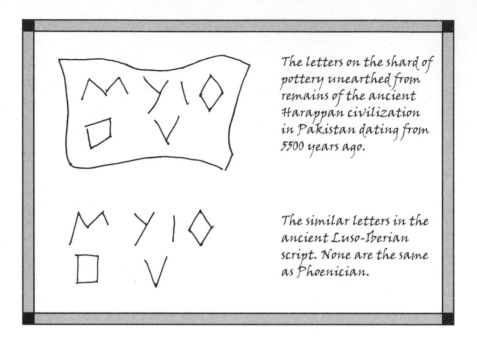

The letters on the shard of pottery unearthed from remains of the ancient Harappan civilization in Pakistan dating from 5500 years ago.

The similar letters in the ancient Luso-Iberian script. None are the same as Phoenician.

(IMAGE 42) *A drawing of the 5,500-year-old piece of decorated pot unearthed in a Harappan city in Pakistan, compared with the same letters in the Algarve "Southwestern Script." It dates from over 2,000 years before the Phoenicians even existed, and none of the letters are the same as the Phoenician alphabet.*

Further research on the BBC site revealed the same photograph popping up to illustrate finds made recently in a 3500 B.C. Pakistani city from the Harappan civilization. I have not been able to ascertain which it relates to, although I suspect it is the latter, but in a way it doesn't much matter. Both sites are far older than Phoenician, Greek, and even the accepted dates that historians stubbornly maintain for Egyptian civilization. This considerably extends the area of influence for this enigmatic alphabet. One cannot rule out that the pottery arrived at the site as a result of trade, but then that does not affect its age. Maybe the inscription reads "a souvenir from Atlantis" (tongue in cheek).

Some scholars have suggested that Phoenician was the model for scripts developed in such far-flung places as Southeast Asia, Tibet, Mongolia, and, particularly, the Brahmin script of India. The date of the pottery shard shown on the BBC web site contradicts that and shifts the spotlight onto the Algarve script. The Phoenicians did not even exist then—yet the Algarve script bears distinct similarities to the inscription, so it was apparently known in the Indian subcontinent at that time.

Anyone who begins to research old civilizations and legends will quickly come across assertions that the whole world once spoke the same language and used the same alphabet. Bearing this out, far afield in the opposite direction from India, samples of the alphabet have been found in North America—the Grave Creek Tablet mentioned in the last chapter, for example. Elsewhere, the Spanish recorded a form of writing possessed by the Aymara Indians living on the shores of Lake Titicaca in South America. Some of the characters match others in the Southwestern Script.[94]

Is there an echo here of the biblical account of the Tower of Babel, which begins by saying that originally the whole world had just one language and goes on to imply that this had enabled mortals to develop their civilizations and technology? Quoting from Genesis 11:1-9:

"But the Lord came down to see the city and the tower that the men were building. The Lord said: 'If as one people speaking the same language they have begun to do this, then nothing they plan to do will be impossible for them. Come, let us go down and confuse their language so that they will not understand each other.' So the Lord scattered them from there all over the earth, and they stopped building the city."

Note that the Lord was not alone. He said "Come, let *us* go down. . . ." It also implies that man was becoming technologically advanced. The Tower of Babel is most likely a metaphor for this, and the biblical account, in a rather folksy way, hides the true nature of an event of truly disastrous proportions that almost annihilated that civilization just as it was acquiring the height of technology.

2500 B.C. to 400 B.C.

Until a few years ago, most of the *herouns* discovered in the Algarve and engraved with the old script were scattered amongst local museums, with a few appropriated by others elsewhere in Portugal. Now a superb, purpose-built museum in a southern country town called Almodôvar has successfully gathered around twenty of them together. It is seen as a tourist attraction, as several impressive *heroun* examples were found in that neighborhood. Unfortunately, the museum is adhering to the establishment view and, although they are all beautifully displayed, the samples are dated as being from the first millennium B.C. I questioned the museum authorities on this point, specifically asking on what evidence some original dates had been adjusted to more recent ones. I received no answers.

As many as forty letters, maybe more, have been identified in the local Algarve script; but, since it evolved over thousands of years, Carlos Castelo points out that many of the letters represent the same character, several times having evolved from one to the other. An example is a letter that looks like "Y," which later became "X."

The Phoenician alphabet has twenty-two characters, the Greek has twenty-four, and the Iberian sources vary from twenty-two to twenty-seven. Of the Algarve letters, eleven are the same as Greek and thirteen appear to be the same, or very similar, to Phoenician. If the local script had developed from Phoenician and Greek, why did the local people go to the trouble of developing so many new characters when they were already presented with completed alternatives? They certainly wouldn't have done so for a few grave-stones, and there is no evidence of its being used for more than that during the Phoenician era. The crude, uncraftsmanlike execution of the work suggests a relic language—largely forgotten, but perpetuated by a priestly class to impress its flocks for ceremonial purposes. In ancient times, the ability to read and write was often restricted to rulers and priests. It was used as an instrument of power and to inspire awe in the ordinary people.

Interestingly, the spread of the script discoveries matches many of the areas where Cro-Magnon man lived. These people were characteristically well built with blond hair. Examples often cited are the Guanches from the Canary Isles and the blond Berber tribes from the Atlas Mountains in Morocco. No evidence has been found to show where this particular race originated. They seem to have almost simultaneously appeared along the western seaboard of Europe and Morocco more than ten thousand years ago. It has frequently been suggested that they must have come from somewhere else and fanned out from their original homeland when it was destroyed or became uninhabitable. It is not surprising that many have suggested that that homeland was Atlantis.

Some linguistic experts have also maintained that the ancient Basque language, thought to be the oldest in Europe, is derived from a once-great Iberian race that extended all over the western seaboard, to areas of France including Brittany, to Iberia, to the Celtic areas of the British Isles, and to the Berber areas of North Africa. They maintain that even today the Basque and Berber languages have very close affinities.[95] If there was one root language, they would also initially have had one root alphabet.

I have laid out just some of the evidence indicating that variations of the same archaic script existed as far back as the end of the last Ice Age. Many other examples from Portugal extend from 6000 B.C. right up to the last millennium B.C. It appears to have also been known in predynastic Egypt, Minoan Crete, Israel, and even the Indian subcontinent, as far back as 3500 B.C.; proof of its use exists in many other cultures. It is accepted that our current Western alphabet was derived from Phoenician and Greek, yet clearly these had both imported many characters from this earlier, much older alphabet.

There is, therefore, a strong case for reassessing the real origin of our alphabet. Could we even have found the form of writing used on Atlantis? It cannot, of course, be claimed conclusively to be so; more evidence will be needed, but it is an extraordinary set of coincidences:

1. This book has, I hope, proved that southwest Iberia was where Plato indicated Atlantis once existed.
2. Academics generally acknowledge that the script emanated from southwest Iberia.
3. Ancient Greek records state that the region already had a script as far back as 6000 B.C., and samples of one exist that are at least six thousand years old.
4. There is at least one verifiable, dated archaeological find proving that the script was in existence before the time given by Plato for the destruction of Atlantis in 9600 B.C. There are others, but, as they are controversial, I have not included them here.

So, what do you think? There is a welter of more detail and evidence from Carlos Castelo and others who have investigated the subject, but I don't think it necessary to bore you with it to make my point. I feel that I have laid out enough to prove that there was a very ancient script, that it emanated from southwest Iberia but eventually spread over a considerable area, and that it existed before the destruction of Atlantis. If you agree that I have made a case for Atlantis having existed in the same region of Iberia, then the script must be from Atlantis.

Irrespective of Atlantis, there is also a watertight argument for rewriting the history of our Western alphabet.

I rest the case and pass on to another of those fascinating questions hanging over those Atlanteans: What were they like? Could they be in your family tree?

CHAPTER EIGHTEEN

The Atlanteans . . . Are You Related?

His long red hair and beard contrasted strikingly with the ankle-length white robe. He sat in the prow of the ship, his brilliant blue eyes fixed steadfastly ahead. There could be no looking back. His heart was heavy.

So many years, so much work. The city behind him, disappearing around the river bend, was where his family had lived for generations. The recent disaster affecting mainly the southern part of the kingdom, in which a major part of the fertile land had been flooded, then swallowed by the sea, had been a demoralizing blow. Although the sea level had been rising very slowly for centuries, this sudden disaster had convinced him that he must locate elsewhere if the great experiment was to survive and prosper. The homeland was too unstable. This was not the first time it had been shaken and reshaped by a huge earthquake. The next one might destroy everything that was left. He had decided that he could not take that risk.

He had lingered long enough to help his son rebuild and repair the major damage. Much had been achieved, and the remaining work could safely be left in the younger man's hands.

Now focus must be concentrated on the future, and on plans for a new life to the east at the far end of the great confined sea beyond Gades. The area had been carefully chosen. It was unlikely to be affected by the writhing that kept repeating itself in the tormented land of his forebears: it would be far removed from any new inundation from the great ocean.

He was sure that they would be welcome there. The small indigenous population led a simple, hard life hunting and collecting natural vegetation. His little band had much to offer: seeds and cultivation, irrigation systems, animal husbandry, pottery and weaving skills, the ability to build stable homes and shelter. This was a chance to start afresh; a new challenge for him and his followers and a healthier, more contented life for the natives.

What happened to them? Who were those Atlanteans, and what did they look like? Who now carries their genes? Could their blood be coursing through your veins? The questions and uncertainties tumble over themselves.

If, as I hope it does, this book prompts archaeological work, particularly on the seabed, it should reveal some definitive answers. For now, though, we can only speculate and form hypotheses from the limited existing evidence, which, I must emphasize, is all that the following amounts to.

Plato wrote: "They all of them by just apportionment obtained what they [the gods] wanted . . . and peopled their district" (clues 19 and 20).

Also "He [Poseidon] begat children by a mortal woman and settled them in part of the island" (clue 22).

Clue 22 also tells us about the five pairs of male twins that Poseidon sired with this mortal woman. We can assume that, as Plato informed us, these then became the elite, each ruling a different part of the kingdom; they would have intermarried with their own kind to preserve the purity of the line. However, from Plato's chronology, it would appear that the ordinary people were installed first (clues 30 and 31) and, if this is what Plato meant, the population was, somehow, put in place remarkably quickly—certainly before all the original twins were ready to govern part of the kingdom and "rule over many men." Logic dictates, however, that it would have taken a few hundred years to reach significant numbers, even if everyone produced large families. So what on earth was Plato alluding to?

Poseidon did not organize mass immigration from elsewhere, as, toward the end of *Critias*, we are informed that the DNA of these subjects was a mixture of Poseidon's and that of existing mortals.

Plato wrote: "For many generations, as long as the divine nature lasted in them, they were obedient to the laws, and well-affectioned toward the god, whose seed they were; for they possessed true and in every way great spirits, uniting gentleness with wisdom in the various chances of life, and in their intercourse with one another. They despised everything but virtue, caring little for their present state of life, and thinking lightly of the possession of gold and other property, which seemed only a burden to them; neither were they intoxicated by luxury, nor did wealth deprive them of their self-control; but they were sober, and saw clearly that all these goods are increased by virtue and friendship with one another, whereas by too great regard and respect for them, they are lost and friendship with them. By such reflections, and by the continuance in them of a divine nature, the qualities which we have described grew and increased among them but when the divine portion began to fade away, and became diluted too often and too much with the mortal admixture, and the human nature got the upper hand, they then, being unable to bear their fortune, behaved unseemly, and to him who had an eye to see grew visibly debased, for they were losing the fairest of their precious gifts; but to those who had no eye to see the true happiness, they appeared glorious and blessed at the very time when they were full of avarice and unrighteous power."

That sounds ominously like a comment on today's world with its maniacal pop and celebrity worship and magazines flaunting and publishing "richest-people lists" as though the amassing of wealth is blessed.

Note the words "whose seed they were." Plato is implying that parts of the gods' genes were used. This is emphasized by the mention of "the continuance in them of a divine nature"—an unmistakable allusion to the better traits inherited from the gods. Note, too, "and became diluted too often and too much with the mortal admixture," in this case referring to the traits of the humans they were partly created from. The people of Atlantis were, obviously, a combination of the two.

You can draw your own conclusions as to just what he was implying. It does seem to reflect another familiar story—the creation account in

Genesis. It may explain why a DNA helix ended up carved on a monumental stone egg.

As to the original physical characteristics of these Atlanteans, we can only make assumptions from communities that may have resulted from Atlantean survivors, based on the premise that they fanned out from southwest Iberia.

It would be logical that each different set of "gods" ensconced in their domains in different parts of the world had spawned their own individual recognizable races, with some physical characteristics unique to each: skin tone or hair color, for example.

The "sleeping prophet," Edgar Cayce, indicated in one of his trances that the world's five races of man evolved in different parts of the globe: "The Yellow race in Mongolia and Gobi areas, the White race in the Caucasian mountains, the Brown race on the American Pacific coast and western Andes, the Black race in Africa and, finally, the Red race in Atlantis."

In another trance, Cayce said that Atlantis originally existed from the western end of the Mediterranean to the Bahamas. What he meant by the "Red race" is unclear. He could have been referring either to a combination of the ruddy complexion most red-haired and blond people have, or that caused by exposure of their skin to the sun. Blonds or people with straw-colored hair are found side by side with redheads.

The scraps of information about the Atlanteans that can be gleaned from such places as the Canary Islands indicate tall red- or blond-haired individuals with blue, gray, or green eyes.

Intriguingly, as well as remains of ancient blonds, those of red-haired individuals have been unearthed over a wide area. Along with the Canary Islands, pertinent examples have been found in Egypt and in South and North America, areas recorded to have received visitations from tall white strangers.

Today, the places where a significant percentage of the population has red or blond hair are Scandinavia, Finland, Scotland, Ireland, and, to a lesser degree, Wales. Surprisingly, there are also substantial numbers in the Middle East. All shades of blond hair, from straw to almost white, are prevalent in Germany.

Other evidential strands regarding the blond/red hair gene are:

- The ancient Irish book *Lebor Gabata Erre* ("The book of the taking of Ireland"), compiled in the twelfth century A.D., describes a group of early invaders. They were called the *Tuatha de D'anann,* meaning "Tribe of Dan (or Danu)," and comprised people with long red hair and high foreheads who were tall and had blue eyes. There were two classes. Members of one, the elite, were adept in medicine, metal-working, and communication (presumably writing); in the other, ordinary, class were such basic occupations as farmers and shepherds.
- The Book of Judges records that the people of the Goddess of Danu were a mighty seafaring tribe.
- The Guanches on the Canary Islands were tall with red or blond hair and blue/gray/green eyes.
- The same traits, particularly blond hair, can still be seen in some Berber tribes in the Atlas Mountains.
- The ancient Thracians reputedly had red hair and blue eyes. This race was one of the most populous in Eastern Europe, but it failed to unite as one nation. It has never been conclusively established where they originated. I will discuss them further a little later.
- There are red-haired people among the population in northern India. Early archaeologists who unearthed the first ancient cities in India and Pakistan reported that the rulers' remains showed that they were tall with red hair.[96]
- Naturally preserved red-haired giants with Western features have been unearthed in China. A step pyramid without precedent in that country exists in the same area, at Xian in the Qui Chan Province.[97] Some historians maintain that these people, who were known as the Tocharians, were responsible for building the Silk Road and the cities along it. Although the odd mummy remains on display, others have been locked away in stores and the Chinese government has not encouraged further exploration.
- Elena Wishaw referred to the facially distinctive tall blonds, quite unlike the indigenous Spaniards, still found in parts of Andalucía around 1920.

- "Aztec" is the local Nahuatl word for "people of Aztlan," indicating where they came from. Their ancestors were described as having red hair and were thought to have migrated south from northern Mexico. That is remarkably close to the Antilles Islands, part of what I suggest was the Atlantis Empire. They were also described as having very straight noses extending immediately down from their foreheads. Mrs. Wishaw gave exactly that description for the blond Spaniards in Andalucía.

- "Aztlan" is reputed to have meant "the place of herons" or "whiteness." One of the most common birds in the Algarve is the white egret heron. This description also sounds remarkably similar to that of Atala, the homeland of a race recorded in ancient Vedic literature as the great enemy of India. It is described as being a "white island" in the great western ocean on the other side of the world that eventually disappeared below the sea. Not surprisingly, it has often been associated with Atlantis. The Berbers have a similar legend.

- A red-haired mummy was recovered from Nevado Ampato in Peru, near the famous mountaintop remains of Machu Picchu. Other finds of mummies in South America have included a mixture of those with the stiff, black hair of the indigenous Indians, and others with long, silky, wavy red hair; tall bodies; and long skulls (Thor Heyerdahl).

- An ancient and sadly desecrated cemetery near Nazca in Peru, famous for the "Nazca lines," had dozens of partly exposed red-haired corpses.

- Spaniards reported seeing red-haired Incas in South America. Francisco Pizarro, the famous Spanish conquistador, was told by locals that the remaining tall white men with beards and red or blond hair were the last survivors of the Viracochas, who had suddenly appeared from the eastern ocean and taught them so much. Heyerdahl is also reported as saying that the Inca rulers were tall with much lighter skin than the small, dark locals.

- In his book *Aku-Aku: The Secret of Easter Island*,[98] Heyerdahl recounted how the leading family largely comprised fair-skinned redheads with long, thin noses—quite unlike the rest of the islanders, who were darker-skinned and had black hair and flat noses. These redheads were the remnants of the earlier ruling class who had arrived on the island by boat a long time before. Significantly, the Viracochas had eventually left South America from the west coast by boat. Could they have reached Easter Island? These rulers were almost totally obliterated in a rebellion by the indigenous locals. Heyerdahl also found red-haired people on the Marquesas Islands, close to Easter Island. The famous statues on the island originally had red hairpieces, made from a separate red stone, on the tops of their heads.

- Remains of red-haired people have even been discovered in New Zealand. One theory is that these, too, were remnants of the same Viracochas who had eventually left South America from the west coast.

- Many Egyptian mummies have been found to have red hair. The very early ruling demigods were installed in Egypt by the original gods who came from the west.

None of these offers firm evidence that the original Atlanteans had the same characteristics, but the likelihood is that people with such distinctive features would have evolved in one place. The dispersal of people with these characteristics around the world is often associated with civilizers appearing in foreign lands and imparting their knowledge. Their point of departure appears to have been someplace in the center. They appeared in South America from the east, in Egypt from the west, and in northern Europe from Iberia.

The most well-known and often trumpeted dispersal relates to those tall, bearded, long-haired white people who visited South America. They arrived by boat, and in one legend the boat is described as shining, as though covered in fish scales. It sounds like metal.

Similar accounts existed all over that continent. Although the names vary, the most well known were Viracocha and Quetzalcoatl. The former was said to have started his own civilizing mission immediately after the great flood, and he was linked to the mysterious city of Tiahuanaco on the Bolivian Altiplano, for which the locals claim immense age. He came in a time of chaos to set the world right. A great scientist and architect, he was noted for constructing irrigation channels so that agriculture could flourish. That sounds remarkably like duplicating Plato's account of Atlantis.

The story of Quetzalcoatl follows an identical pattern. He arrived in Mexico after it had been overwhelmed by a deluge, bringing agriculture to the area together with seeds for crops, and teaching the arts of mathematics, astronomy, and how to build a refined culture.

Graves containing tall people with extended skulls have also been found in the northern part of Egypt—a race quite different from the later Egyptians.

Osiris was revered as being one of the first gods and is said to have ruled in Egypt for a long period, initially having to contend with banishing cannibalism among the primitive natives. You will recall a mention that Thoth, who appeared on the scene afterward, was said to have come from a distant land, which he had ruled, in the west. He was credited by the ancient Egyptians as having invented mathematics and astronomy, as well as schooling them in land surveying, medicine, reading, and writing. There are extraordinary similarities here with the South American accounts.

At what period these gods appeared in Egypt is mired in controversy and conflicting views. Preserved in Turin's Egizio museum, however, is what is considered to be the oldest map of topographic interest surviving from the ancient world. It was drawn by an Egyptian scribe in 1160 B.C. for Rameses IV, to help in a quarrying expedition. Apart from the map of the area, it shows geological information and includes numerous annotations. It states that the first demigods in Egypt were installed by the original gods to rule on their behalf around 9850 B.C. That is remarkably close to the time given by Plato for the demise of Atlantis. The fact that they were called "demigods" (i.e., literally half gods) presumably meant they were not from the pure lineage of the original gods, but offspring from mating with the native population, so they retained some of the "divine nature" and physical characteristics of the gods that set them apart.

If any of these people came from Atlantis, it would explain how the Egyptians knew about the tragic lost civilization—another piece in the jigsaw puzzle.

The ruling elite of Atlantis may have had prior warning of the eventual overwhelming disaster and have left before it struck or, possibly, survived in their citadel and left afterward. There could well have been a preceding period of seismic activity. Some may have left as a result of an earlier major earthquake that sank part of the plain. Not all of the empire would have been affected at the same time, so these "civilizers" could also have departed to other countries from various parts of the Atlantean kingdom at different times. It is likely, for instance, that some of those who visited South and North America would have come from the Antilles/Bahamas region.

In both South America and Egypt, these seemingly identical people arrived complete with the same knowledge that had been developed in the place from whence they came.

Author Andrew Collins, in his books *Gods of Eden* and *From the Ashes of Angels,* proposes that these "gods," who were responsible for this much-earlier culture in Egypt, for whatever reason left there and resettled in the Lake Van region of Kurdistan.[99] Much later, the remnants of this group descended from that base onto the plains of the Fertile Crescent and kick-started the Sumerian civilization.

Plato indicated that Atlantis also ruled well into the Mediterranean. Did some of those ruling elite strike out to the east and northeast, eventually penetrating as far as India, and then establish the Silk Road all the way to China?

Let us consider what we know:

- Many thousands of years ago, tall, blond or red-haired, blue-eyed, and bearded civilizers arrived by sea in South America, having voyaged from the east.
- Others, physically identical, arrived in Egypt from the west and again introduced the arts of civilization. Indications are that this could have happened as long as fourteen thousand years ago.
- The installation of the first demigods as rulers of Egypt corresponds with Plato's date for the destruction of Atlantis.
- Both groups are described as having the same mastery of agriculture, mathematics, astronomy, building, irrigation, and writing.

Many commentators have pointed out the obvious: that this indicates a dispersal of the same people from the same place, somewhere between the two destinations, a place where they had already developed their knowledge and skills. Atlantis and its island empire in southwest Iberia fit that hypothesis perfectly.

This would, however, only appear to account for the ruling elite group, who were small bands of select, knowledgeable individuals. The destination of any survivors from the ordinary population is best gleaned from the current placement of the blond/red hair gene and the ancient alphabet. That would indicate Scandinavia, Scotland, Ireland, Wales, and pockets in the eastern Mediterranean. The blonds of the Atlas mountains in Morocco and the Canary Islands were likely there all along as part of the empire. Most of those down on the North African coastal plains would have been annihilated by the disaster; only pockets in the mountains survived and remained fiercely loyal to their territory and tribe. Some among the North American tribes have blond hair, and they have preserved legends that their ancestors came from a foreign land.

This proposed migration from southwest Iberia to the Celtic areas of Great Britain has received support from research recently carried out in Wales. Professor John Koch from the University of Wales at Aberystwyth says that archaeological inscriptions on those large stones found in the Algarve show that the Celts came from southern Portugal and southwest Spain—not from central Europe, as previously accepted. He maintains that the Southwestern Script in Chapter Seventeen can be deciphered as Celtic.

Another expert on Welsh history, Dr. Raimund Karl from the University of Wales at Bangor, has said: "In the last couple of years there have been a number of genetic studies of human DNA indicating that the population of much of the western part of the British Isles is related to other communities along the Atlantic seafront. These include Brittany, northern Spain, Portugal, and the French Atlantic coast. That's their genetic origin."

Even earlier, Professor Sykes of England's Oxford University had carried out DNA research that established that ancient Britons originated from the Iberian peninsula many thousands of years ago. In 2001, research by Oxford University combined with the University of California found that the Basques of northern Spain were genetically linked to the Celts of Ireland and Wales. Other research has also shown that the Berbers of the Atlas Mountains fall into the same group and, in 2009, a paper in *BMC*

Evolutionary Biology recorded that research had found that the Berbers were of the same lineage as the Guanches on the Canary Islands. Other work has also shown a link with the Balkans.

How, though, does one then account for the many dark-haired Celts? Most likely, it is because the Poseidon family was the blond/red-haired lot, whereas the original ordinary mortals were dark-haired. The combination of their DNA would have spawned a mixture. Also to be considered is the well-ingrained local legend that the south Walians arrived there under their leader Brutus, fleeing from Troy.

But who were the Trojans from Troy? Japheth was Noah's third son, and Japheth's seventh son was called Tiras. He is held to be the ancestor of the Tiracians, more generally known by their Greek name, the Thracians. Troy was reputedly named after Tiras. When founded around 1900 B.C., it was known as Troas, and subsequently Troi, then Troy, with the Thracian inhabitants called Trajans or Trojans. Apart from Brutus, who was related to the old Trojan royal family and who escaped with his followers to Wales, others migrated northeast through Europe and became the ancestors of the Swedes. Many Bulgarians also claim to be descendents of these ancient Thracians—not the Slavs, who only arrived in the region around A.D. 600. The Thracians were described as having ruddy complexions, red or blond hair, and blue eyes.

There has also been much "coming and going" of groups between Ireland, Wales, and Scotland, as well as Scandinavia. The seeds have been well and truly intermingled.

The indications are that the Conii from southwest Iberia were also dark-haired. Where do they fit into the puzzle? Were they the remnants of the ordinary Atlanteans, or were they Celts who migrated there from elsewhere in central Europe, as many historians have maintained? This previously accepted history of the Celts is currently undergoing a complete reappraisal. The theory that they came from central Europe is now broadly accepted as being a mistake, resulting from a misunderstanding by ancient chroniclers. The latest genealogical research indicates they were Iberian.

The original Atlanteans most likely evolved into different tribes or clans, all living harmoniously together. Some had more of the gene producing the red or blond hair, while others, with increasingly less of the gods' DNA, inherited the original humans' black hair. Plato said that the "admixture" of the gods had diminished.

It seems increasingly likely that the Conii and the Celts were one and the same and were the early migratory ancestors of some of the south Walians as well as the Basques.

It is pertinent here to take up Carlos Castelo's theory that the ancient southwest Iberian language was carried from that area to the Middle East by the populace fleeing a disaster. If that was the case, these people would have been absorbed into the confused racial mixing bowl there, although the physical characteristics of some—tall, with red/blond hair and blue eyes—were significantly different from those of the indigenous Sumerian and Semitic population. It would certainly explain the frequent occurrence of red hair in that area. Some Israeli scholars have painstakingly linked the Tribe of Dan that invaded Ireland with one of the lost tribes of Israel, also called the Tribe of Dan, after one of Jacob's sons. The tribe's journey northwest, overland from Israel, and the areas they settled or migrated through can, claim the scholars, be traced by the names left behind. The Danube and Don Rivers and Denmark (*Danemark*) are a few examples. This version of history is disputed by others, who maintain it is a bid to enlarge the area of influence of Judaism. Irish records, however, state that these invaders had red hair and blue eyes. Could Dan, who reportedly had red hair and was one of Jacob's sons, have had a red-haired mother?

There is a report that Moses's father-in-law was the head of the Kenites, a group that joined with Moses's Israelites. An alternative name, frequently used in ancient reports, for the Conii/Kunii people from the Algarve was the Cynetes or Kynetes.

The Tribe of Dan—or Dana—was also reported to have worshipped the goddess Diana, also a well-known Greek deity. The large river that forms the border between the Algarve and Spain, now called the Guadiana, used to be known as the Ana. I have read that the whole region was once known as the country of Ana (D'Ana?).

If all this is confusing, I apologize. I have tried to pull together many, many strands that cover thousands of years. Modern genetic research, such as that involving DNA and Haplogroup X, is undoubtedly helping to unravel the tangled web and indicates that the various dispersals of people discussed here are broadly correct.

No matter how complicated the path all these blonds or red-haired people took, however, if we could follow them back it is likely they would all lead to southwest Iberia and Atlantis.

So, do you carry the Atlantean gene this hypothesis about hair color would indicate? If you have blond/red hair, or any of the shades in between, then you probably do. No matter where you now live, somewhere in the ancient past, one of your ancestors with these unique distinguishing features probably struck out from Atlantis. Welcome to the club.

This book started with that huge stone egg. I have not revisited it so far as, in itself, it did not provide any evidence to prove that Atlantis was in Iberia. Now, with Atlantis firmly nailed down, I decided that it was time to further research this extraordinary object. Might it be the first relic ever found to support Plato's legend?

CHAPTER NINETEEN

The Great White Egg

She had deliberately chosen this very night. The old woman had said it would be auspicious for her mission. The full moon created an eerie combination of flat light and deep shadows.

She drifted up the gentle slope past the houses, with their slumbering occupants, and the almond trees, with the perfume from their delicate white blossom hanging heavily in the air, until the monument suddenly loomed stark on the skyline, its glistening, white surface beckoning. Willing herself not to recoil against the chill surface, she loosened the robe and pressed her naked body to the stone. She moved gently, massaging against the strange symbol sculpted onto it, her arms widespread in a fervent embrace. She ached for a child but, after several years with her man, pregnancy still eluded her. Now she fervently prayed to the gods to make her fertile.

The old woman had said that this great white egg, representing the very essence of birth, had worked its magic in the past. Why not for her?

It was powerful. Legend had it that the gods erected it long ago to mark the beginning.

That's not a recorded event, but one that I suspect could well have happened quite regularly many thousands of years ago. The stone egg still exists, having survived every calamity the Algarve's torrid history could

throw at it. As recounted in the first chapter, it has been lying unappreci-
ated for some thirty years in a corner of a delightful museum in Lagos,
an old coastal town famous as a port for many of Henry the Navigator's
caravels that sailed forth to discover uncharted parts of the world. If this
book's hypothesis for Atlantis is correct, then this object could be highly
significant.

The museum houses an eclectic variety of remains from the Neolithic,
Roman, and Moorish periods, together with ethnic examples from life
in the area during the last few centuries. The largest object there, the
stone egg, is not from Lagos but from land near Silves. I knew the general
area where it had been found, but not the exact position. The museum
could not help, nor could the local archaeology department; but a spot of
amateur sleuthing eventually enabled me to track down one of the local
men involved in the discovery. He obligingly took me to the very place.
To my amazement, it was overlooking the area I have already suggested
was the port for Plato's Atlantis capital, ancient Silves. He had helped
unearth it three decades before, when the land was being prepared for
agriculture. A new well was being dug when, at a depth of between four
and five meters, the workmen hit the top of a huge, curved, smooth
rock. At first they thought it was the back of a carved stone pig, but,
as the sides were excavated, it became obvious that it was a large egg.
Together, the workmen succeeded in hauling it to the surface with ropes.
I had originally been told of its existence more than twenty years ago by
an eyewitness who had seen it lying by the side of the road before being
moved to its new home in Lagos (Silves did not then have a suitable
museum to accommodate it).

The Lagos museum describes it as a *menhir* (standing stone), but I
believe it is too sophisticated for that and was designed for another specific purpose—although it could have served as a *menhir* later in its life,
as suggested in the opening cameo of this chapter. It is made from local
limestone—the same white stone that Plato indicated was among those
used extensively in the Atlantis citadel and which is freely available very
close to where the relic was found.

It has been sculpted to represent a large egg, about six feet in height—or
length. Unfortunately the side it lies on in the museum has been broken

either during its discovery or, more likely, at some stage when it was toppled over from wherever it was erected.

Sculpted down the three visible sides of the egg is the same large motif. The images stand proud of the surface, indicating that great care had been taken in the stone's preparation, especially if the workers had only stone tools. It would have been far easier to finish the whole surface, then carve the images into it. (SEE IMAGES 44, 45, AND 46 IN THE PHOTO INSERT.)

What could the motif possibly mean, or represent? It immediately struck me that it had an astonishing resemblance to the DNA helix but, before jumping to sensational conclusions, further research was called for.

Carlos Castelo informed me that each segment of the motif was identical to the fertility symbol of the Kunii people, assumed to have been adopted because of its similarity to the female vulva. It would, however, be illogical to stack a whole pile of segments on top of one another. That would be confusing. One symbol standing alone is more easily recognizable and has greater impact.

The similarity to the DNA helix is masked by a central rod. Is it possible, though, that there are two elements combined? One element could be the central rod or wand, and the other a simplified version of the DNA helix to make it possible to carve it on stone.

Throughout ancient history, the rod has represented power, the staff of office, the scepter of kings and queens. Historical records are littered with other references, including:

- Author Zecharia Sitchin, an expert on ancient Sumerian tablets, believed that the rod or wand traditionally represented "the Lord of the manufacture" or "implement of life."
- Ancient Egyptian priests were depicted with rods.
- Stone Age paintings show figures holding rods, thought to be symbolic of power.
- Moses had a wand—as did his brother Aaron—that supposedly had magical powers.
- Druids had a wand that represented "the tool and vehicle of the power of the heavens."
- Some scholars believe the rod has roots as a phallus—always a good fallback for bemused experts.

In 1910, archaeologist Dr. William Hayes Ward wrote that he thought a well-known symbol called the caduceus had originated in Sumeria between 3000 and 4000 B.C. The oldest known example is on a Sumerian cylinder seal. This is uncannily similar to the carving on the Algarve "egg." It depicts two snakes coiling up the rod and is sometimes shown with wings at the top. (SEE IMAGE 43 BELOW.)

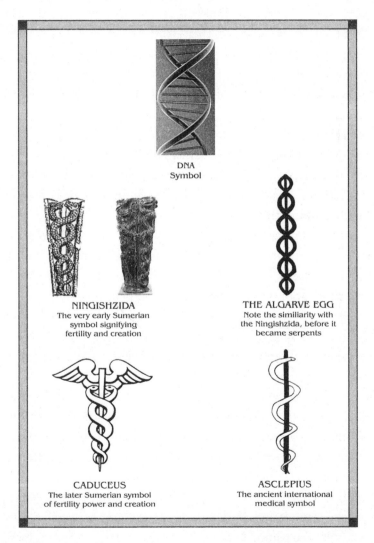

(IMAGE 43) *Chart depicting the DNA symbol, the carving on the stone egg, and other similar symbols of ancient Sumerian origin dating from between 4,000 and 2,000 B.C.*

It is unclear exactly what the caduceus originally represented or stood for, but the most widely accepted explanation is that it was a symbol of fertility and wisdom. Later, the Greeks associated it with their god Hermes (or Mercury), who was known as "the messenger of the gods." Among his more dubious credentials, Hermes was the god of thieves, but he was also the protector of merchants. I suppose the latter would have been apt for a monument overlooking a bustling harbor front devoted to trade, although there are no wings or snakes on the Algarve stone. He is also thought to have been the Greek equivalent of the Egyptian god Thoth, who originally ruled in the West.

The caduceus has also become confused with another ancient motif, the asclepius, which shows a single snake around a rod and was the original medical symbol. Confusion still reigns, with the caduceus wrongly appearing on the badge of the American medical corps.

Yet another similar symbol predates the caduceus by about a thousand years: the Ningishzida. It represented a Mesopotamian deity who was the god of nature and fertility.

That the symbol on the egg appears to have evolved into something slightly different in Sumeria but still stood for fertility and wisdom supports the DNA hypothesis. The gods/rulers who influenced the founding of the Sumerian civilization were known as the "serpent people." If they introduced the symbol into Sumeria, it's easy to see how it could have evolved into two intertwining serpents. The Sumerians were not the only ones to depict versions of it; an intertwined snake version appears on frescoes on the tombs of Egyptian pharaohs Seti and Rameses VI.

The age of the Algarve "egg" is critical here. It is thought that the many *menhirs* and assorted standing stones scattered around the Algarve date from around 3500 to 2500 B.C. As mentioned in the last chapter, the established view is that the Kunii people migrated from the northeast to the Algarve after that period. Carlos Castelo, supported by the latest genetic research, might disagree; but if that is correct, and the "egg" dates back as far as the other *menhirs*—to around 3500 B.C.—then the original symbol could not have come with the Kunii. They must have extracted just one segment from the egg's carving, knowing that it was locally associated with fertility and because of its unmistakable similarity to the female vulva.

I strongly suspect, however, that the stone egg is even older. It was found at a depth of between four and five meters, in arable land at the brow of a hill. It is unlikely that soil would have been naturally washed down onto it: the opposite is far more likely.

In their book *Uriel's Machine*, Robert Lomas and Christopher Knight detailed a strong scientific case for Noah's great flood occurring in 7640 B.C.[100] This also concords with the last great glacier melt. Apart from the host of worldwide legends, the evidence is supported by research. The measurable results point to the cause being a large ice meteorite breaking into pieces and plunging into the oceans around the world. Large chunks of the ozone layer would have been destroyed, leading to an increase in the production of carbon-14. Nitric acid would have been formed by nitrogen being burned by the sheer energy of the impact. This has been measured in worldwide ice cores, demonstrating that an event of this magnitude happened in about 7640 B.C.

That some ten thousand species became extinct around that time is strong supporting evidence.

The inevitable result would have been gigantic tsunamis crashing over all the world's landmasses at speeds of around 640 miles per hour. Even worse, their height would have reached five kilometers. Only those on the highest mountains or hundreds of miles from any coast could have survived the initial calamity. The equivalent of a nuclear winter would have followed, with the sun blotted out in most areas. There would also have been unprecedented deluges of rain.

Colossal amounts of mud, rock, and debris would have been tossed around before being dragged back out to sea or deposited on land as the waters subsided. The world's great saltwater lakes—the Dead Sea and that in Utah, for example—would have been formed as the ocean water remained trapped in large valleys.

The many *menhirs* that can still be seen all over the western Algarve are, almost certainly, still in their original standing positions. They must, therefore, have been erected since this flood, otherwise they would have been flattened and buried. Archaeologists concur in dating them back to between 3500 and 2500 B.C. The great egg, however, was buried under thirteen to sixteen feet of soil. It is tempting to presume that this was a result of this last great flood. It must have been buried sufficiently deep to have disappeared. If it had just lain toppled on the ground and even partly visible for centuries, its significance would almost certainly have led to any superstitious new populace reerecting it to an upright position.

The specific area where it was discovered is called *Vale de Lama*, which translates as "Valley of Mud." The precise spot on which it was found is too high to have been affected by the great tsunami of 1755. The land on each side of the Arade River, near its mouth at Portimão, was then temporarily flooded to a height of around thirty-six feet. The egg site is nine kilometers upriver, but not on its banks: it is on a rise overlooking the old harbor and is elevated more than thirty-six feet.

If it was erected before Noah's flood, then it must be more than 9,640 years old. But even a perfunctory examination reveals that before being buried, it had been subjected to eons of weathering. This is particularly obvious on the symbol.

Could it be from Atlantis? Could it even have been toppled and buried in the disaster that crippled the civilization? Plato stated that the disaster was caused by earthquakes and floods.

There is no way of knowing, unless archaeologists were to undertake new, deep exploratory digs in the immediate area of the discovery where it is possible that artifacts might be found that can be dated. Plato wrote that the area was densely populated, all the way down the waterway between the harbor and the coast. Nowhere would there have been a greater concentration of people than in this area overlooking the ancient harbor. If the town just upriver was the original Atlantis capital, then discoveries could at last start putting flesh on the Atlantis skeleton.

Let us reconsider all the known information:

- We have what appears to have been a large, meticulously carved stone egg, the ancient worldwide creation/fertility symbol. A world or cosmic egg, a mythological symbol in many other cultures, has long signified the beginning. The account of it in the Hindu *Vayu Purana* is but one example from distant shores.

- The Algarve stone is very old. Although it is now impossible to be emphatic about an exact date, it is almost certainly at least fifty-five hundred years old, from the period when the ancient megalithic necropolis was built at Alcalar, about twenty kilometers to the west. Most *menhirs* or dolmens are found either still standing, toppled over on the land, or just partially buried. Since this stone egg was buried so deep in a location where soil was unlikely to be deposited on top of it, it could be considerably older. One of the events that could have caused that was a great flood, possibly in 7640 B.C. The weathering on the egg would indicate that it had already been subject to the elements for a few thousand years before becoming buried. Alternatively, it just might have been toppled and initially buried by the very disaster that befell Atlantis.

I believe that this last astounding hypothesis is worthy of consideration. Its association with the site of the capital of Atlantis described in such detail by Plato, and with the hints he gives regarding the creation of the Atlantean population, justifies drawing that conclusion.

That nobody has ever made those connections until now is, perhaps, the reason why its significance has never been considered and the stone egg has been dismissed as just another Neolithic *menhir*.

Memory of the symbol on its shell could have survived and ultimately found its way to Sumeria with the fleeing Atlanteans, perhaps first via Egypt—or even with ancient mariners. There, because of its powerful symbolism, it was eventually adopted as their creation/fertility motif and subtly altered to become the Ningishzida and eventually the caduceus. The Sumerians were fascinated with serpents, one of them being featured in their creations myth and, of course, another in the Bible.[101]

Displayed alongside the "egg" in the museum is a smaller item. It is a stone with the same motif, also labeled a *menhir*—although, strangely, nowhere near the usual height of one. It appears to be much more recent than the "egg," as its condition is much better. It is probably an example of how memory of the powerful symbol had been preserved locally, as they knew it was hugely significant and related to fertility and the creation of life. Tradition had it that barren women would approach and embrace standing *menhirs*, in the belief that this would help them conceive.

The same symbol was probably taken by the survivors of Atlantis to other areas of northern Europe. Consequently, other *menhirs* and assorted megalithic monuments may well feature it.

In 2005, the author Frank Joseph published an encyclopedia full of references and terms that might concern Atlantis.[102] In it, he gives an explanation of the name Alatuir. The Slavic people have a legend that they migrated to central Europe from a sunken island kingdom in the western ocean called Buyan or Bouyan. The Alatuir was a big, egg-shaped object of white stone. It had magical properties and was the source of ultimate power at the very center of their kingdom. Joseph claims that it was the egg-shaped symbol of the primeval mystery cult in Atlantis, but does not give any explanation for this. Is there a connection between this story and the egg found by the ancient capital in the center of what this book identifies as the Atlantis kingdom, or is it just another of the scores of bewildering coincidences?

I also cannot help wondering if there has been confusion in the real origin of this legend between the Slavs and the Thracians. The Slavs did not occupy the Balkans till the fifth or sixth century A.D., and it is generally accepted that they migrated there from the north, perhaps central Russia. Prior to that, the Balkan region and its fringes were largely occupied by Thracians, who were discussed in the last chapter. They are recorded by various ancient writers as being a bawdy, drunken, rowdy lot but fierce warriors. They would probably have figured much larger in history in the last two millennia B.C. if they had managed to put their tribal animosities aside and unite. Interestingly, they were also described as being tall and blue-eyed, with blond or red hair and ruddy complexions, remarkably similar to the Guanches in the Canaries, living in a great western ocean. You can see what I am alluding to.

It is not at all clear, but quite possibly these Thracians stemmed from the very old and little-appreciated Vinca civilization. This is not a recorded historic name but that of the village where, in 1908, the largest Neolithic settlement ever found in Europe was excavated. It is fourteen miles from Belgrade, on the river Danube. This unique archaeological site showed it was from an organized society with wooden homes, orderly rows of streets, advanced agriculture, and developed trades such as ceramics. They were particularly expert in working with gold and silver, as clearly demonstrated by the stunning, exquisitely detailed jewelry unearthed in Bulgaria. Some of these discoveries have been reliably dated to approximately 5000 B.C.[103] Nothing of such quality has been unearthed anywhere else in the world that is remotely near that age. It unambiguously indicates an advanced society. It would have taken many centuries for any race to arrive at such high pinnacles in craftsmanship and technique. The Sumerian civilization has generally been accepted as the world's oldest, but it was barely stirring at that time.

Not a great deal is known about this impressive Vinca culture, apart from the fact that it flourished over a wide area of central Europe, including the Balkans, from 6000 to 3000 B.C. One earlier site has even been dated to 7000 B.C. The area the culture covered included that part of Bosnia where controversy rages over claims of the ancient pyramids that exist there. Some experts, often after a very cursory inspection, dismiss them as completely natural formations. Others believe they are indeed natural hills but that they have been modified to the pyramid shape. More recent discoveries of a hard conglomerate previously laid over the surface but now just below that of the main hill would seem to settle the argument, confirming that the latter version is correct. The dates so far arrived at for these "pyramids" are for many thousands of years before the arrival of the current Slavic population.

Were the Thracians the remnants of the Vinca culture? If so, did they fashion these pyramids? If that was the case, the legend of the "egg" and its homeland way to the west in the great ocean assumes an even greater significance. It could have been a legend of the Vinca civilization, absorbed into the overall community with the Slavs as the two races intermingled. Incidentally, some historians believe the Sumerian culture was triggered, or at least influenced, by the Vinca culture. It would explain how the Sumerians had, puzzlingly, managed to reach such a high level of sophistication so quickly. Many figurines of people with weird serpentine faces are wrongly attributed to the Sumerians—they were Vinca. These have resulted in wild theories that lizardlike aliens were the gods who kick-started the Sumerian civilization. If the Vinca came from the western ocean (Atlantis), the "helix"-style symbol could have arrived in Sumeria via them.

Returning to the Algarve egg, I have been unable to find references to other ancient monuments sculpted to this perfect shape, although I would not be surprised if there are some, considering how the Atlantis tribes appear to have spread. It truly is a piece of sculpture, not just an adaptation from a chunk of naturally formed rock, as *menhirs* usually are. There is another group of standing stones farther north in Portugal; they are also described as egg-shaped but are far too elongated to be realistically considered as "eggs."

The Egyptians saw the universe in the image of the egg, associating it with one of their earliest deities, Knefu. He was credited with being the creator of the bodies of human children, which he then placed in mothers' wombs. He was given the title of "Lord of created things from himself." His depiction often featured a ram's head with an egg between its horns.

Eggs were also at the center of the creation myth of the Persians, who kept carved eggs in their temples as symbols of everything that is born.

Michael Tellinger, in his book *Temples of the Ancient Gods*, recounts his dramatic discovery of ancient habitats in the Swaziland and Zululand areas of South Africa.[104] A team of international experts using the latest dating techniques came to the conclusion that the sites dated from 8,000 to 11,500 years ago. Close by were equally ancient gold mines. Zulu legends assert that these mines were worked by artificially produced flesh-and-blood slaves created by the "First People."

This seemingly unbelievable account mirrors those given by Zecharia Sitchin in several books on his translations of some of the tens of thousands of inscriptions on clay tablets unearthed in Sumeria.[105] Some people dispute his controversial interpretations, which are that the original rulers, long before the Sumerians, are recorded as doing exactly the same: creating a race, initially to work mines for them. You may have already noted that these accounts bear a passing resemblance to the creation account in Genesis. It would all have been laughed out of court fifty years ago, but hardly a week passes now without a new report about scientists manipulating genes, duplicating life-forms, and generally "playing God."

Why was this Algarve egg sculpted with an emblem that resembled the basic building block of life, combined with the rod variously recorded as indicating "the Lord of manufacture," "the implement of life," and "the tool and vehicle of the power of the heavens"?

Did Plato hint at the answer? In clue 20, he wrote: ". . . then the gods peopled their districts."

The egg's unique shape, the enigmatic symbol on its shell, where it was found, the depth at which it was buried, the indication of long weathering on its surface, and that astonishing similarity to the Slavic legend all amount to an extraordinarily potent combination.

You can imagine it yourself, the egg standing proudly on the brow of a small rise in the center of a heavily populated area overlooking the ancient port and its environs, on a suitable plinth, possibly created and installed there by Poseidon, Atlas, or one of their heirs as a permanent monument to their creation of Atlantis . . . perhaps even the very creation of its people. The myriad of visitors from other parallel civilizations and from all over the sprawling Atlantis Empire docking at the port could have been told this. That could have been an intrinsic and crucial aspect of the hold the gods had over them. There was nothing to be lost and everything to gain by making sure that their subjects and visitors knew it.

This is a highly speculative theory, but it would explain this extraordinary object and where it was found.

It may be minute compared to the Great Pyramid, but could this egg encapsulate a message even more significant than the pyramid is thought to convey?

On the subject of pyramids, where did they originate? They can be found in slightly differing forms and sizes in most parts of the world where those Atlanteans would appear to have lived or visited. Is there a connection?

CHAPTER TWENTY
The Pyramid Connection

nother author, Jim Allen, in his book *Lost Kingdom of the Andes*, claims to have found a site on the Bolivian Altiplano that matches Plato's description of the Atlantis Citadel.[106] It sits on a large plain surrounded by mountains, but he admits he had to adjust Plato's measurements for it all to hang together.

My analysis of the geographic and other clues detailed in earlier chapters makes the above claim groundless. Atlantis, as described by Plato, could not have been in South America. Nevertheless, Mr. Allen could well have discovered an important link. Did those tall, white visitors to South America have an agenda, other than simply helping the locals to advance? Did they yearn to replicate their successful homeland civilization to the extent that they discovered a site that lent itself to reproducing the same configuration as their ancient capital? We know their experiments included setting up a model of their original agricultural system with its extensive use of irrigation, as well as divulging knowledge that they had previously acquired about astronomy, mathematics, and construction. Could they have also contemplated creating a duplicate of their old capital as well as other aspects of their original civilization?

There are several clues that this was so. One is embodied in some of the huge buildings and walls they constructed thousands of years ago and that still exist in South America. These have survived to this day because of their polygonal style of construction. This method entails the use of large blocks of stone cut into irregular shapes, then so perfectly fitted together that it's impossible to get a cigarette paper into the joints. The buildings withstood serious earthquakes because this form of construction effectively dissipates any tremors. The tall strangers appear to have brought this knowledge with them—an indication that it had evolved in their homeland. Taking the logic a stage further, they could only have done that if that original country was subject to serious tremors, so allowing experimentation . . . borne out of necessity. That would certainly have been the case if they had come from southwest Iberia. Elena Wishaw discovered several surviving examples of this style of construction in and around Niebla. Some were in the earlier walls of the town, while others were in the ancient construction of the *desembarcadero*. She also quotes Dr. Oric Bates, an eminent archaeologist of the period who worked with her for a while at Niebla, as saying that he had personally inspected several similar examples at sites in Morocco, at Lixus near Larache, for example. Both indicate that this method of building was practiced in the Atlantis kingdom.

In Chapter Three, when discussing the remains that were seen briefly from the top of the cliff on the Algarve coast as the sea withdrew just before the 1755 tsunami struck, I made the point that they had most likely been built in the polygonal style. They would not otherwise have survived the huge quakes and raging seas.

Another significant clue is that in South America, these visitors appear to have even gone to the length of reproducing the unique Atlantis metal alloy of gold and copper, orichalcum. In all probability, this was because it maintained the appearance of gold and was the ideal material from which to make fine jewelry. This is the very alloy Plato mentioned, which had previously caused so much head-scratching but was finally identified in an earlier chapter. It has not been found elsewhere.

The case does not rest there. The most famous, ancient monuments in the world are the Egyptian pyramids. They have fired imaginations, spawned speculation, and inspired awe for thousands of years. Numerous theories swirl around them—some considered, serious, and exhaustively researched; others preposterous. Debate and argument rage between alternative thinkers and the rigid establishment.

If you carefully analyze all the evidence with an open mind, I think you will come to the conclusion that at least the Great Pyramid, together with the Sphinx and a couple of the Egyptian temples, are far older than the current accepted dating. The sheer weight of evidence cannot be ignored. Yet this is what the establishment does, dubbing any dissenters "pyramidiots." These "experts" are like a man ambling down a road, whose leg is suddenly severed by a skidding motorcycle, but tries to carry on walking as if nothing had happened. If you are interested in sifting some of the most compelling facts, then *Fingerprints of the Gods*,[107] written by Graham Hancock, and *Keeper of Genesis*,[108] co-authored by Hancock and Robert Bauval, provide a thorough grounding and an appetite for more.

Egypt does not, however, have a monopoly on pyramids. South America has more than its share. Surprisingly, the earliest there were circular and not built from cut and dressed stone but from heaped-up earth and rock. Others were oval, and one at La Venta is a fluted conical shape.[109]

Some are proven to be of a great age. A circular step pyramid between Mexico City (site of the Aztec capital) and Cuernavaca, for example, had been partly covered in lava from a volcanic eruption that devastated the whole surrounding area after the pyramid had been constructed. Geologists concluded that the lava was deposited there at least seven thousand years ago. The American archaeologist who examined the pyramid was convinced that it had fallen into ruin around eighty-five hundred years ago.[110] This surely proves that the Aztecs, who arrived on the scene more than seventy-five hundred years later and built their famous capital Tenochtitlan "down the road" in the middle of water, were not the first to construct pyramids here; they copied them! It also suggests that the four-sided shape evolved later, possibly because it was much more suited to stone construction than a circular one and lent itself more to other uses. But how do the ancient pyramids figure in this debate about migrating Atlanteans?

Well, isn't it somewhat odd that there are such visually similar structures in several countries that are otherwise totally unconnected: South America, an island in the Canaries, Egypt, and even China, for example? The same analysis applies to the distribution of mummies. The only common strands connecting them all are those tall white visitors with such distinctive individual characteristics and that some places may have a relic population of Atlanteans answering to the same physical descriptions.

There may be more to add to the list. As explained in Chapter Nineteen, it has been claimed, comparatively recently, that some pyramids exist in Bosnia, a Slavic nation that was part of the Vinca culture eight thousand years ago. These pyramids have caused consternation and disbelief among archaeologists, but that has not stopped the nearest town from becoming a tourist attraction. They have been examined by several experts who dismissed them as natural phenomena, whereas others agree but say they have quite obviously been enhanced by a little extra shaping and reworking by man. This makes them credible—and they would not be the only hills to have been "shaped," as will be revealed later. Why were they shaped? Does it provide another Slavic link to add to the stone egg and paradise homeland in the western ocean?

South America is not the only place with a round pyramid, although some English archaeologists will find this view very controversial. There is a site in southwest England that is part of the UNESCO World Heritage complex, encompassing the famous Stonehenge and Avebury sites. In addition to these more famous monuments, there is a round mound sitting in isolation on a flat plain. It is estimated that its construction started around 4,750 years ago. To the best of my knowledge, there has never before been a suggested connection to round pyramids, yet no one knows why it was built or what it was used for. At 120 feet high, it is thought to be the tallest human-made mound in Europe, and the perfectly circular base is 548 feet in diameter. The center at the top is directly over the center of the base. Known as Silbury Hill, it was a huge undertaking involving an estimated eighteen million man-hours (equivalent to five hundred men working fifteen years) to cut and stack in place the 248,000 cubic meters of chalk. This could not have been achieved by individuals showing up when they felt like it to do their charitable stint. It must have been a highly organized society, with an elite power firmly in control. It was no loose-knit pastoral farming community.

Despite several tunnels being dug into the mound in recent times, nothing significant has been found apart from some organic remains that facilitated the dating. There must have been an all-consuming, overriding purpose to sustain such a massive undertaking. What was it? The hill is on a flat plain and at one stage was surrounded by a substantial ring of water. Archaeologists do not rule out the possibility that it may have had a structure on its flat top. The area is close to South Wales, and the same people who lived there also inhabited the Silbury area before being forced back into the South Wales stronghold by invaders. The famous "blue stones" used in Stonehenge came from South Wales, confirming that people with a common purpose were common to both areas. Could they have been the same immigrants from southern Portugal—referred to in the research from the University of Wales? Why, though, would they want to build a round pyramid surrounded by water? And what inspired all the other constructions in this unique format—round or four-sided—elsewhere around the world?

When an inquisitive Spanish historian inquired who had built the pyramids, the local South Americans replied that they were built by the Viracochas, the tall, white, bearded men, as they reminded these gods of their homeland. Thor Heyerdahl was told by locals living in the vicinity of the mysterious city of Tiahuanaco that the Viracochas had fashioned the first step pyramid there from an existing hill. I have already mentioned that the area around Silves in the Algarve is notable for its innumerable distinctive small, conical hills about the same height as pyramids, providing an unforgettable, unique landscape. When terraced, they can eerily resemble step pyramids. Another coincidence, or an illuminating insight into why they may have been the inspiration for the pyramids? Perhaps, but I think those emigrants from Atlantis had a far more compelling reason. (SEE IMAGES 12D, 47, 48, AND 49 IN THE PHOTO INSERT.)

Why would they want to replicate a part of the distinctive topography of their heartland? Surely it was not because they were homesick. There had to be another, much stronger drive. I think the answer is revealed by analyzing the traditions of other civilizations.

Ancient people are frequently recorded as worshipping the place or object that signifies "the beginning" or "first place." To the Sumerians, the concept of the pyramid-shaped ziggurat symbolized the "Mountain of Paradise" that rose from the center of the "Lost Paradise." The first man was referred to as the "Sky Father" and his wife as the "Earth Mother."

That sounds uncannily like Atlantis, where the ancient mother of their race was Cleito, who lived on the original hill in the center of the kingdom that later became the capital. It existed in the middle of the small, flat plain and inevitably would have been of the same conical configuration as the many other hills that still exist around it today. Poseidon, a god, took Cleito, an earth woman, as his wife and made his home there, and it was there that the five sets of male twins were conceived and first saw the Atlantean sun. They represented the birth of their race, the primeval beginning. This supports the link established in Chapter Nineteen between the Sumerians, the Ancient Vinca culture, the Balkans, and Atlantis.

At the summit of the hill, Poseidon constructed a temple dedicated to Cleito. Later, the simplicity of the hill would have been lost as it was quarried and developed with Poseidon's palace and other habitations; but the memory would have been retained, with the mirror images of the original all around as permanent reminders. It was the symbolic heart of the whole sprawling empire and where the ten rulers, all descended from those first twins, returned every five to seven years to touch base and renew their vows and allegiance.

Was the original simple hill, topped by the temple, the first pyramid? Were the later pyramids all over the world duplicating and commemorating this original point of creation, and did they eventually evolve into more sophisticated, geometric, and astronomic structures?

It would explain why some émigrés went even further and created memorial cities in the same image. Apart from the one claimed on the Bolivian Altiplano, a photograph is purported to exist of one on the seabed off Cuba.

There is no hard proof of these theories. I doubt if we will ever find "patented in Atlantis" carved on a South American or Egyptian pyramid. But neither have I heard of any other plausible hypothesis. Perhaps future expeditions prompted by this book, particularly on the seabed in front of southwest Iberia, may throw light on the mystery and give it some substance. It was quite likely that other Atlantean cities had their own pyramids, complete with temples.

But while we're waiting for that, I would like to throw a little light on one last aspect of Atlantis. It is one that has prompted many wild stories. Did the Atlanteans possess any advanced technology?

CHAPTER TWENTY-ONE
Shocks and Centenarians

Plato gave the merest of hints that, although Poseidon was operating in the Stone Age, he did possess some very advanced knowledge. Some examples: ". . . and peopled their district" (clue 20) and ". . . himself being a god, found no difficulty in making special arrangements for the center island, bringing up two springs of water from beneath the earth. . . ." (clue 27). There were also those massive feats of engineering such as the canals and the embankments.

A very intriguing theory was put forward by Dr. Roger Coghill, the noted British expert on electromagnetism mentioned earlier. He is a fellow believer that Atlantis was in the Algarve.[111]

He pointed out that as the walls encircling the Atlantis citadel and the surrounding embankments were clad in different metals and were separated by water, it could have functioned as a huge simple electric cell. All that metal cladding on the walls of the embankment had always seemed a huge, unnecessary extravagance unless it was to emphasize wealth and power. Coghill's insight might explain why. It would have been the perfect use of simple slow technology to produce electricity. Those silver-clad upper walls may well also have shone and dazzled by night.

There is also a very well-known find of a primitive electric battery that surfaced in a Baghdad museum decades ago, indicating that the ancients knew of the technology, although we have no record of what it was used for. It is also claimed that ancient illustrations in the Hathor temple in Dendera, in Egypt, show examples of electrical equipment and light bulbs.[112] Archaeologists describe the "bulbs" as "snake stones"; but, when shown pictures of the paintings, professional electrical engineers found that explanation hilarious. (SEE IMAGES 50A AND 50B BELOW.) Several eminent archaeologists have commented that when previously untouched Egyptian tombs have been opened, they have shown no signs of how the pitch darkness was illuminated to allow the considerable work and decoration to have taken place. Oil lamps and the like invariably leave telltale stains and marks. Do the illustrations in the Hathor temple provide the answer?

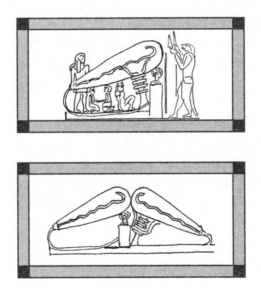

(IMAGES 50A AND 50B) *Drawings of two of the paintings in the hall of the Hathor temple at Dendera in Egypt. A group of electrical engineers examined them and claimed they clearly represented electrical equipment, insulators, and lamps. Inevitably, archaeologists disagree and say they are snake stones.*

There are other genuine historical testimonies of "shining lamps" in ancient times, from Egypt to Jerusalem. Just one example is found in the second century A.D. writing by Lucian of Samosata, which refers to a statue of a goddess in a Syrian temple as follows: "She bears on her head a stone called a lamp, and it receives its name from its function. That stone shines in the night with great clarity and provides the whole Temple with light, as with [oil] lamps. In the daytime, it shines dimly, but has a very fine aspect."[113]

It has been conjectured that the batteries could have been used in the process of electroplating, since well-documented examples of the end products exist in several museums. Another suggestion has been that low-voltage batteries had medical uses such as for a quick temporary anesthetic. It is known that electric eels were used for that purpose.

A recent press report prompted my imagination to come up with another alternative use for those canals around the capital, but with the same result as Coghill's suggestion. Researchers had found a way of generating electricity by simply exploiting the differences in the salinity of fresh- and seawater. I quote: "Stanford researchers have developed a rechargeable battery that uses seawater and freshwater to create electricity. Aided by nanotechnology, the battery employs the difference in salinity between fresh and seawater to generate a current. A power station might be built wherever a river flows into the ocean." As discussed earlier, the Arade River is tidal as far as the west side of Silves with its remnants of ancient embankments, whereas the town was constantly supplied from the east with freshwater flowing down the river. Could those inner rings of water have been engineered to harness this natural rhythm of the incoming tide and outgoing freshwater? It could have operated with a simple system of tidal sluice gates. Perhaps boats only penetrated as far as the outer harbor, with access to the citadel only possible over the connecting bridges.

If the Atlantis rulers were generating some form of electricity, what were they using it for, apart from a little nighttime illumination? One of the most astonishing aspects of ancient records and legends about old civilizations is the life spans given for the rulers. You have to look no farther than the Bible for examples. Those old kings didn't live for decades, but centuries! Historians just ignore this as though the records are not there. If they were about mother goddesses or phallic worship, they would embrace them without a murmur. (Not literally, I would hasten to add!) The historians offer no logical explanations, other than that they are all exaggerations or mistakes due to different ways of calculating years. However, the records are far too frequent to dismiss in such a glib way; they have to be addressed. How come, thousands of years ago, life spans were so long for a select few; yet with all the advanced paraphernalia and drugs of our medical industry, only a very small minority of us makes it past ninety?

In 1987, Dr. Hulda Clark, an American, invented a machine now known as the "Zapper." It followed much earlier controversial work in the 1930s by Royal Raymond Rife. The theory behind the inventions was that practically all diseases and ailments are caused by microorganisms or viruses, and a low-voltage current passed through the body, individually tuned to each virus, kills them. Increasingly, research is proving the virus part of this theory true. Recently there was a press report that fifteen percent of cancers are now proven to be caused by viruses. It is claimed that in 1934, in a landmark study, Rife used his machine to cure all of sixteen advanced cancer and tuberculosis patients given to him for the experiment. He was immediately attacked by the American medical authorities and industry on the basis that they could not duplicate his results. Presumably, he was not prepared to divulge information he regarded as his property. This hardly makes sense if he really did cure the sixteen patients, but one way or another his technology was suppressed. Today, thanks largely to the Internet, it has again become better known. His machine, and Dr. Clark's more advanced model, allegedly work by passing a low-voltage current through the body at exactly the same frequency as that resonated by the pathogens. It destroys them but does not damage other body tissue. Thousands of these machines are now being used throughout the world, and they can be bought on the Internet for relatively very little.

Arguments, counterarguments, and conspiracy theories abound. Rife's case has not been helped by charlatans who produced and sold machines claiming to mimic his discoveries but that in fact were useless. Court cases and prison sentences followed. I hold no brief for Zappers, although I admit that the explanation of the science behind them seems eminently sensible. The debate could easily be resolved if some openly monitored public trials were held involving people who are expert in pinpointing the virus responsible and in operating the machines. I have merely mentioned the matter here as a possible example of simple alternative technology that could have helped those gods to live longer, and as a reason why they may have needed to generate electricity.

If so, it is likely that they would have kept it for themselves. Their subjects would have been in awe of their supernatural power that allowed them to live to such a trouble-free long age. Another recent media report, which some readers will also have seen, concerned our old friend DNA. Scientists have apparently discovered that after a certain age, something stops being renewed in certain specific DNA, and this is what kicks in the ageing process. Now they can turn their attention to reversing it. We are on the very cusp of being able to prevent our bodies' deteriorating and ageing. Combine that with conquering disease, and we will have life spans of centuries as well, providing we are allowed access to it. Could the world cope with massive populations of multicentenarians? It would mean massive adjustments, and you can see why in ancient times it would have been limited to a very select few.

Did Poseidon and his fellow gods have the ability to manipulate DNA, whether it was for their own benefit or for creating subservient, god-worshipping races of humans? If so, they must have known all about it before creating their kingdoms and "peopling" them. They would have possessed some sort of technology—and, unless they were tapping into another power source undiscovered by us, they would have needed electricity for it.

CHAPTER TWENTY-TWO

The Next Challenge

This extremity of Europe—southwest Iberia—has long been overlooked when contemplating man's ancient past. It is as though there has been a huge collective amnesia. This book, though, demonstrates how the key to unlocking a radically different perception of civilized, human activity in ancient times could lie in this very region.

The unearthing of the extraordinary facts relating to the 1755 quake, thought to have been between a hundred and a thousand times bigger than the one that flattened Port-au-Prince in Haiti in 2010, causing more than 220,000 fatalities, and at least as strong as—or even stronger than—that in Japan in March 2011, was one of the main elements in springing the lid on the Pandora's box and prompted this investigation.

Geological research on the seabed in the Bay of Cádiz has confirmed that a quake of similar magnitude also occurred there at a time closely approximating the date given by Plato for the final destruction of Atlantis (9600 B.C.). Since then, at intervals of 1,250 to 2,250 years, there have been more seismic upheavals of similarly gigantic proportions.

Scientists now have a much better understanding of how plate tectonics causes temblors such as these. The fault line in front of southwest Iberia is the site of a titanic struggle between the European and African plates.

They are inexorably moving head to head, resulting in enormous pressures that are suddenly and catastrophically released when one or both eventually submit and, in seconds, displace millions of tons of the earth's crust. It is not only a disaster waiting to happen, but one that has occurred repeatedly over millennia! Indeed, at one stage the Atlantis coast could have extended to the point where the two great tectonic plates are currently battling it out.

The event that destroyed Atlantis could well have been triggered, and even dramatically magnified, by the huge quantities of meltwater now calculated to have been released from the ice caps at that time.

Many books have claimed to have discovered Atlantis somewhere else in the world, but most were prone to ignoring those clues given by Plato that did not support their theories. One example is the proposition about the Minoan civilization on the Greek island of Santorini. It is currently basking in a bout of publicity as a result of programs on TV and recently published books. Yet it meets few of Plato's clues and falls woefully short on many others. Arguments continue to be paraded regarding alternative whereabouts of the Pillars of Hercules, while arbitrarily adjusting Plato's timescale by a factor of up to ten, despite the theories being comprehensively discredited. Yes, Santorini blew up with an almighty bang, although Plato makes no mention of a volcanic eruption. Yes, it caused a huge tsunami and yes, the Minoans were undoubtedly a great maritime power; but their destruction happened around eight thousand years *after* the dates given by Plato for Atlantis. There is a possibility that their civilization was grafted from resurgent elements of the original Atlantis culture and that, in much earlier times, the island might have been an outpost of the Atlantis Empire. Samples of the ancient Iberian alphabet have been found on Crete, the main Minoan power base. That's about as close to Atlantis as it could possibly have been.

Conversely, the exhaustive analysis of Plato's clues detailed on these pages has revealed that the overwhelming majority point to southwest Iberia. None of the clues have been shirked or dodged, even if there wasn't an immediate obvious explanation for a few of them. Incredibly, even the ancient capital Plato described in such exacting detail has been pinpointed. You can go and walk its streets today and gaze down over the surrounding area from the current castle ramparts, imagining how it looked when surrounded by water and embankments, a hive of Atlantean activity.

The awesome Atlantis wealth is traced to the phenomenal amount of metals mined in the area for thousands of years. The mountains, the site of the great "bustling harbor," and the huge sunken plain all exist. Even the approximate position of one set of unaccountable, submerged ruins is known. Conundrums that have baffled researchers for years have been resolved—the nature of the mysterious metal "orichalcum," for example.

Plato's vast Atlantis island-based empire has been reunified and all the dots joined up across the Atlantic islands to America. The pieces of the puzzle now fall into place.

What else might we learn? Chapters Eighteen and Nineteen give an indication of the riches that could await us. That ancient alphabet and the great white stone egg, with its enigmatic symbol, hint at something sensational about our past. Were the gods in possession of knowledge that we are only currently acquiring—the manipulation of DNA and the creation of life-forms? Controversial translations of ancient Sumerian text and Zulu legends support that hypothesis.

Thankfully for those of us fortunate to live in this small paradise, the next big seismic orgasm to hit southwest Iberia is not scheduled for at least a thousand years. If, however, appropriate research is undertaken, metaphorical quakes could soon be shaking the very foundations of current historical and archaeological thinking. This could yield huge bounty in terms of artifacts, as well as knowledge about this fabled civilization that, toward the end of the Ice Age, bestrode the Western world. This was but one part of a worldwide mix of civilizations whose existence is denied by the establishment—largely because they refuse to acknowledge the great age of many colossal remains. Even when extreme age is not a contention, in cases such as the ancient sites on the Mediterranean island of Malta and the odd pyramid in South America, they offer no credible explanation as to how they could fit into their configuration of history.

It is left to writers and researchers such as Graham Hancock, who have devoted their lives to the subject, to continue to probe and question. These are not armchair researchers but motivated people who have traveled widely and investigated—not just sites on land; they have also thrown light on colossal remains on the seabed. Some are at depths that, as the world-famous "sea-level unit" at England's Durham University points out, could only have been above water approximately eleven thousand years ago. Ah, but there are perfectly natural explanations, say the cynical, professional doubters. Come on! Natural explanations for massive stone blocks, precisely cut, fitted together, and stacked one above the other; explanations for pillars, arches, doorways, and steps laid out over huge areas of the seabed! Such remains are increasingly being found in Asia, particularly off the coasts of India and Japan, indicating that advanced civilizations once existed worldwide, concurrently with Atlantis.

Plato alluded to this in clues 18, 39, and 82:

"In the days of old, the gods had the whole earth distributed among them by allotment."

"For because of the greatness of their empire, many things were brought to them from foreign countries."

"The largest of the harbors were full of vessels and merchants coming from all parts."

Cataclysmic inundations and upheavals have engulfed our vulnerable planet at least three times during the melting of the great glaciers around fifteen to sixteen thousand, eleven to twelve thousand, and seven to eight thousand years ago. Inevitably, they will have destroyed most tangible and dateable evidence for these huge stone remains, although some artifacts found off the coast of India in one such giant city have been scientifically dated between 7000 and 9000 B.C. We may yet strike gold. Exploration of the relatively shallow seabed in front of the Algarve and Andalucía may well reveal something sensational.

Religious bigots among the Spaniards who invaded South America destroyed masses of recorded, critical local history. One pious and proud Catholic bishop boasted of making a bonfire of tens of thousands of manuscripts and other items. Fortunately, the Spaniards never conquered India, so Plato's Atlantis story is not the only account of ancient civilizations to have survived. The Indian Vedic literature records India's distant past, with the gods wielding weapons uncannily similar to hydrogen bombs and death rays, and gadding around in a varied fleet of airplanes. The descriptions are too accurate for this to be coincidental fiction.

There is now too much plausible evidence to continue in denial. It is time the establishment embraced serious alternative researchers and started rigorously examining their discoveries and theories, instead of instantly dismissing and insulting them for daring to challenge the establishment's own dogmatic beliefs.

Over the last twenty-four hundred years, many have also dismissed Plato's story as fictitious. This book has proved that much of the detail from his accounts was indeed factual. Certainly he added a little "top dressing" here and there, but the basic legend is proven to be true.

Circumstantial clues indicate that the original rulers who created Atlantis were tall, with blond or red hair. As time passed, they were not content to stay there, just sunning themselves in the balmy climate. Whether they were righteously inspired to spread civilization and improve mankind's lot, or were forced to emigrate by natural disasters, we will never know. It was probably a combination of both.

Apart from many legends, actual physical remains of people answering to this description have been found all over the globe. Invariably they were visitors who often became rulers and imparted their vastly advanced knowledge for the benefit of the indigenous populations. They were the builders of the earliest pyramids in South America, as well as gigantic cities such as Tiahuanaco. Many researchers have suggested that some of the exceptional remains in Egypt were built in a much earlier epoch than that officially attributed. Some readers will already be familiar with these theories that particularly relate to the Great Pyramid and the Sphinx, as well as a few of the temples. The latter exhibit a building style unlike other local temples, and are completely devoid of the usual hieroglyphics and decorations. Discoveries of the remains of people with red hair support the legends of tall white people ruling Egypt long before the great dynasties. One logical conclusion is that these earlier gods or rulers were responsible for the construction—or at least the planning—of these great monuments, just as they were in South America.

Pyramids elsewhere in China and the Canary Islands are also connected to people with these physical characteristics. Discoveries are slowly completing a picture to match the prose in the Indian Vedic accounts. The great ancient cities such as Mohenjo-daro and others from the Harappan culture, plus huge underwater sites recently found off the Indian coast, support the written record of an advanced civilization. Early archaeological finds again indicate that the original rulers were red-haired people.

Recent genetic research has proven that the population in Celtic Wales came from the Algarve and southwest Andalucía. Red-haired people are still much in evidence among the current Welsh population, and even more so in other Celtic societies. Pockets of redheads still exist in some Portuguese villages. It has been assumed that these were the outcome of liaisons between the locals and the Duke of Wellington's troops who had been sent to kick out Napoleon. The analysis in this book leads to the possibility of their having remnant genes of the Atlanteans.

It is apparent from Plato's account that Atlantis was a great maritime power; so, logically, it would have mapped the planet. Is it surprising that "atlas," the name of the first king of Atlantis, is still given to a book of maps?

A whole new template for man's ancient past is now emerging. A powerful civilization called Atlantis existed at the end of the last Ice Age, its trading tentacles stretching around the world. If they did not already exist, civilizations on other continents were likely spawned toward the end of its existence, a process that was continued out of necessity when the homeland disappeared below the sea. The movers and shakers were all from the same highly individual stock. Later survivors from the empire's outposts probably infiltrated even farther, confirming North American Indian reports of red-haired invaders.

Atlantis was where it all started, and Atlantis was in southwest Iberia on land now largely below the Atlantic.

The potential now exists for truly exhilarating discoveries that could shatter the current paradigm of history.

PART THREE

Stop Press

CHAPTER TWENTY-THREE
Astounding Confirmation

By the time this manuscript was completed, I was convinced that I had exhausted all avenues for evidence to support my hypothesis. Indeed, having matched sixty of Plato's exacting clues, I hardly deemed any more as necessary. All that remained was for serious archaeological digs and underwater surveys to start, hopefully revealing historical riches.

Then I came across some astounding further confirmation. I was aware of the ancient Indian Vedic book the *Mahabharata*, which was written long before Plato's time. It gives information about a much earlier Indian civilization ruled by gods who possessed immensely powerful weapons and flying machines. They are described in great detail, including graphic descriptions of the terrible devastation wrought by this armory. Hard as it is to believe, it appears to describe atomic warfare. Here is an example:

> ". . . a single projectile
> charged with all the power of the Universe
> an incandescent column of smoke and flame
> as bright as the thousand suns
> rose in all its splendor . . .
> a perpendicular explosion with its billowing smoke clouds . . .

. . . the cloud of smoke rising after its first explosion
formed into expanding round circles like the opening of giant
parasols . . .

. . . it was an unknown weapon,
an iron thunderbolt,
a gigantic messenger of death,
which reduced to ashes
the entire race of the Vrishnis and the Andhakas
. . . the corpses were so burned
as to be unrecognizable.
The hair and nails fell out;
pottery broke without apparent cause,
and the birds turned white.

After a few hours
all foodstuffs were infected . . .
. . . to escape from this fire
the soldiers threw themselves in streams
to wash themselves and their equipment."

This civilization's implacable enemy was ruled from an island on the other side of the world in the great western ocean. India was threatened as this enemy's forces conquered area after area, inexorably moving ever closer.

The island was called Atala and, since it consisted of three concentric cities encircling each other and separated by water, the capital city was known as Tripura. Does that sound familiar? It was eventually destroyed by a dreadful weapon created by the Indians' gods. After the city was destroyed, the land sank into the sea.

I also knew that in a Moroccan Berber legend, Atala was the name given for a fertile land to the north, occupied by a nation of people expert in mining gold, silver, copper, and tin. They launched eastward in conquest across North Africa; but shortly afterward, their homeland also disappeared in a huge conflagration.

These Indian and Moroccan references to Atala have frequently been cited as evidence for Atlantis that has survived from ancient times, although only Plato supplied any detail.

One day, while poring over a Google Earth image of the Atlantis capital's harbor area, west of Silves, my son spotted that the large hill overlooking it was called Atalaia. It set my heart pounding. Investigation immediately confirmed that this was the local name for the whole substantial hill, and had been so as far back as records existed. The word has been adopted into the Portuguese language to mean a "lookout point," hardly surprising when the top of this hill was a perfect lookout point and already called Atalaia as part of the whole capital complex. It had been assumed to have been introduced by the Moors; but in fact Atala was originally a Sanskrit word and also meant "lookout" in ancient India, as well as referring to its implacable enemy. A similar word, Atalaya, is used across the border in Andalucía.

The great white limestone egg, called Alatuir in Slavic legend and detailed in Chapter Nineteen, was unearthed at the very side of the Atalaia hill.

The *Mahabharata* also described Atala as "The White Island." It has been widely assumed that this was because the inhabitants were described as having white skin. Now I suggest that there is a more logical explanation, as the Atalaia hill mostly consists of white limestone and, a little upriver, the top of the hill upon which Silves is built had also consisted of white limestone before it was quarried (or blasted) away.

I explored the top of the Atalaia hill and, to my amazement, rather than the usual summit there is a very large saucer-shaped depression like a shallow crater. It is a good five hundred meters in diameter. The rim is broken on the western edge and the side of the hill below it is scattered with variously sized lumps of rock.

These incredible similarities in association with the ancient capital of Atlantis cannot be dismissed as mere coincidence. It is the ultimate confirmation that Atlantis and Atala were the same place and have been identified. Coupled with my discovery of Atlantis, it also gives credibility to the *Mahabharata*, as it proves that it was also describing somewhere that actually existed on the other side of the earth.

There is more, however. As mentioned earlier in this book, large cities have recently been discovered submerged on the seabed off the coast of India, as well as in Japanese waters. One, in India's Gulf of Cambay, has been reliably dated to the same period as Plato gave for Atlantis. It verifies Plato's statement that Atlantis was but part of a worldwide civilization and underpins the research of other authors who have painstakingly assembled evidence to prove that such a civilization once existed but was destroyed by cataclysmic natural events.

A whole new vista for the history of humankind, from more than twelve thousand years ago, is beginning to reveal itself.

APPENDIX ONE

Mistranslations from Plato's Dialogues

Nesos

- As far as I can trace, the first to question the accepted translation "ISLAND" was OLOF RUDBECK (1630–1702), a famous rector from UPPSALA UNIVERSITY in SWEDEN. He pointed out that Greeks of Plato's era commonly used the word "NESOS" when referring to PENINSULAS.

- In the 1920s, ADOLF SCHULTAN—the well-known German archaeologist—wrote that the ancient Greeks also used "NESOS" in connection with the mouths/deltas of rivers such as the Nile, Indus, Tiber, and Tartessos. He spent many years searching unsuccessfully for the kingdom of Tartessos.

- Some think that Plato used the plural "NESSON" rather than "NESOS." If that was the case, his intention could have been to imply "ISLANDS." This chimes with his use of the word "PEL-AGOS" to describe the area starting outside the Straits of Gibraltar. Spartel was the principal island of a group in the Atlantic that was very close to the mouth of the straits. There is a possibility that the numerous islands and lagoons, now existing farther west along the Spanish coast and in front of the Algarve in Portugal, may have existed at that time. Allowing for rising sea levels and other quakes, there could have been more of them and they could have been larger. It is therefore possible that Plato could have been referring to a part-mainland and part-island empire in the gulf in front of Gibraltar.

Meson

- Plato used the Greek word "MEZON" in relation to the size of ATLANTIS. It has been translated as implying that Atlantis was "bigger than Asia and Libya combined." JURGEN SPANUTH was one of the first to point out that it could also mean "greater in authority or power."
- Among many other historians, EDWARD GIBBON believes that the ancient Greeks and Romans were referring to just modern-day Turkey when talking of Asia.
- MICHAEL GRANT has gone further and put forward the view that the ancients were really only referring to their kingdom of LYDIA, merely a small region in eastern Turkey.
- Other commentators such as FELICO VINCE have suggested that ancient mariners measured the size of territory by its coastal perimeter rather than its total area. If this formula was applied to the Atlantis alluded to by Plato, it could result in a variety of sizes—especially if it also took into consideration the empire of Atlantic islands, the north coast of Morocco, and even the land they ruled inside the Mediterranean.

Georgeos Diaz-Montexano

This is a Hispanic-Cuban researcher who has ruffled more than a few feathers with his seemingly prickly nature, and has been dismissed by some as a mere amateur. This is unfortunate, as he has made important contributions to interpreting what Plato wished to imply. Being a nonacademic does not preclude one from carrying out a deep study of a subject. Professors do not have a monopoly on brains or application. Georgeos has unearthed versions of Plato's two Dialogues that predate those used for the previously accepted translations. The original versions, penned by Plato, no longer exist, so there are only various versions that were initially translated into Latin and then, later, into modern Greek.

Despite the furor Georgeos has generated, I was agreeably surprised to find that his conclusions were similar to mine: that the Iberian Peninsula and parts of Morocco were Atlantis. We diverge in that he centers his beliefs principally on Spain, not Portugal's Algarve.

Among the misinterpretations that he claims to correct are the words Plato originally used to describe its size. Georgeos maintains that when the older texts are translated, the meaning is "an island/peninsula almost joined to Morocco [Libya] and bigger than Turkey [Asia]."

Iberia is almost connected to Morocco at Gibraltar, and the straits would have been narrower and extended farther into the Atlantic in 9600 B.C. The Iberian Peninsula is bigger than Turkey, and of course, significantly larger than "Lydia."

The Relevant Parts of Plato's Dialogues

Timaeus

Many great and wonderful deeds are recorded of your state in our histories. But one of them exceeds all the rest in greatness and valor. For these histories tell of a mighty power which unprovoked made an expedition against the whole of Europe and Asia, and to which your city put an end. This power came forth out of the Atlantic Ocean, for in those days the Atlantic was navigable; and there was an island situated in front of the straits which are by you called the Pillars of Heracles; the island was larger than Libya and Asia put together, and was the way to other islands, and from these you might pass to the whole of the opposite continent which surrounded the true ocean; for this sea which is within the Straits of Heracles is only a harbor, having a narrow entrance, but that other is a real sea, and the surrounding land may be most truly called a boundless continent. Now in this island of Atlantis there was a great and wonderful empire which had rule over the whole island and several others, and over parts of the continent, and, furthermore, the men of Atlantis had subjected the parts of Libya within the columns of Heracles as far as Egypt, and of Europe as far as Tyrrhenia. This vast power, gathered into one, endeavored to subdue at a blow our country and yours and the whole of the region within the straits; and then, Solon, your country shone forth, in the excellence of her virtue and strength, among all mankind. She was preeminent in courage and military skill, and was the leader of the Hellenes. And when the rest fell off from her, being compelled to stand alone, after having undergone the very extremity of danger, she defeated and triumphed over the invaders, and preserved from slavery those who were not yet subjugated, and generously liberated all the rest of us who dwell within the pillars. But afterwards there occurred violent earthquakes and floods; and in a single day and night of misfortune all your warlike men in a body sank into the earth, and the island of Atlantis in like manner disappeared in the depths of the sea. For which reason the sea in those parts is impassable and impenetrable, because there is a shoal of mud in the way; and this was caused by the subsidence of the island.

I have told you briefly, Socrates, what the aged Critias heard from Solon and related to us. And when you were speaking yesterday about your city and citizens, the tale that I have just been repeating to you came into my mind, and I remarked with astonishment how, by some mysterious coincidence, you agreed in almost every particular with the narrative of Solon; but I did not like to speak at the moment. For a long time had elapsed, and I had forgotten too much; I thought that I must first of all run over the narrative in my own mind, and then I would speak. And so I readily assented to your request yesterday, considering that in all such cases the chief difficulty is to find a tale suitable to our purpose, and that with such a tale we should be fairly well provided.

And therefore, as Hermocrates has told you, on my way home yesterday I at once communicated the tale to my companions as I remembered it; and after I left them, during the night, by thinking, I recovered nearly the whole of it. Truly, as is often said, the lessons of our childhood make wonderful impression on our memories; for I am not sure that I could remember all the discourse of yesterday, but I should be much surprised if I forgot any of these things which I have heard very long ago. I listened at the time with childlike interest to the old man's narrative; he was very ready to teach me, and I asked him again and again to repeat his words, so that like an indelible picture they were branded into my mind. As soon as the day broke, I rehearsed them as he spoke them to my companions, that they, as well as myself, might have something to say. And now, Socrates, to make an end to my preface, I am ready to tell you the whole tale. I will give you not only the general heads, but the particulars, as they were told to me. The city and citizens, which you yesterday described to us in fiction, we will now transfer to the world of reality. It shall be the ancient city of Athens, and we will suppose that the citizens whom you imagined were our veritable ancestors, of whom the priest spoke; they will perfectly harmonize, and there will be no inconsistency in saying that the citizens of your republic are these ancient Athenians. Let us divide the subject among us, and all endeavor according to our ability gracefully to execute the task which you have imposed upon us. Consider then, Socrates, if this narrative is suited to the purpose, or whether we should seek for some other instead.

Critias

Yet, before proceeding further in the narrative, I ought to warn you that you must not be surprised if you should perhaps hear Hellenic names given to foreigners. I will tell you the reason of this: Solon, who was intending to use the tale for his poem, inquired into the meaning of the names, and found that the early Egyptians in writing them down had translated them into their own language, and he recovered the meaning of the several names and when copying them out again translated them into our language. My great-grandfather, Dropides, had the original writing, which is still in my possession, and was carefully studied by me when I was a child. Therefore if you hear names such as are used in this country, you must not be surprised, for I have told how they came to be introduced. The tale, which was of great length, began as follows:

I have before remarked in speaking of the allotments of the gods, that they distributed the whole earth into portions differing in extent, and made for themselves temples and instituted sacrifices. And Poseidon, receiving for his lot the island of Atlantis, begat children by a mortal woman, and settled them in a part of the island, which I will describe. Looking toward the sea, but in the center of the whole island, there was a plain which is said to have been the fairest of all plains and very fertile. Near the plain again, and also in the center of the island at a distance of about fifty stadia, there was a mountain not very high on any side.

In this mountain there dwelt one of the earth-born primeval men of that country, whose name was Evenor, and he had a wife named Leucippe, and they had an only daughter who was called Cleito. The maiden had already reached womanhood, when her father and mother died; Poseidon fell in love with her and had intercourse with her, and breaking the ground, enclosed the hill in which she dwelt all round, making alternate zones of sea and land larger and smaller, encircling one another; there were two of land and three of water, which he turned as with a lathe, each having its circumference equidistant every way from the center, so that no man could get to the island, for ships and voyages were not as yet. He himself, being a god, found no difficulty in making special arrangements for the center island, bringing up two springs of water from beneath the earth, one of warm water and the other of cold, and making every variety of food to spring up abundantly from the soil. He also begat and brought up five pairs of twin male children; and dividing the island of Atlantis into ten portions, he gave to the first-born of the eldest pair his mother's dwelling and the surrounding allotment, which was the largest and best, and made him king over the rest; the others he made princes, and gave them rule over many men, and a large territory. And he named them all; the eldest, who was the first king, he named Atlas, and after him the whole island and the ocean were called Atlantic. To his twin brother, who was born after him, and obtained as his lot the extremity of the island toward the Pillars of Heracles, facing the country which is now called the region of Gades in that part of the world, he gave the name which in the Hellenic language is Eumelus, in the language of the country which is named after him, Gadeirus. Of the second pair of twins he called one Ampheres, and the other Evaemon. To the elder of the third pair of twins he gave the name Mneseus, and Autochthon to the one who followed him. Of the fourth pair of twins he called the elder Elasippus, and the younger Mestor. And of the fifth pair he gave to the elder the name of Azaes, and to the younger that of Diaprepes. All these and their descendants for many generations were the inhabitants and rulers of divers islands in the open sea; and also, as has been already said, they held sway in our direction over the country within the Pillars as far as Egypt and Tyrrhenia.

Now Atlas had a numerous and honorable family, and they retained the kingdom, the eldest son handing it on to his eldest for many generations; and they had such an amount of wealth as was never before possessed by kings and potentates, and is not likely ever to be again, and they were furnished with everything which they needed, both in the city and country. For because of the greatness of their empire, many things were brought to them from foreign countries, and the island itself provided most of what was required by them for the uses of life. In the first place, they dug out of the earth whatever was to be found there, solid as well as fusile, and that which is now only a name and was then something more than a name, orichalcum, was dug out of the earth in many parts of the island, being more precious in those days than anything except gold. There was an abundance of wood for carpenter's work, and sufficient maintenance for tame and wild animals. Moreover, there were a great number of elephants in the island; for as there was provision for all other sorts of animals, both for those which live in lakes and marshes and rivers, and also for those which live in mountains and on plains, so there was for the animal which is the largest and most voracious of all. Also whatever fragrant things there now are in the earth, whether roots, or herbage, or woods, or essences which distill from fruit and flower, grew and thrived in that land; also the fruit which admits of cultivation, both the dry sort, which is given us for nourishment, and any other which we use for food—we call them all by the common name pulse, and the fruits having a hard rind, affording drinks and meats and oint-ments, and good store of chestnuts and the like, which furnish pleasure and amusement, and are fruits which spoil with keeping, and the pleasant kinds of dessert, with which we console ourselves after dinner, when we are tired of eating—all these that sacred island which then beheld the light of the sun, brought forth fair and wondrous and in infinite abundance. With such blessings the earth freely furnished them; meanwhile they went on constructing their temples and palaces and harbors and docks. And they arranged the whole country in the following manner:

First of all, they bridged over the zones of sea which surrounded the ancient metropolis, making a road to and from the royal palace. And at the very beginning they built the palace in the habitation of the god and of their ancestors, which they continued to ornament in successive genera-tions, every king surpassing the one who went before him to the utmost of his power, until they made the building a marvel to behold for size and for beauty. And beginning from the sea they bored a canal of three hundred feet in width and one hundred feet in depth and fifty stadia in length, which they carried through to the outermost zone, making a passage from the sea up to this, which became a harbor, and leaving an opening sufficient to enable the largest vessels to find ingress. Moreover, they divided at the bridges the zones of land which parted the zones of sea, leaving room for a single trireme to pass out of one zone into another, and they covered over the channels so as to leave a way underneath for the ships; for the banks were raised considerably above the water. Now the largest of the zones into which a passage was cut from the sea was three stadia in breadth, and the zone of land which came next of equal breadth; but the next two zones, the one of water, the other of land, were two stadia, and the one which surrounded the central island was a stadium only in width. The island in which the palace was situated had a diameter of five stadia. All this including the zones and the bridge, which was the sixth part of a stadium in width, they surrounded by a stone wall on every side, placing towers and gates on the bridges where the sea passed in. The stone which was used in the work they quarried from underneath the center island, and from underneath the zones, on the outer as well as the inner side. One kind was white, another black, and a third red, and as they quarried, they at the same time hollowed out double docks, having roofs formed out of the native rock. Some of their buildings were simple, but in others they put together different stones, varying the color to please the eye, and to be a natural source of delight. The entire circuit of the wall, which went around the outermost zone, they covered with a coating of brass, and the circuit of the next wall they coated with tin, and the third, which encompassed the citadel, flashed with the red light of orichalcum.

The palaces in the interior of the citadel were constructed in this wise: in the center was a holy temple dedicated to Cleito and Poseidon, which remained inaccessible, and was surrounded by an enclosure of gold; this was the spot where the family of the ten princes first saw the light, and thither the people annually brought the fruits of the earth in their season from all the ten portions, to be an offering to each of the ten. Here was Poseidon's own temple, which was a stadium in length, and half a stadium in width, and of a proportionate height, having a strange barbaric appearance. All the outside of the temple, with the exception of the pinnacles, they covered with silver, and the pinnacles with gold. In the interior of the temple, the roof was of ivory, curiously wrought everywhere with gold and silver and orichalcum; and all the other parts, the walls and pillars and floor, they coated with orichalcum. In the temple they placed statues of gold: there was the god himself standing in a chariot—the charioteer of six winged horses—and of such a size that he touched the roof of the building with his head; around him there were a hundred Nereids riding on dolphins, for such was thought to be the number of them by the men of those days. There were also in the interior of the temple other images which had been dedicated by private persons. And around the temple on the outside were placed statues of gold of all the descendants of the ten kings and of their wives, and there were many other great offerings of kings and of private persons, coming both from the city itself and from the foreign cities over which they held sway. There was an altar too, which in size and workmanship corresponded to this magnificence, and the palaces, in like manner, answered to the greatness of the kingdom and the glory of the temple.

In the next place, they had fountains, one of cold and another of hot water, in gracious plenty flowing; and they were wonderfully adapted for use by reason of the pleasantness and excellence of their waters. They constructed buildings about them and planted suitable trees; also they made cisterns, some open to the heavens, others roofed over, to be used in winter as warm baths; there were the kings' baths, and the baths of private persons, which were kept apart; and there were separate baths for women, and for horses and cattle, and to each of them they gave as much adornment as was suitable. Of the water which ran off they carried some to the grove of Poseidon, where were growing all manner of trees of wonderful height and beauty, owing to the excellence of the soil, while the remainder was conveyed by aqueducts along the bridges to the outer circles; and there were many temples built and dedicated to many gods; also gardens and places of exercise, some for men, and others for horses in both of the two islands formed by the zones; and in the center of the larger of the two there was set apart a racecourse of a stadium in width, and in length allowed to extend all around the island, for horses to race in. Also there were guardhouses at intervals for the guards, the more trusted of whom were appointed to keep watch in the lesser zone, which was nearer the Acropolis, while the most trusted of all had houses given them within the citadel, near the persons of the kings. The docks were full of triremes and naval stores, and all things were quite ready for use. Enough of the plan of the royal palace.

Leaving the palace and passing out across the three, you came to a wall which began at the sea and went all round: this was everywhere distant fifty stadia from the largest zone or harbor, and enclosed the whole, the ends meeting at the mouth of the channel which led to the sea. The entire area was densely crowded with habitations; and the canal and the largest of the harbors were full of vessels and merchants coming from all parts, who, from their numbers, kept up a multitudinous sound of human voices, and din and clatter of all sorts night and day.

I have described the city and the environs of the ancient palace nearly in the words of Solon, and now I must endeavor to represent the nature and arrangement of the rest of the land. The whole country was said by him to be very lofty and precipitous on the side of the sea, but the country immediately about and surrounding the city was a level plain, itself surrounded by mountains which descended toward the sea; it was smooth and even, and of an oblong shape, extending in one direction three thousand stadia, but across the center inland it was two thousand stadia. This part of the island looked toward the south, and was sheltered from the north. The surrounding mountains were celebrated for their number and size and beauty, far beyond any which still exist, having in them also many wealthy villages of country folk, and rivers, and lakes, and meadows supplying food enough for every animal, wild or tame, and much wood of various sorts, abundant for each and every kind of work.

I will now describe the plain, as it was fashioned by nature and by the labors of many generations of kings through long ages. It was for the most part rectangular and oblong, and where falling out of the straight line followed the circular ditch. The depth, and width, and length of this ditch were incredible, and gave the impression that a work of such extent, in addition to so many others, could never have been artificial. Nevertheless I must say what I was told. It was excavated to the depth of a hundred feet, and its breadth was a stadium everywhere; it was carried around the whole of the plain, and was ten thousand stadia in length. It received the streams which came down from the mountains, and winding around the plain and meeting at the city, was there let off into the sea. Farther inland, likewise, straight canals of a hundred feet in width were cut from it through the plain, and again let off into the ditch leading to the sea: these canals were at intervals of a hundred stadia, and by them they brought down the wood from the mountains to the city, and conveyed the fruits of the earth in ships, cutting transverse passages from one canal into another, and to the city. Twice in the year they gathered the fruits of the earth—in winter having the benefit of the rains of heaven, and in summer the water which the land supplied by introducing streams from the canals.

As to the population, each of the lots in the plain had to find a leader for the men who were fit for military service, and the size of a lot was a square of ten stadia each way, and the total number of all the lots was sixty thousand. And of the inhabitants of the mountains and of the rest of the country there was also a vast multitude, which was distributed among the lots and had leaders assigned to them according to their districts and villages. The leader was required to furnish for the war the sixth portion of a war chariot, so as to make up a total of ten thousand chariots; also two horses and riders for them, and a pair of chariot horses without a seat, accompanied by a horseman who could fight on foot carrying a small shield, and having a charioteer who stood behind the man-at-arms to guide the two horses; also, he was bound to furnish two heavy armed soldiers, two slingers, three stone-shooters, and three javelin men, who were light-armed, and four sailors to make up the complement of twelve hundred ships. Such was the military order of the royal city—the order of the other nine governments varied, and it would be wearisome to recount their several differences.

As to offices and honors, the following was the arrangement from the first. Each of the ten kings in his own division and in his own city had the absolute control of the citizens, and, in most cases, of the laws, punishing and slaying whomsoever he would. Now the order of precedence among them and their mutual relations were regulated by the commands of Poseidon, which the law had handed down. These were inscribed by the first kings on a pillar of orichalcum, which was situated in the middle of the island, at the temple of Poseidon, whither the kings were gathered together every fifth and every sixth year alternately, thus giving equal honour to the odd and to the even number. And when they were gathered together they consulted about their common interests, and inquired if any one had transgressed in anything and passed judgment, and before they passed judgment they gave their pledges to one another in this wise:—There were bulls who had the range of the temple of Poseidon; and the ten kings, being left alone in the temple, after they had offered prayers to the god that they might capture the victim which was acceptable to him, hunted the bulls, without weapons but with staves and nooses; and the bull which they caught they led up to the pillar and cut its throat over the top of it so that the blood fell upon the sacred inscription. Now on the pillar, besides the laws, there was inscribed an oath invoking mighty curses on the disobedient. When, therefore, after slaying the bull in the accustomed manner, they had burned its limbs, they filled a bowl of wine and cast in a clot of blood for each of them; the rest of the victim they put in the fire, after having purified the column all around. Then they drew from the bowl in golden cups and, pouring a libation on the fire, they swore that they would judge according to the laws on the pillar, and would punish him who in any point had already transgressed them, and that for the future they would not, if they could help, offend against the writing on the pillar, and would neither command others, nor obey any ruler who commanded them, to act otherwise than according to the laws of their father Poseidon. This was the prayer which each of them offered up for himself and for his descendants, at the same time drinking and dedicating the cup out of which he drank in the temple of the god; and after they had supped and satisfied their needs, when darkness came on, and the fire about the sacrifice was cool, all of them put on most beautiful azure robes, and, sitting on the ground, at night, over the embers of the sacrifices by which they had sworn, and extinguishing all the fire about the temple, they received and gave judgment, if any of them had an accusation to bring against anyone; and when they given judgment, at daybreak they wrote down their sentences on a golden tablet, and dedicated it together with their robes to be a memorial.

There were many special laws affecting the several kings inscribed about the temples, but the most important was the following: they were not to take up arms against one another, and they were all to come to the rescue if any one in any of their cities attempted to overthrow the royal house; like their ancestors, they were to deliberate in common about war and other matters, giving the supremacy to the descendants of Atlas. And the king was not to have the power of life and death over any of his kinsmen unless he had the assent of the majority of the ten.

Such was the vast power which the god settled in the lost island of Atlantis; and this he afterwards directed against our land for the following reasons, as tradition tells: for many generations, as long as the divine nature lasted in them, they were obedient to the laws, and well-affectioned toward the god, whose seed they were; for they possessed true and in every way great spirits, uniting gentleness with wisdom in the various chances of life, and in their intercourse with one another. They despised everything but virtue, caring little for their present state of life, and thinking lightly of the possession of gold and other property, which seemed only a burden to them; neither were they intoxicated by luxury; nor did wealth deprive them of their self-control; but they were sober, and saw clearly that all these goods are increased by virtue and friendship with one another, whereas by too great regard and respect for them, they are lost and friendship with them. By such reflections and by the continuance in them of a divine nature, the qualities which we have described grew and increased among them; but when the divine portion began to fade away, and became diluted too often and too much with the mortal admixture, and the human nature got the upper hand, they then, being unable to bear their fortune, behaved unseemly, and to him who had an eye to see grew visibly debased, for they were losing the fairest of their precious gifts; but to those who had no eye to see the true happiness, they appeared glorious and blessed at the very time when they were full of avarice and unrighteous power. Zeus, the god of gods, who rules according to law, and is able to see into such things, perceiving that an honourable race was in a woeful plight, and wanting to inflict punishment on them, that they might be chastened and improve, collected all the gods into their most holy habitation, which, being placed in the center of the world, beholds all created things. And when he had called them together, he spake as follows:

˙The rest of the Dialogue of Critias has been lost.

NOTES AND REFERENCES

CHAPTER TWO

1. *Fingerprints of the Gods* by Graham Hancock: William Heinemann, 1995.
2. There is confusion about the exact dates of Plato's life. Wikipedia gives 424/423 to 348/347.

CHAPTER THREE

3. *The Antediluvian World*, by Ignatius Donnelly: reprinted by Echo Library, 2006.
4. Books on Atlantis by Charles Berlitz are *The Mystery of Atlantis*: Souvenir Press, 1976, and *Atlantis, the Lost Continent*: G. P. Putnam and Sons, 1984.
5. *Discovery of Atlantis*, by Robert Sarmast: First Source Publications, 2006.
6. *U.S. Geological Survey of Mid-Atlantic Ridge*, by Charles S. Piggot, 1936.
7. *The Sunken Kingdom*, by Peter James: Pimlico, 1996.
8. *The Atlantis Blueprint*, by Rand Flem Ath and Colin Wilson: Little, Brown and Co., 2000.
9. Dr. Sunil Prasannan's article appeared on Graham Hancock's web site. Professor Arysio Santos's book, *Atlantis: The Lost Continent Finally Found*, broadly advances the same theory: Atlantis Publications, 2011.
10. BBC News web site, 19 January 2002. *Underworld. Flooded Kingdoms of the Ice Age*, by Graham Hancock: Michael Joseph, 2002. There is also an excellent article detailing the amount of research on the site on the Graham Hancock web site, headed "Gulf of Cambay, Cradle of Ancient Civilisation."
11. *Underworld, Flooded Kingdoms of the Ice Age*, by Graham Hancock: Michael Joseph, 2002.
12. *Gateway to Atlantis,* by Andrew Collins: Headline Publishing, 2000.
13. *Edgar Cayce's Atlantis*, by Drs. Greg and Lora Little and John Van Auken: ARE Press, 2006.

CHAPTER FOUR

14. BBC Home web site. Edited guide entry. "The Great Earthquake 1755."
15. BBC News web site, August 15, 2005. *Nature* magazine, July 22, 2005. Survey by Dr. Marc Andre Gutscher.
16. Ibid.

CHAPTER SIX

17.   *The Siege and Conquest of Silves in 1189*, by Jonathan Wilson: Mesquita Press, 2009.

18.   The first Roman invasion of the Iberian Peninsula occurred in 219 B.C. Wikipedia, "The History of Portugal."

19.   Wikipedia, Viriathus (Viriato in Portuguese).

20.   The city of Pax Julia was so named by Julius Caesar in 48 B.C. after peace was made with the local Lusitanian tribes. The ruins are very close to the modern town of Beja.

21.   *The Holy Kingdom*, by Adrian Gilbert, Alan Wilson, and Baram Blackett: Bantam, 1998.

22.   *Atlantis in Andalucia*, by E. M. Wishaw: republished by Adventures Unlimited Press, 1997.

23.   Ibid.

24.   Ibid.

25.   The original information came from the Greek historian Herodotus. He wrote that Kolaios reached the capital of Arganthonius after two days' sailing from Gades (Cádiz). This is evidence that the capital could not have been as close as Huelva, or elsewhere in the general area, which is currently accepted by historians for Tartessos. Two days' sailing would have taken him much farther, well along the Algarve coast.

26.   Strabo (The Geographer) lived from 64 B.C. to A.D. 24. He is most famous for his seventeen-volume work *Geographica*, in which he gives much information about southwest Iberia.

27.   *Atlantis in Spain*, by E. M. Wishaw: republished by Adventures Unlimited Press, 1997.

28.   Wikipedia. Rameses III is thought to have reigned from 1186 to 1155 B.C. The Sea Peoples invaded in year eight of his reign.

29.   *Atlantis in Spain*, by E. M. Wishaw: republished by Adventures Unlimited Press, 1997.

30.   Ibid.

CHAPTER SEVEN

31.   *Gateway to Atlantis*, by Andrew Collins: Headline Book Publishing, 2000.

32.   www.atlantisquest.com, the web site of Cedric Leonard.

33.   Harold T. Wilkins was a Cambridge-educated journalist and author, 1891–1960.

CHAPTER EIGHT

34.   *The Greek Lexicon*, by Liddle and Scott. There are many editions.

35.   This mistranslation in the recognized English versions is confirmed by Chalcidius's early translation into Latin.

36.   Wikipedia.

37.   "The deluged civilization of the Caucasus," by Reginald Fessenden (1866–1932). Published in www.radiocom.net/Deluge/Deluge1-6.htm

38. Wikipedia. Universidad Computers de Madrid, Geology of the Iberian Peninsula.
39. Web site: "Plato's Atlantis was a River Delta," by Dr. Ulf Richter, Germany.
40. A detailed study of the use of the word "pelagos" in Plato's era by Georgeos Diaz-Montexano established that it was always associated with "Salt marshes, lagoons, seas of low bottoms with stumbling blocks or Islands." Later, the Greeks used the word to mean "Open sea, high sea, or deep sea," which is what you will find in standard dictionaries of ancient Greek. Interestingly, another earlier use of the word was for a "flooded plain." That could not be more apt for the area in front of southwest Iberia (George Liddle, Robert Scott, Henry Stuart Jones, and Roderick Mckenzie). Chalcidius, who attended Plato's academy, completed the very first translation into Latin and used the "Fretum" for pelagos. This means salt marshes, etc. Much later, Marcilio Ficino used the same word in his translation into Latin.
41. "The ocean beyond the Pillars" in the geographer Scylax's *Periplus,* thought to date from the fourth century B.C.
42. The Phoenician Himlico was the first known sailor to reach the northwest shores of Europe. The oldest recorded source for his voyage is in *Natural History,* by the Roman Pliny the Elder (A.D. 23–79).
43. Pliny the Younger (A.D. 61–113).
44. Plutarch (A.D. 46–120).
45. *Maps of the Ancient Sea Kings,* by Charles H. Hapgood: republished by Adventures Unlimited Press, 1996.
46. The philosopher Chalcidius had been a student in Plato's academy. In 321 B.C., he translated *Timaeus* into Latin.
47. http://www.georgeosdiazmontexano.com. He has several other web sites, some only in Spanish.
48. Jonas Bergman, an Atlantologist from Uppsala in Sweden, has an excellent web site in which he strives to identify Atlantis with Morocco.
49. Eberhard Zangger, a Swiss geoarchaeologist who has written several books on ancient civilizations. While working for Cambridge University in 1989, he advanced the theory that Troy was Atlantis.

CHAPTER NINE
50. Herodotus was shown the statues in the Temple of Thebes. It is detailed in Book 11 of his *History.*
51. The best analysis can be found on www.atlantisquest.com
52. Wikipedia, under "Tumbago."

CHAPTER TEN
53. Wikipedia, under "Younger Dryas."
54. www.atlantisquest.com/taming
55. Ibid.

56.   *New Scientist* magazine, January 3, 1985.

57.   *The Algarve Tiger,* by Siobhan Mitchell and Edwardo Goncalves: Vista Iberics Publicacoes, 2001.

CHAPTER TWELVE

58.   *Atlantis in Spain,* by E. M. Wishaw: republished by Adventures Unlimited Press, 1997.

59.   Ibid.

60.   Ibid.

61.   *The Atlantis Effect,* by Dr. Roger Coghill: Ker Menez, Lower Race, Pontypool, UK.

62.   *Algarve Goodlife* magazine, February 2003.

CHAPTER FOURTEEN

63.   Dr. Frank C. Hibben was a professor of archaeology at the University of New Mexico. He visited Alaska in 1941, and the results were published in his book *The Lost Americans*: Apollo Editions, 1961.

64.   www.atlantisquest.com

65.   Ibid.

66.   The Tunguska explosion. NASA Science News web site. science@NASAnews, 2008.

67.   *The Atlantis Blueprint,* by Rand Flem Ath and Colin Wilson: Little, Brown and Company, 2000.

68.   *Underworld, Flooded Kingdoms of The Ice Age,* by Graham Hancock: Penguin, 2003.

CHAPTER FIFTEEN

69.   Discovered at Largo Velho, Muges, in Portugal. Dated to the Mesolithic period.

70.   Heyerdahl organized several investigations between 1991 and 1998 by teams of archaeologists who eventually contradicted his views. They thought the step pyramids were constructed by Spanish farmers using the rocks they were clearing from the fields. Heyerdahl pointed out that this did not account for the east-west astronomical alignment, the shaped corner stones, staircases, and flat platforms on the tops. The area containing the pyramids is now an ethnographic park devoted to Thor Heyerdahl and his beliefs.

71.   From *Marvelous Things Heard,* one of several books that are attributed to Pseudo-Aristotle authors.

72.   volcanoline.com/madeira. The last volcanic eruptions were in the west-central part of Madeira; they created cinder cones and lava flows.

73.   *The Atlantis Effect,* by Dr. Roger Coghill: Ker Menez, Lower Race, Pontypool, UK.

74.   *Edgar Cayce's Atlantis,* by Drs. Greg and Lora Little and John Van Auken: ARE Press, 2006.

75.   Ibid.

76. *Underworld, Flooded Kingdoms of The Ice Age,* by Graham Hancock: Penguin, 2003.

77. *Edgar Cayce's Atlantis,* by Drs. Greg and Lora Little and John Van Auken: ARE Press, 2006.

78. *Underworld, Flooded Kingdoms of The Ice Age,* by Graham Hancock: Penguin, 2003.

79. *Gateway to Atlantis,* by Andrew Collins: Headline Book Publishing, 2000.

80. The Grave Creek Tablet was discovered in 1838 in West Virginia, U.S.A. It is a small sandstone disc and is inscribed on one side with alphabetic characters. It was found during excavations at the Grave Creek Mound (69 feet high and 295 feet in diameter). Although the tablet is now missing, a plaster cast and a photograph exist in the Smithsonian Museum.

81. ARE (Association for Research and Enlightenment) web site.

CHAPTER SIXTEEN

82. Arganthonius was thought to have lived from 670 to 550 B.C. Although this sea battle is often referred to, I can find no suggested date for when it happened.

CHAPTER SEVENTEEN

83. http://www.whowerethephoenicians.com. Diodorus Siculus, Plato, and Tacitus all subscribed to the belief that the alphabetic letters were brought to Phoenicia from Egypt. Interestingly, Eusebius quotes a fragment from Sanchoniathon that Thoth, the Egyptian, was "the teacher of the Phoenicians in the art of writing." In view of the ancient alphabetic characters found in Egypt by archaeologist William Flinders Petrie, and of the fact that the Egyptian god Thoth originally ruled in a western land, this is very significant.

84. Tacitus was a Roman historian who lived from A.D. 56 to 117.

85. Strabo recorded this, among many other interesting facts about southwest Iberia, in his *Geographica.* His descriptions are uncannily similar to Plato's description of Atlantis.

86. This was carved on reindeer bone. That animal has not populated southern France and northern Spain since the glacial period, so the dating of this discovery can hardly be disputed.

87. Discovered in 1916 at Banca Deta, Corunna, in Galicia, northern Spain.

88. www.antiquos.com Georgeos Diaz Montexano.

89. William Flinders Petrie (1853–1942) was the pioneer of methodology in archaeology. He lived in Egypt for long periods and explored extensively throughout the country. The British Museum has a special Flinders Petrie section.

90. Manetho was an ancient Greek who lived in the third century B.C. and wrote the famous *Aegyptiaca* (History of Egypt).

91. The Turin King list is thought to date from the reign of Rameses II. It is now in the Egizio museum in Turin. It covers the period from the ancient god–kings of Egypt to the seventeenth dynasty.

92. Discovered in 1878 by Dr. Rene Verneau.
93. *The Atlantis Effect*, by Dr. Roger Coghill: Ker Menez, Lower Race, Pontypool, UK.
94. *Mysteries of Ancient South America*, by Harold T. Wilkins: Rider & Co., 1945.
95. *Researches into the Early Inhabitants of Spain*, by Wilhelm von Humboldt, 1821. *The Basque Language*: University of Pennsylvania Press, 1957.

CHAPTER EIGHTEEN

96. The ancient Indian book *The Mahabharata* records that the leaders of the Adityas, the very ancient Indian rulers, were white with light red or light brown hair.
97. There are many pyramids around Xian in Qui Chan Province in China. The pyramids are officially thought to be mausoleums of the Quin Dynasty. They are close to the Tarim Basin, where two tall, red-haired mummies were found, one female and one male. *The Tarim Mummies*, co-authored by Professor Victor Mair of the University of Pennsylvania.
98. *Aku Aku, the Secrets of Easter Island*, by Thor Heyerdahl: Penguin, 1972.
99. *From the Ashes of Angels*, by Andrew Collins: Michael Joseph, 1996.

CHAPTER NINETEEN

100. *Uriel's Machine*, by Robert Lomas and Christopher Knight: Element Books, 2000.
101. *From the Ashes of Angels*, by Andrew Collins: Michael Joseph, 1996.
102. *The Atlantis Encyclopedia*, by Frank Joseph: New Age Books, 2005.
103. *Treasures of Lost Races*, by Rene Noobergen: Teach Services, 2001. *Ancient Bulgaria's Golden Treasures*, by Colin Renfrew: National Geographic. Wikipedia: "Varna Necropolis."
104. *Temples of Ancient Gods*, by Michael Tellinger: Zulu Planet Publications, 2010.
105. *The 12th Planet*, by Zecharia Sitchin: Avon, 1976. (Book 1 of "The Earth Chronicles" series.)

CHAPTER TWENTY

106. *Atlantis, Lost Kingdom of the Andes*, by Jim Allen: Floris Books, 2009.
107. *Fingerprints of the Gods*, by Graham Hancock: William Heinemann, 1995.
108. *Keeper of Genesis*, by Robert Bauval and Graham Hancock.
109. *Fingerprints of the Gods*, by Graham Hancock: William Heinemann, 1995.
110. Ibid.

CHAPTER TWENTY-ONE

111. *Atlantis Effect*, by Dr. Roger Coghill: Ker Menez, Lower Race, Pontypool, UK.
112. These reliefs are referred to in many books and web sites, such as: "A Short History of Ancient Electricity," www.bibliotecapleyades.net/; harunyaha.com/en/works/13770/light-bulbs-were-used-for
113. Ibid.

ACKNOWLEDGMENTS

I would like to thank the following who have assisted greatly in putting together over twenty years of research into what I hope is a persuasive and enjoyable book:

My Algarve editor, Elaine Edgely, and Jonathan Veale for his encouragement and sound advice. Neil Simpson for his invaluable help with the final shaping of the manuscript and my agent, Andrew Lownie, for his wise counseling, patience, and perseverance.

Particularly my wife, Margaret, for her help and tolerance.

INDEX

Page references in *italics* refer to illustrations.